Mediated Political Realities

Mediated Political Realities.

Dan Nimmo   James E. Combs

Longman
New York & London

Mediated Political Realities

Longman Inc., 1560 Broadway, New York, N.Y. 10036
Associated companies, branches, and representatives
throughout the world.

Developmental Editor: Irving E. Rockwood
Editorial and Design Supervisor: Ferne Y. Kawahara
Manufacturing Supervisor: Marion Hess
Printing and Binding: Fairfield Graphics

"Journalese," from *Safire's Political Dictionary* by William Safire
(New York: Ballantine Books, 1978) © Random House, Inc. Reprinted with
permission.

Excerpts from "The Iceman Cometh," from *Selected Plays of Eugene O'Neill*
(New York: Vintage Books, 1957) © Random House, Inc. Reprinted with
permission.

The definition of "fantasy" © 1981 Houghton Mifflin Company.
Reprinted by permission from *The American Heritage Dictionary of the English
Language.*

Library of Congress Cataloging in Publication Data
Nimmo, Dan D.
  Mediated political realities.

  Bibliography: p.
  Includes index.
  1. Communication in politics.   I. Combs, James E.
II. Title.
JA74.N54   302'.12   82-151
ISBN 0-582-28309-4   AACR2
ISBN 0-582-28310-8 (pbk.)

Manufactured in the United States of America

To Dick Chase
Minister of Plenty

Man is essentially a dreamer,
wakened sometimes for a moment
by some peculiarly obstrusive
element in the outer world, but
lapsing again quickly into the
happy somnolence of imagination.

Bertrand Russell
Sceptical Essays

Contents

Contents   xi

Preface

The behavioral movement that reached political science after World War II left many marks on the discipline, i.e., a heightened emphasis upon the search for testable theories explaining human conduct, an avid interest in new techniques of data gathering and analysis, a greater interdisciplinary focus, and a desire to rebuild the discipline along the lines of a more positivist science. All the while, in a fashion reminiscent of the development of a new nation-state or the emergence of a self-conscious identity among newly independent peoples, political scientists searched for their roots, their founding fathers, and notable landmarks in the historical development of the discipline. And, although not all political scientists might agree upon whom to honor with the title "Father of Modern Political Science," most do concur that certain figures from the scholarly past merit admission to the discipline's pantheon of prime progenitors.

Of such figures few ignored Arthur F. Bentley. Early treatises on the growth of the behavioral movement cited Bentley's contributions, especially his effort to remove "mind stuff" from the study of politics, define the "raw materials" of the study of government, and stress the key role played by group activity and pressures in the "process of government." More rarely, however, political scientists recognized Bentley's contributions to, and advice for, studying what the authors of this work regard as its basic subject, namely, the mediation of political realities through communication.

Faced with what he called a "dead political science," Bentley asked, "What can there possibly be to a political science with the very breath of life left out?" Bentley suggested what he thought that breath to be: "He who writes of the state, of law, or of politics without first coming to close quarters with public opinion is simply evading the very

central structure of his study." Since those words appeared in 1908 in
Bentley's *The Process of Government*, political science has changed considerably. The study of public opinion, for instance, may not be "the
very central structure" of the study of politics, but it certainly occupies a
major place in the discipline. However, two of Bentley's recommen-
dations for the study of public opinion have received far less attention.

First, Bentley regarded "language activity" as a primary focus of
political inquiry generally and of public opinion. More precisely, he
argued that "it is what is reflected in language that demands primary
attention." Perhaps because he worked fifteen years as a journalist
Bentley never lost sight of the key relationship between communication
and politics, and between communication and social activity. He elabo-
rated on that focus, first introduced in *The Process of Government*, in later
works, notably *Relativity in Man and Society* and *Behavior Knowledge Fact*.

Yet, later generations were not quick to follow Bentley's lead. Studies of the relation of communication and politics were more likely to
derive from working journalists or sociologists than political scientists.
And when studies of voting and campaigning did examine the relationship, the verdict was that communication had "minimal effects" on
political behavior. Only recently have political scientists started to take
seriously the role played by mass and group communication. But here
too there has been a tendency to dismiss a second of Bentley's prescrip-
tions. Writing of "the raw material of government" Bentley asked in
The Process of Government, "Ought we not to draw a distinction in advance between it and other varieties of social activity, so that we can
have our field of study defined and delimited at the outset?" He
answered with a resounding "No." Political scientists should not be
like children making paper toys, using their scissors too confidently,
thus cutting themselves off from the material they need. Rather, "We
shall plunge into any phenomena or set of phenomena belonging to
the roughly recognized field of government."

The "roughly recognized field of government" did not include
communications for a long while, at least as recognized by much of
mainstream behavioral political science. Once it did, communications
was quickly delimited to include public affairs journalism, then communication in electoral campaigns, but little else. Excluded were such
phenomena of popular culture as entertainment programming on radio
and television, the popular film industry, celebrity magazines, sports,
religious movements, conspiratorial movements with popular appeal,
etc. Popular culture, it seemed, was important only to the populace
comprising American democracy, not to the students of the democratic
polity.

This book is an effort to heed Bentley's advice in the study of politics generally, and in the "language activity" of political communica-

tion particularly. Our argument is straightforward: Few people learn about politics through direct experience; for most persons political realities are mediated through mass and group communication, a process resulting as much in the creation, transmission, and adoption of political fantasies as realistic views of what takes place. We pursue that argument, as Bentley advised, along "interesting paths we shall be prepared to follow." Consequently, readers will find subjects treated in this work not frequently encountered in political science texts. Because those subjects have generally been ignored, or at least deemphasized in political inquiry, much of our argument is necessarily exploratory and speculative. Nonetheless, we have drawn upon such research findings from the communication sciences as offer insights into how various media portray politics to Americans. How Americans respond on the basis of those portrayals is, given the state of research, even more elusive a topic for discussion.

Portions of this book report original research into the rhetorical visions contained in the mass media, especially in nightly television network newscasts. We wish to acknowledge grants from the following that made such research possible: the Television Studies Program, George Washington University; the Valparaiso University Alumni Association; and the Faculty Research Award Program, University of Tennessee-Knoxville. We are grateful to the Television News Archive, Vanderbilt University, for cooperation in supplying compiled videotapes of network news coverage. Professor Thomas Hood, Department of Sociology, University of Tennessee-Knoxville, and Professor Thomas D. Ungs, Department of Political Science, University of Tennessee-Knoxville, made it possible to secure required video playback equipment. Ann Norris and Barry Kolar assisted in the tedious tasks of coding and analyzing the content of televised public affairs programming. We thank Maxine Martin for her prompt and efficient typing of the draft manuscript. Jan Trice provided valuable assistance in indexing. We thank Irving Rockwood of Longman Inc. for taking the study of Thumb's Second Postulate seriously, David Estrin for his assistance, and Ferne Kawahara for seeing the book through production. Finally, Dick Chase, to whom this volume is dedicated, merits another acknowledgment for providing required space within friendly confines, thus affording opportunities for reflection and planning of the book's contents. By bringing the fantasies of 1879 into the present, he has substantially eased anxieties about what 1984 may really be like.

Dan Nimmo
James E. Combs

Introduction

How Real Is Politics?

The Mediation of Political Realities

Miss Sherwin of Gopher Prairie never lived, yet she is immortal. Her name is unknown to most, yet her fame is enduring. Her residence is fictional, yet we all live there. She will never die because, at least in politics, each of us is Miss Sherwin of Gopher Prairie.

Writing in 1922 after the close of World War I, journalist Walter Lippmann reflected on Miss Sherwin and her understanding of that great conflict.[1] Miss Sherwin, he wrote, "is aware that a war is raging in France and tries to conceive it." But she has never been to France and "certainly she has never been along what is now the battlefront." All she has seen are pictures of soldiers, and it is impossible for her to imagine three million of them. "No one, in fact, can imagine them, and the professionals do not try," wrote Lippman. Instead, "they think of them as, say, two hundred divisions." Miss Sherwin thinks not of masses of soldiers, but of a personal duel between the French General Joffre and the German Kaiser. Her mind's eye pictures an eighteenth-century painting of a great soldier, a hero: "He stands there boldly unruffled and more than life size, with a shadowy army of tiny little figures winding off into the landscape behind." Miss Sherwin is not alone in this fantasy. Indeed, great men themselves are not "oblivious to these expectations." So, a photographer visits the French General Joffre and finds him in a drab office at a worktable without papers where he is preparing to sign his name to a single document. Someone notes that there are no maps on the walls. Surely it is impossible to think of a general without maps. So, maps are quickly put in place. The photograph is snapped. The maps are immediately removed.

There is a moral in this little tale about innocent Miss Sherwin of Gopher Prairie. Lippmann believed that people act on the basis of pictures they carry around in their heads, pictures of the way they think things are. These pictures derive from, and are changed by, two sources or a combination thereof. One is direct experience. People's

1

daily lives consist of direct, firsthand experiences with events, places, other people, objects, and so on. They eat and sleep, work and play, argue and relent, worry and relax. The pictures in their heads help them give meaning to all of that and everything adds up to a portion of each one's reality. But a lot of things happen with which people do not deal directly. They hear, read, or see pictures of these things, imagine what took place, give them meaning, and incorporate these indirectly experienced things into their pictures of the world, a second portion of their reality.

For Miss Sherwin of Gopher Prairie, direct experience of the war in France was unthinkable. She could only conceive of that war on the basis of what she was told or expected to be told. Her reality was not a firsthand, direct involvement in the Great War but a product of second-hand, indirect accounts. It was, in sum, a *mediated*, not a direct, reality. Miss Sherwin was not alone in this respect. Unable to conceive of three million soldiers plagued by the agonies of combat, professionals relabeled the three million, changing them into two hundred depersonalized, impersonal divisions. And the mediated realities of both Miss Sherwin and the generals must conform to expectations. If a general is expected to have battlemaps, supply them, take the photograph, remove them. Mediated realities are thereby self-fulfilling: accounts of the way things are conform to the pictures people have of those things, reinforcing not challenging the pictures in our heads.

This is a book about such mediated realities, specifically, mediated realities of politics. Its argument is straightforward, namely, the pictures we have of politics are not the products of direct involvement but are perceptions focused, filtered, and fantasized by a host of mediators —the press, entertainment programming on television, movies, popular magazines, songs, and group efforts in election campaigns, political movements, religious movements, and government policymaking. To introduce the argument, we first pose the question "How real is politics?" by considering how real is real, how real is fantasy, and the logic of mediated politics—real and fantastic.

HOW REAL IS REAL?

There is a Japanese fable so venerable that over the course of many centuries it has been related in song, narrative, and dramatic form. Indeed, by transferring the setting of the tale to the American West, an enterprising producer made it into a moderately successful movie (*The Outrage*). Briefly, it involves a group of people who cross paths after separately witnessing a common event. Each renders an account of what he or she saw. Although each person saw precisely the same things happen, each interprets those happenings in such different ways that no two persons' accounts are the same. Each person's imagination results in a different picture in his or her head.

The point of the story is that we all live in a common world, but no two people live in the same one. Each of us forges our own reality. What is real to one of us may be illusion to another and vice versa.

How real, then, is real? Philosophers have debated that question for centuries and are probably no closer to a consensus than on that first day when one of them stubbed a toe on a rock and pondered whether the pain came from a real stone or an imaginary one. For purposes of this volume, little is to be gained by summarizing all the philosophic arguments over the nature of reality. Rather, we shall simply state a position on that question that is in keeping with our basic purpose of describing mediated political realities.

Our view derives from a line of thinking summarized in a provocative, anecdotal book by Paul Watzlawick entitled *How Real is Real?*[2] Watzlawick's training and professional experience are in the fields of psychiatry and psychotherapy. His career experience has led him to conclude that many alleged mental, emotional, and social disorders grow out of faulty communication between people, discourse that places people in different worlds constantly talking past one another. *How Real Is Real?* argues simply that "communication creates what we call reality." At first blush many may dismiss that proposition as obvious, even trivial. After all, humans must communicate with one another; it stands to reason that they will influence one another's views by doing so. Hence, is it not obvious that one's impressions of things flow from communication? Perhaps, but Watzlawick is saying something more. He is saying that insofar as *things* make any difference to us at all—that is, real things, or reality—communication creates them. Watzlawick admits this is a "most peculiar" view, "for surely reality is what is, and communication is merely a way of expressing or explaining it." *Not at all*, he urges, and, then, summarizes his position neatly:

[O]ur everyday, traditional ideas of reality are delusions which we spend substantial parts of our daily lives shoring up, even at the considerable risk of trying to force facts to fit our definition of reality instead of vice versa. And the most dangerous delusion of all is that there is only one reality. What there are, in fact, are so many different versions of reality, some of which are contradictory, but all of which are the results of communication and not reflections of eternal, objective truths.[3]

There are three points here: (1) our everyday, taken-for-granted reality is a delusion; (2) reality is created, or constructed, *through* communication not expressed *by* it; (3) for any situation there is no single reality, no one objective truth, but multiple subjectively derived realities. The world is *Rashomon*.

Reflecting on the implications of these points can yield discomfort. Granted we are generally willing to accept limits to our understanding, that there are few things we can *really* know. But does that deny there is a concrete, palpable "real world" that exists and is knowable? Watzlawick implies as much. The trouble, as he understands it, is that whether a real world exists or not, the only way we can know it, grasp it, make sense of it, is through communication. Even when we are directly involved in things, we do not apprehend them directly. Instead, media of communication intervene, media in the form of language, customs, symbols, stories, and so forth. That very intervention is a process that creates and re-creates (constructs and reconstructs) our realities of the moment and over the proverbial long haul. Communication does more than report, describe, explain—it creates. In this sense all realities—even those emerging out of direct, firsthand experience with things—are mediated. Looking back we can speculate that Miss Sherwin's reality of Gopher Prairie was no less mediated than was her conception of the war raging in France.

One other point should be underscored: in any situation there is more than one reality, or version of reality, and some are contradictory. We scarcely need reminding that countless millions have died extending or defending a particular version of reality in the face of other versions, seeking often to impose a single objective truth on all. More peaceful political debates are also clashes of competing versions of what is real. In 1980 Jimmy Carter and Ronald Reagan squared off in a televised presidential debate. Was one clearly right, correct, and honest? Was the other wrong, stupid, and evil? Avid supporters of either candidate might have thought so. But perhaps contradictory pictures of the world were merely dancing through each candidate's head.

What accounts for multiple, contradictory realities? If we accept Watzlawick's basic premise, that communication creates multiple realities (i.e., all realities are mediated), then any means of communication that intervenes in human experience is a potential mediator of reality. Our focus in this book, however, is not on all such means, but only on two. The first consists of the role that group communication plays in mediating realities (what we shall later refer to as group-mediated politics); the second consists of the part mass communication plays (what we shall speak of as mass-mediated politics).

Whether "birds of a feather flock together" or "opposites attract," we know not which, nor if either, adage is correct. But we do know that it is characteristic of the human species to congregate in groups. It forms all kinds: families, neighborhoods, villages, work groups, play groups, churches, crowds, and many others. Rewarding or not, group life apparently serves needs for companionship, camaraderie, cooperation, defense, and so forth. Certainly one attribute of any group is communication among its members. Through communication members define situations, problems, and the means of coping with difficulties—it simply makes living together possible. And in the process, the members create realities for the group. Differing groups (and differing groups within groups) frequently create contrasting pictures of the world. As we shall argue in Part II, group-mediated politics lends a special quality to government realities in this nation, particularly in defining relationships among politics and religion, conspiracies, the press, and policymaking.

It could be argued, as it has, that in an earlier era groups were the center of life for people. Tightly bonded, intimate family gatherings, for instance, were surely important in defining the realities for several generations of Americans. Today, however, there is another reality-creating means of communication, sometimes complementing and sometimes competing with groups. That, of course, is mass communication, or what we often refer to as mass media. *"Social reality is constituted, recognized, and celebrated with media,"*[4] write the authors of a recent work on the role of the mass media in shaping American understandings of the way things are. We share the view that much of what passes for social realities in contemporary America is what the mass media fashions. We examine the quality of mass-mediated politics in Part I.

However, before discussing the specific sources of mediated political realities, we need to consider a problem thus far brushed aside in asking "How real is real?" To say that communication creates realities, that there are different versions of what is real in a given situation, that common-sense notions of eternal, objective truths are deluding implies that reality is an iffy matter. Few of us care to live our lives in a continuous state of doubt. Indeed, we would be regarded as strange if we went around constantly asking: "What did you really mean by that?" "Did I really see what I think I saw?" "Do you see what I see?" In our everyday lives we simply take certain things for granted. If not reality, then what?

WELCOME TO FANTASY ISLAND

Humans are not passive creatures. The things that reach them in their everyday lives—whether through direct, firsthand experience or indirectly by way of groups and mass media—have no inherent meaning. People must take such messages, interpret them, and act. Some things impress people, others they forget, others they avoid. People are active mediators, or interpreters, of their worlds. They are a part of a communication process that creates realities.

Human imagination is essential to that process. We employ our imagination for every conceivable purpose. It helps us frame a picture of the way things are. But imagination does more. As philosopher David Hume wrote, "imagination extends experience."[5] Lacking imagination, the pictures in our heads would be limited. But with imagination we can conceive of things that we have never experienced. Indeed, perhaps no one has ever experienced what can sometimes be imagined.

Now imagination can take many forms. Suppose one is taking an extended vacation in a foreign land. It takes some hardheaded planning to decide what clothes to take, lodging to arrange, meals to prepare or buy, transportation to schedule, perhaps a language to learn, and a myriad of other details, not to mention finances to obtain. A person must anticipate the problems that can come up in such a venture. Not having made the trip before, one's experience is only a partial guide to what can happen. Here imagination is indispensable in adjusting, in formulating expectations of possible happenings. But perhaps some of us do not plan. Instead we daydream, another form of imagining. The planning of concrete activities takes second place to drifting off into a dream world of what our trip will be like—visits to exotic places, encounters with exciting strangers, titillating experiences.

Whatever form imagination takes—planning, anticipating, forming expectations, dreaming, sensing déjà vu experiences, extrasensory perception, remembering, and so on—the process is essential to the construction of our realities, the pictures of the world in our heads. In dealing with the question of sources of mediated realities, especially the group and mass communication sources of political realities, we single out a particular type of imaginative activity, that of fantasy. As this book will show, the vast bulk of political reality that most of us take for granted (whether we are private citizens or public officials) consists of a combination of fantasies created and evoked by group and mass communication. Preliminary to that argument, we need to delve into the nature of fantasy, its necessity, and its origins.

How Real Is Fantasy, How Fantastic Reality?

In common usage the word fantasy is plagued by many meanings. If trying to decide how real is real is perplexing, consider a standard dictionary's efforts to state how real is fantasy. Here are six meanings attributed to fantasy:[6]

1. The realm of vivid imagination, reverie, depiction, illusion, and the like; the natural conjurings of mental invention and association; the visionary world; make-believe.
2. A mental image, especially a disordered and weird image; an illusion; phantasm.

3. A capricious or whimsical idea or notion.
4. Literary or dramatic fiction characterized by highly fanciful or supernatural elements.
5. An imagined event or condition fulfilling a wish.
6. Can mean literally apart from reality, but it more often describes what seems to have slight relation to the real world because of its strangeness or extravagance.

In sum, fantasy involves imagination, its relationship to reality is problematic, and it is often dramatic in content. It may be vivid or illusory, natural or supernatural, visionary or capricious, believable or make-believe, real or unreal.

Recognizing that fantasy involves imagination and thought and trying to answer the question "Where does reality end and fantasy begin?", many researchers and scholars try to distinguish fantasy as a way of thinking. Psychologists, for example, contrast fantasizing with reality-testing. The former involves imagining events or conditions, usually pleasant and satisfying experiences, that permit a person to achieve wants and wishes blocked in the "real" world—one escapes into a world of one's own imagination. Reality-testing involves exploring and experimenting with one's environment to learn the nature of things, people, and events, in short, probing for evidence to support one's thoughts. In this view psychosis consists of an impairment of reality-testing and a retreat into a world of fantasy.[7] But because all of us fantasize to some degree (how many are daydreaming as they read these lines), the activity extends well beyond the psychotic.

Other scholars endeavor to distinguish between serious and nonserious activity.[8] Taking something seriously demands concentration, application of acquired skills, and work. Nonserious activity is more playful, demanding less focused attention and permitting reverie. One writer[9] extends a similar analysis to contrast what he calls directed and fantasy thought. Directed thought, he writes, concerns itself with immediate goals formed in coping with the environment (such as whether to carry an umbrella if it is cloudy). It involves both short-term memory (Has it rained a lot lately?) and long-term memory (Have I been wet without an umbrella under similar conditions in the past?). Directed thought arouses a person to action, to a decision—to take the umbrella or to leave it. Finally, directed thought can be tested, checked for its accuracy or inaccuracy: Did I need the umbrella or not? Directed thought, then, is volitional. That is, it is the serious activity in which one voluntarily focuses attention on the problem at hand and does something about it.

Fantasy differs in several respects. Fantasy concerns goals that are less immediate, perhaps extending to wishes and desires one has had for a long time but whose fulfillment were interrupted by the demands of the here-and-now. Attention to the immediate external environment is much more perfunctory in fantasizing than in directed thought. Fantasy is more internally focused, more self-centered. Research suggests that during fantasizing this self-centered concern is reflected in ocular fixation, that is, a tendency to ignore other people and one's surroundings, to acquire the blank stare that we have all experienced in talking with someone whose attention is miles away from the conversation. Fantasizing relies largely on long-term memory, on a reliving of the past, and on an imagination of how things will be the same or different in the future. Fantasizers act on the basis of what is running through their heads more rarely than do persons in directed thought; the thought is not father to the deed but is enjoyed purely for its own sake. Finally, because fantasy seldom arouses one to act, the correctness of the fantasy cannot be checked against what happened when one behaved in accordance with it. More frequently the fantasy's accuracy is gauged by whether holding it yields satisfaction, not what happens by living it out. A nonvolitional reverie substitutes for a voluntary focusing of attention and effort.

The above distinctions are useful for they assist us in formulating an understanding of fantasy that will flow throughout our discussion. On one point, however, we take issue with those who hold these views. We suspect more people act out their fantasies than the preceding account suggests. But, because the authenticity of that fantasy is more likely to be judged by the mental and emotional satisfaction that it gives to the one holding it than by the consequences of acting on it, people doggedly cling to their fantasies, often learning little from experience.

Living in Fantastic Worlds

What then is fantasy? A *fantasy* is a credible picture of the world that is created when one interprets mediated experiences as the way things are and takes for granted the authenticity of the mediated reality without checking against alternative, perhaps contradictory, realities so long as the fantasy offers dramatic proof for one's expectations. Consider the main points in this definition. First, a person has a fantasy not because it is demonstrably true or false but because it is believable, that is, credible. The young man fantasizing he is a handsome, desirable lover or the young lady visualizing herself as a femme fatale may not be easily dissuaded, acne or bad breath notwithstanding. Or, if either fantasizes that a facial lotion or a mouthwash will do the trick, correct the fatal flaw disrupting their love life, contradictory results go ignored. Second, if communication creates realities, given the fine line between the real and the fantastic, it is no shock to think that communication creates fantasies as well. Third, the delusion that there is a single reality for any given event rather than many different versions of reality is precisely the substance on which fantasy feeds. A fantasy world substitutes a simplified, single reality for the complex, overlapping, and contradictory versions possible through communication. Fourth, the proof of a fantasy's worth (i.e., whether it is true for its holder) lies not in its correspondence to what happens in the world but whether it conforms to what one expects, perhaps even wants, to be so. In this sense the previously listed definition of a fantasy as an imagined event or condition fulfilling a wish is relevant. Finally, a fantasy has dramatic qualities, that is, for the person creating it, the fantasy is a story with a plot, actors, scene, and ways of expressing things, acts, and motives. Either in the mind or with other people, fantasies are rehearsed and enacted—a key point we return to later in this chapter.

Who has not had an argument with another—be it friend, spouse, bank teller, auto mechanic, teacher, tax collector, or the thousands of others who frequent our daily lives—come out on the short end and, then, rehearsed a mental scenario of getting even next time? Who has not fantasized what it would be like living in another house, having another car, going on a trip, living lavishly—or even adequately? How many Americans tried to imagine the plight of the U.S. hostages held in Iran for 444 days in 1979–1981? All such flights of fancy put us into fantastic worlds, but why do we do it?

There are a number of reasons. As Eric S. Rabkin writes in *Fantastic Worlds*,[10] what we take to be the real world "is a messy place where dust accumulates and people die for no good reason and crime often pays and true love doesn't conquer much." And in the real world things make no sense, occurring randomly; they are "indifferent to the shape we try to sense in our lives."[11] Fantasy is an alternative. Our fantasies can be neat and tidy. Through them we can impose an order on the messy, dirty, chaotic world. We can bend things to our liking through imagination or, if not to our liking, at least to our understanding. Fantasy provides a way out of grappling with contradictory realities. We can transcend the here-and-now, relieve our boredom, and substitute a single reality for multiple ones. Finally, in addition to simplifying, and perhaps comforting us, fantasies provide a way for each of us to know who we are; they provide a self-identity and, if we try to live our fantasies, a way of expressing it. Even in the face of refuting evidence from our daily lives, we reluctantly yield the fantasy of a self-image, even avoiding or ignoring the contradictory claims of others' alleged realities.

In the end, however, it is a matter of human capacities and limits.

We are Miss Sherwin, not omnipresent and not omniscient. We cannot be everywhere, taking part in everything firsthand. Instead, we accept mediated, secondhand accounts of what happens; we interpret them and, because we are unable to check their authenticity, unconsciously take most such accounts for granted. In short, in most aspects of our lives—especially politics—we have little choice but to be Mr. Roarke's guests on "Fantasy Island."[12]

Building Sand Castles

As our definition implies, fantastic realities flow from the work of human imagination interpreting mediated accounts. The social construction of fantasy involves an interplay of group and mass communication. The sequence runs roughly as follows. To begin with, something happens that people find sufficiently novel, perplexing, threatening, amusing, or interesting in some fashion to take note of it. It may be something seen firsthand—an auto accident, bank robbery, political speech, someone scaling the side of a skyscraper, indeed, anything. Or it may be something reported in the news. In either case it is sufficiently provocative, out of the ordinary, and untoward so that people want to know about it, to understand it. The American philosopher Charles S. Peirce believed that humans confronted with novel situations or problems experience an "irritation of doubt" and engage in a natural process of relieving the tensions produced by the ambiguities and anxieties in such a state.[13] If Peirce is correct, this is the beginning of fantasy.

Normally one's striving for clarification leads to personal sampling. This is an unsystematic process of sorting through one's own thoughts and comparing them to what other people think by gleaning tidbits from conversations with friends, acquaintances, coworkers, and others as well as from following the news, watching TV talk shows, and perhaps simply overhearing random comments.[14] Gradually a picture emerges as to "what people think" and "that's the way it is" (as CBS anchor Walter Cronkite used to close his evening network TV news program).

But different people paint different pictures of what happens. Different clusters and groups of people exchange ideas but have no way of knowing whether the version of reality they have fashioned matches that of other groups. They may think everyone shares their version or they may think reality unique to them, that they alone know the truth. In either case a state of "pluralistic ignorance" emerges, a "situation in which individuals hold unwarranted assumptions about the thoughts, feelings, and behavior of other people."[15] Pluralistic ignorance promotes a tendency for individuals to share their private fantasies, form group fantasies, and, then, either communicate those fantasies more broadly under the assumption that other groups share them or insulate the group from people holding seemingly contradictory, threatening pictures of the world.

Because it is shared, a group fantasy takes on an aura of truth that the private fantasies of individuals do not have. To have one's private views shared by others constitutes a social validation of a person's image of things. Laboring under the deceptive assumption that, "If others believe what I believe, it must be true," the proof of the validity of a group fantasy lies simply in the fact that it *is* shared. Similarly, when group members think other groups hold an identical picture of the world, that is added proof that the fantasy is valid.

A person needs only to think of her or his everyday life to spot examples of this fantasy-building process. There is a strong impulse in most of us to want to get along with others. When we come in contact with them—in casual conversation, classroom discussion, working together, playing, or whatever—we seek common ground. Strangers thrust together, for example, probe for a common interest to break the ice. Add to this another impulse: to entertain one another, usually by relating stories of personal experiences or of things happening in the world. If, for instance, family members at dinner hear a tale about welfare cheaters, this may inspire other anecdotes about public morality that conjure up a fantasy of·corrupt politicians, the underworld, disliked minority groups, even the decline and fall of civilization. The group's fantasy sharing enlivens the dinner by interweaving exploits of heroes, villains, fools, ironic twists in the plot, a moral, and so forth.

Granted, then, that people run into situations (either directly or indirectly) that pique their interest, sample thoughts of others, paint a picture frequently shared with others, and, then, assume that other groups either do or do not share the same understanding. In a state of pluralistic ignorance groups have no way of knowing how widely their versions of reality extend. If the situation that prompted the fantasizing in the first instance is of sufficiently widespread interest, conditions are ripe for another stage in fantasy development. At this stage mass communication enters the process, making possible a diffusion of a single fantasy shared by broad segments of a population.

Ernest G. Bormann, a communication scholar, has taken note of the group-fantasizing process. Bormann believes that "dramatizing communication creates social reality for groups of people." By "dramatizing communication" he means the type of tale-telling and storytelling noted above. He believes that such dramatizing occurs in all types of groups. When it begins, the tempo of the conversation picks up, people get excited, are less self-conscious, and the tone of the group meeting becomes lively, intense, interesting. The dramatizing promotes fantasy building and what Bormann calls fantasy chaining, that is, the fantasy chains out to all group members and they share it. The result is a group fantasy of which "the content consists of characters, real or fictitious, playing out a dramatic situation in a setting removed in time and space from the here-and-now transactions of the group."[16]

Bormann does not limit his argument to small, face-to-face groups. Fantasy building and fantasy chaining occur in larger, less intimate groups where people do not even know one another, as in an audience listening to a public speech or viewers scattered nationwide watching a TV news or entertainment program. In short, masses of people can enter the fantasy process. Fantasy themes, Bormann's designation of the dramatic elements of a group's fantasy, constitute the *reality* for a group faced with a problematic situation. That reality, fantasy theme, is replete with symbols describing the actors, means of expression, acts, scenes, and motives of the drama that constitutes the fantasy. When people get caught up in this symbolic reality, they possess what Bormann calls a rhetorical vision, that is, they all respond the same way emotionally to the key symbols that make up fantasies:

A rhetorical vision is contructed from fantasy themes that chain out in face-to-face interacting groups, in speaker-audience transactions, in viewers of television broadcasts, in listeners to radio programs, and in all diverse settings for public and intimate communication in a given society.... [Moreover,] once such a rhetorical vision emerges it contains dramatis personae and typical plot lines that can be alluded to in all communication contexts and spark a response reminiscent of the original emotional chain.[17]

Bormann's analysis thus completes the sequence of building fantastic worlds. Something happens. Individuals take account of it, try to make sense of it. They sort out their own thoughts and sample others. They exchange notes on their preoccupation in small groups. They spin tales; some strike a common responsive chord. They grow excited and involved, a shared symbolic reality builds, a single fantasy filled with dramatis personae chains out to all group members. To relieve a state of pluralistic ignorance, the group goes public, communicating their rhetorical vision to larger audiences. Some visions reach the mass media—TV, radio, movies, magazines, popular songs, popular sports, and so on. These visions penetrate other small groups and stimulate conversation, storytelling, and more fantasy. The fantasy spreads to ever larger audiences and, if potent enough, constitutes the single symbolic reality created for an entire population. Who, for instance, can forget the national fantasy of the return of the U.S. hostages from Iran in January 1981, symbolized by thousands of yellow ribbons tied to auto antennas, light poles, and every other public object?

Thus are fantasies created and propagated. *For those who share them, fantasies are real, the fantasy reality.* So described, the process of group and mass fantasizing is similar to the spread of rumor. Like fantasy, a rumor is a story in general circulation without certainty as to its truth. Rumors help us explain confusing situations and relieve uncertainties; they supply neat, tidy, simplified accounts. And like fantasy, the more importance that people deem the topic of the rumor and the ambiguity of the situation that stimulated it, the wider the spread of the rumor.

Unlike fantasies, however, there frequently are efforts to check the authenticity of rumors. If verified, rumors take on the aura of fact; if contradicted with concrete evidence, they die out. When a rumor cannot be verified or lives on despite mountains of contradictions, it is scarcely distinguishable from fantasy—fulfilling deeply felt emotional needs shared by large numbers of people and, hence, it is real for them.

The Great Cabbage Hoax exemplifies a rumor of fantastic proportions.[18] In the 1940s a rumor started that a federal agency in Washington, D.C., had issued a memo on the regulation of cabbage prices—a memo just short of twenty-seven thousand (26,911) words long! The memo embarrassed bureaucrats charged with regulating food prices during World War II; with the close of the war, the rumor died out. Or so it seemed. Then, in 1951 a toastmaster, at a gathering where the director of the federal price-regulating agency was to speak, again related the rumor, drawing odious comparisons between the rumored memo and the Gettysburg Address (266 words), the Ten Commandments (297 words), and the Declaration of Independence (1,348 words). The rumor chained out to newspapers, sometimes substituting the price of fog horns for cabbages. The rumor persisted, then again apparently died. But no, in 1977 a major oil company in an advertisement in the nation's leading newspapers resurrected the cabbage version of price regulation. This caught the attention of Walter Cronkite who reported it as fact on his "CBS Evening News." An international version reached the *London Times*; this time the alleged memo was a European Common Market directive on duck eggs, 26,911 words long. And, as recently as 1980, Republican congressional candidate Lynn Martin of Illinois, seeking the congressional seat once held by John B. Anderson, made a televised commercial that pictured her looking across a field of soybeans. She told her viewers how her district's soybean farmers had been damaged by a federal "regulation on soybean gradations 18,000 words long," when the Declaration of Independence had only 463 words, the Ten Commandments but 165! (Apparently these were abridged versions of the latter two documents.) The Great Cabbage Hoax is not alone as a fantasy rumor. It joins such legends as that of the woman who died of snakebite while inspecting imported carpets at K-Mart, the $50 Porsche, and the worm meat in McDonald's Big Macs as venerable rhetorical visions.

A fantasy that simply will not die, that endures through generations of chaining, enters the realm of myth. A myth is a credible, dramatic, and socially constructed picture of things that people accept as permanent, fixed, unchanging reality.[19] The genius of the Founding Fathers, the greatness of Abraham Lincoln, the Manifest Destiny of America—are all examples of myths. Fantasy themes may combine to support enduring myths or, at the same time, fantasies conforming to a nation's mythology endure and continue chaining out because of it.

SOAP OPERA POLITICS:
THE LOGIC OF MEDIATED, FANTASTIC REALITY

The creation and chaining out of fantastic worlds from individuals to groups to mass audiences involve storytelling. When something happens that is ambiguous in meaning, provokes people's interest, and raises doubts demanding resolution, the popular urge is to represent *what really happened* in dramatic ways. Dramatic representation of what goes on in the world constitutes the inherent logic of mediated realities, whether those realities are the products of group or mass communication. In the chapters that follow we shall explore how the media of group and mass communication portray reality in dramatic fashion —through news and entertainment programming on television, popular magazines, movies, art, sports, popular movements, and group life. To make the going easier, it will help us to clarify at this point the logic of dramatic representation.

To say something is logical is simply to note that its parts relate to one another and to the whole in a reasonable, systematic fashion. A scientific account, say Einstein's theory of relativity, possesses a logic; each portion of the explanation complements and does not contradict the other portions. Similarly, the classic example of syllogistic reasoning (all men are mortal; Socrates was a man; therefore, Socrates was mortal) is logical. Dramatic communication also has a logic. Think of any story, movie, or stage play. What are its elements?[20]

1. *Dramatis personae*, or *actors*: the characters of the drama, frequently portrayed as heroes, villains, and fools.
2. *Acts*: what the actors do and say.
3. *Style*: the way the actors portray themselves, through their tone of voice, gestures, expressions, and so on.
4. *Plot line*, or *scenario*: the unfolding story that relates what is happening, to whom, and how.

5. *Scene*: the setting wherein the drama takes place.
6. *Motives*: the aims and purposes attributed to the actors that allegedly cause them to do what they do.
7. *Sanctioning agent*: the principal source that justifies the events, actions, and conclusion of the drama.

In any given drama one or more of these elements may be emphasized, others minimized. For instance, the plot lines of the exploits of Superman—whether in the original comic books, the radio serial, the TV series, or the more recent feature films—have always been less important to the drama than the heroic qualities of the lead character and the virtue of the sanctioning agent, "Truth, justice, and the American way." Acts and styles take a back seat to hero (Luke Skywalker), villain (Darth Vader), and breathtaking scenic effects in *Star Wars* and *The Empire Strikes Back*.

Regardless of emphasis, however, dramatic logic requires a sense of unity in the relationship of these elements. This is achieved primarily through the unfolding of the drama itself, a progression that conforms to the necessities of developing dramatic conflict. Conflict is the struggle emerging from the interplay of opposing forces in the plot, for example, between the villainous J. R. Ewing and virtually every other character in the popular nighttime TV soap opera "Dallas." The ancients, Greeks and Romans, who originated drama compared the plot, or logical sequence, of a drama to the tying and untying of a knot.[21] The tying and untying has a five-part structure: introduction, rising action (or complication), crisis (or turning point), falling action, and denouement (or resolution). The introduction creates the tone, sketches the characters, details the setting, establishes opening events, and supplies nuances necessary for understanding the drama. The pace of the plot picks up, action rises, and opposing forces join the dramatic conflict (the Southern gentry ride off to war in *Gone with the Wind*). Then something happens (as when the temptress Delilah coaxes from Samson the secret of his strength) to provoke a crisis. Action subsides (the aliens from Krypton take control of the world in *Superman II*). But there must be a final resolution in keeping with the overall rhetorical vision evoked by the drama (as when, in TV situation comedies, after laughing for twenty minutes, crying for five, we smile through our tears at the end).

Such are the basics of dramatized communication. But mediated realities unfold before audiences in a particular dramatic format, melodrama. Melodrama emerged as the most popular dramatic form of the nineteenth century. As attested to by soap operas on television ("General Hospital," "All My Children," "Guiding Light" in the daytime, "Dallas" and "Dynasty" at night), comic strips (Dick Tracy, Mary

Worth), adventure novel series (James Bond, Travis McGee), and movies
(*Superman*), the popularity of melodrama is undiminished. Moral justice is at the heart of most melodrama—trials of the virtuous, calumny
of the villainous, good rewarded, evil punished. Suspense is the key—
from certain death to miraculous safety, disgrace to vindication, paradise lost to paradise regained, vanquished to victor. Anxiety is provoked—unrelenting dangers, unexpected threats, hairbreadth escapes.
And characters are clearly labeled—good are good, bad are bad. Finally, happy endings are preferred but not essential (once things have
been put right again on the ranch, we ask, "Who was that masked
man, anyway?"). Tragic endings suffice; as trivia buffs know, even
John Wayne died in some (how many?) of his movies! Or there may be
no clear-cut resolution at all. This is especially the case in serialized
melodrama for, as the popularity of "Dallas" demonstrates, the audience left hanging is the audience kept, even enlarged.

These characteristics are more than qualities of melodrama, they
are requirements. Related as they are to the elements and structure of
dramatic logic, they define what an account must have to be melodramatic. They add up to a "melodramatic imperative."[22] That imperative is a set of requirements frequently imposed by people on events as
they try to account for what really happened. Those requirements fix
the content and structure of fantasy themes and rhetorical visions.
Mediated realities, thus, often carry the aura of soap operas. Is this the
case with mediated *political* realities? The chapters that follow contend
that this is precisely the case. The political world that unfolds daily before our eyes is presented in group and mass communication in melodramatic ways. The realities of political events—presidential campaigns,
the Iranian hostage crisis, the 1979 accident at the Three Mile Island
(TMI) nuclear plant, assassination attempts on public figures, Watergate, the conduct of war, the rise and fall of political dynasties, political
conspiracies, political movements, policy decisions—reach us in
accounts that impose the melodramatic imperative on human events.
T. S. Eliot wrote that we understand nothing until it is dramatized for
us; Shakespeare, that "the play's the thing." If so, we add that mediated politics is soap opera politics. Perhaps in some cases, again to
quote Shakespeare, they may be tales "told by an idiot, full of sound
and fury, signifying nothing."

MEDIATING THE REALITIES OF MEDIATED POLITICS

The idea that political realities are mediated through communication is
not new. It did not originate with Lippmann's concern over Miss Sherwin of Gopher Prairie. It is a theme that runs through much of political
theory, although often muted in modern political science. An early

progenitor of that academic discipline, Arthur F. Bentley, argued that the principal raw materials of political inquiry were linguistic. Bentley was interested in describing government as the *activities* of people, not as static institutions nor as the hidden motives of men. Government for Bentley was always in process—changing, dynamic, in flux. The only way to observe that process was by studying the activities of the politically involved. And the key activity was communication: "Actions, not of individual men, but as wave motions of the linguistic behaviors of men, advancing and receding across the centuries."[23]

In the chapters that follow we examine these "wave motions" as they manifest themselves in political fantasies, rhetorical visions, and melodramas. We shall look first at mass-mediated political realities. Specifically our focus turns initially to the principal source of mediated politics for most Americans, television news. In Chapter 1 we explore the fantasy themes, rhetorical visions, and melodramas in televised news coverage of domestic and foreign crises. In Chapter 2 we examine the mediated world of the political campaign, noting that politicians tailor their appeals to melodramatic requirements. Political history was once something people read about in textbooks. They still do. But much of our political history is now mediated through the art forms of popular culture, something we describe in Chapter 3. Americans love to celebrate their heroes and heroines, political as well as any other; in Chapter 4 we describe the national soap opera of political celebration. Consciously or not, countless people fashion their images of politics through politics as it is depicted in the movies; thus, in Chapter 5 the politics of Hollywood's mediation is the topic. Chapter 6 looks at the politically relevant rhetorical visions in popular sports and closes the discussion of mass-mediated politics. Then, we shift our attention to four areas of group-mediated political fantasies. In Chapter 7 groupthink is the topic, that is, the tendency of people to fantasize in coming to a group consensus on courses of action. Chapter 8 examines the phenomenon of pack journalism, the remarkable consensus in the news media on what is real. There has always been an overlap of religion and politics in this nation, and Chapter 9 describes the politicoreligious visions in that area. Chapter 10 examines the recurring tendency of many groups to explain our politics in conspiratorial ways, fashioning fantasy worlds of friends and enemies. Finally, in a concluding chapter we look back on the fantasyland that is Americans' mediated politics.

In his *Republic* Plato relates the tale of human beings living in an underground den, bound so that they cannot turn their heads. They can see nothing that goes on around them, only the shadows of those things that the fire throws on the cave wall. When they converse they give names to and talk about the shadows of things, thinking they are

naming the real things and not shadows. Suddenly one prisoner is released. The objects that produced the shadows are passed before his
eyes. He is perplexed. He thinks the shadows he formerly saw are
truer than the objects shown to him. Compelled to look at the piercing
light of the fire, he turns away from the objects to the images on the
wall. The shadows are clearer than the objects, again more real. Finally, hauled out to the sunlight, slowly the prisoner adjusts to seeing the
objects for what they are. Yet, pushed back into the cave, blinded by
the sudden darkness, he sees even less than his fellow prisoners who
were not released. The prisoners conclude it is better not to ascend to
the light and would kill anyone forcing them to do so.

Mediated, secondhand reality is one's politics. There is little people
can do about that. But they can examine political fantasies and by recognizing them be more skeptical and wary of what they otherwise take
for granted. There is at least some liberation from the cave of fantasy in
that. But what if no one wants to ascend? We think the risk worth taking in spite of the fate of Plato's prisoner. We hope readers will find
that to be the case as well. Otherwise they may get restless, a prospect
not too bright in light of Plato's little tale.

NOTES

1. Walter Lippmann, *Public Opinion* (New York: Macmillan, 1922), pp. 12–
13. In writing about Miss Sherwin of Gopher Prairie, Lippmann borrowed
from the 1920 novel of Sinclair Lewis, *Main Street*.
2. Paul Watzlawick, *How Real Is Real?* (New York: Random House, 1976).
(Vintage Books)
3. Ibid, p. xi.
4. David L. Altheide and Robert P. Snow, *Media Logic* (Beverly Hills,
Calif.: Sage Publications, 1979), p. 12. The emphasis is in the original.
5. David Hume, *A Treatise of Human Nature* (London: Noon, 1739).
6. *American Heritage Dictionary of the English Language* (New York:
American Heritage Publishing Co., Inc. and Houghton Mifflin Co., 1969), s.v.
"fantasy."
7. Robert M. Goldenson, *The Encyclopedia of Human Behavior* (Garden City,
N.Y.: Doubleday & Co., 1970), s.v. "fantasy"; George A. Theodorson and
Achilles G. Theodorson, *A Modern Dictionary of Sociology* (New York: Thomas Y.
Crowell Co., 1969), s.v. "fantasy." These definitions exemplify the contrast between fantasy and reality-testing.
8. Dennis K. Davis and Stanley J. Baran, *Mass Communication and Everyday Life* (Belmont, Calif.: Wadsworth Publishing Co., 1981), chap. 5. Offers a
full discussion of the distinction between serious and nonserious activity.
9. Thomas L. Lindlof, "Fantasy Activity and the Televiewing Event," in
Dan Nimmo, ed., *Communication Yearbook IV* (New Brunswick, N.J.: Transac-
tion Books, 1980), pp. 277–291.
10. Eric S. Rabkin, ed., *Fantastic Worlds* (New York: Oxford University
Press, 1979).
11. Ibid., p. 3.
12. The reference, as with the title of this section, derives from the popular
ABC television show "Fantasy Island," a fictional place where people go to act

out their fantasies with the aid of the island's proprietor, Mr. Roarke, played by the venerable actor, Ricardo Montalban.

13. Charles S. Peirce, "The Fixation of Belief," in Philip P. Wiener, ed., *Values in a Universe of Chance: Selected Writings of Charles S. Peirce* (Garden City, N.Y.: Doubleday & Co, 1958), pp. 91–112. (Anchor Books)

14. W. Phillips Davison, "The Public Opinion Process," *Public Opinion Quarterly*, 22 (Summer 1958): 93.

15. Hubert J. O'Gorman, "Pluralistic Ignorance and White Estimates for Racial Integration," *Public Opinion Quarterly*, 39 (Fall 1975): 314; Robert K. Merton, *Social Theory and Social Structure* (Glencoe, Ill.: Free Press, 1957), p. 377; Floyd H. Allport, *Social Psychology* (Boston: Houghton Mifflin Co., 1924).

16. Ernest G. Bormann, "Fantasy and Rhetorical Vision: The Rhetorical Criticism of Social Reality," *Quarterly Journal of Speech*, 58 (December 1972): 397.

17. Ibid., 398.

18. Ralph L. Rosnow and Allan J. Kimmel, "Lives of a Rumor," *Psychology Today* (June 1979): 88–92. The definition of rumor used in this discussion is that of Rosnow and Kimmel. See also Tamototsu Shibutani, *Improvised News* (Indianapolis, Ind.: Bobbs-Merrill Co., 1966).

19. Dan Nimmo and James E. Combs, *Subliminal Politics* (Englewood Cliffs, N.J.: Prentice-Hall, 1980). (Spectrum Books)

20. Donald C. Shields, "A Dramatistic Approach to Applied Communication Research," in John F. Cragan and Donald C. Shields, eds., *Applied Communication Research* (Prospect Heights, Ill.: Waveland Press, 1981), pp. 5–13; Kenneth Burke, "Dramatism," in Lee Thayer, ed., *Communication: Concepts and Perspectives* (Washington, D.C.: Hayden Book Co., 1967). (Spartan Books)

21. William Flint Thrall, Addison Hibbard, and C. Hugh Holman, *A Handbook to Literature* (New York: Odyssey Press, 1960).

22. Paul H. Weaver, "Captives of Melodrama," *New York Times Magazine*, April 29, 1976, p. 6.

23. Arthur F. Bentley, "Epilogue," in Richard W. Taylor, ed., *Life, Language, Law: Essays in Honor of Arthur F. Bentley* (Yellow Springs, Ohio: Antioch Press, 1957), p. 212.

Part I
Mass-Mediated Politics

As individuals, people live in the private world of their own hopes and dreams, fears and anxieties, joys and sorrows. But few people exist as isolated individuals. Most of us also live in groups, sharing with others the pleasures and discomforts of group life. In both their private and group lives people depend on the mass media—to inform, entertain, guide, and yield a sense of a larger world than the everyday experiences that private and group matters offer. A large portion of their daily lives thus derives from the mediation of mass communication as well as their personal and group contacts. As noted in the book's introduction, it is not always clear just how much of the mass-mediated world is real, how much fantasy. In Part I we deal with several of the mass-mediated worlds where Americans reside—worlds of crises, electoral conflict, the historical past, filmland fiction, celebrities, and sports. Obviously some of these worlds are of explicit political importance. Others may seem less so, yet readers will find that they too mediate realities of political relevance.

Six decades ago noted political journalist Walter Lippmann wrote that, "Universally it is admitted that the press is the chief means of contact with the unseen environment." Hence, he continued, "It is almost inexplicable that no American student of government, no American sociologist, has written a book on newsgathering." Social scientists are today no longer guilty of ignoring the press and its part in mediating "the unseen environment." Few studies, however, look beyond the news media to the role of TV entertainment programming, Hollywood films, celebrity magazines, and popular sports in creating and mediating politically relevant worlds, real and fantastic. Studies that do exist equivocate, ranging from claims of omnipotence to claims of impotence for the mass media. To the degree that relevant studies

exist, we cite them in Part I. But we warn readers that the state of the art
in the political and communication sciences gives rise to a larger body
of speculations than of tested propositions. Some of our assertions in
Part I—especially in Chapters 3 through 6—are of that nature. They
speak not to the *effects* of the mass media but to the *content* of media
messages that bring to individuals and group members visions of "the
unseen environment" of politics. We trust the good judgment of readers who will remember that the legitimate scientific enterprise consists
of paired activities, that is, the proposing of plausible explanations and
the testing of such ideas. One does not proceed without the other. It is
to that initial task that we now turn.

1

What's Happening?

TV News Reports the Unexpected

Few old enough at the time to recall the event would today fail to remember precisely where they were and how they felt on hearing that the Japanese had bombed Pearl Harbor, December 7, 1941. The same holds for November 22, 1963, the day President John Kennedy was assassinated, or for April 4, 1968, the date of Martin Luther King Jr.'s assassination. Critical, unexpected events mediated through the news etch themselves into our memories for all time. We never forget where we were and what we were doing when we found out about such events.

March 30, 1981 was such a day for many Americans. Again there was an attempt on the life of a president. Once more a bullet found its mark. President Ronald Reagan was wounded while leaving a Washington, D.C., hotel after completing a speaking engagement. But unlike many other unexpected events that provide the raw material of news, this one was unique. Accompanying the president as he departed the hotel that day were cameramen from the nation's television news networks. They captured on film details of the assassination attempt: a glimpse of a suspect being grabbed by security officers, a glance at the gun pointed at the president's limousine, the grimace on the president's face when struck, the blood-soaked head of the president's press secretary, the shouts, confusion, and sounds of pistol fire. Four minutes after the first shot, ABC–TV relayed the news to the nation, shortly thereafter all three TV networks began continuous coverage of the event and its aftermath.

What vision emerged from televised coverage of the crisis surrounding the attempt on Ronald Reagan's life on March 30, 1981? In some respects the vision conformed to what political scientist Doris A. Graber calls the three stages of crisis coverage.[1] When unexpected critical events occur, notes Graber, the news media first transmit uncoordinated messages, often preempting regular programming to report directly from the scene. As time passes reporters find out more information, begin to discern patterns, and develop a coherent story. This constitutes the second stage. Finally, there are efforts to put the event into larger perspective, to discern its long-range consequences.

Although on the scene at the time of the assassination attempt on President Reagan, TV journalists nonetheless provided uncoordinated, confusing messages conforming to Graber's first stage. For forty minutes viewers were assured that the president had not been wounded by the gunfire. Then followed conflicting reports about the seriousness of the injury (one network reported the president was undergoing open-heart surgery when it was open-chest surgery), the caliber of the bullets, the type of weapon, and the character of the alleged assailant. All three networks erred in reporting the death of the president's press secretary, James Brady, from a head wound. Later, learning the report was incorrect, ABC's anchor Frank Reynolds demanded irately of his colleagues, "Let's get it nailed down, somebody!" But even as details came into perspective hours later, confusion remained. Again, the seriousness of the president's injury was a case in point. Network anchors, probing in interviews with surgeons, aired conflicting views of the risks involved in the injury, how it could be handled, and prospects for the president's recovery. On yet another front the networks offered differing views regarding who was in charge of government in the president's absence and the precise details of presidential succession. Finally, even the third stage of coverage of this crisis raised doubts and confusion. The day following the assassination attempt and after the president's surgery, reporters attended a press conference. Presidential aides briefed them on the president's condition, giving assurances that the president was recovering well. Indeed, the president had signed a major government order that very morning. Reporters viewed the signature. One network questioned that it was, in fact, the president's signature. Leslie Stahl of CBS pronounced the signature "shaky," but ABC's Sam Donaldson found it "firm."

In short, the rhetorical vision emerging from TV's coverage of the assassination attempt on President Reagan was one of confusion, contradiction, and at times chaos. This is not an indictment. Coverage of a breaking news story of such magnitude requires quick, often questionable reporting without the luxury of the time to authenticate sources and information. What is the key is not the reasons underlying the fantasy chained out from crisis coverage but the nature of the fantasy itself. For people do act on the basis of such fantasy. In doing so they reinforce the fantasy itself. Again, the Reagan assassination attempt is a case in point. One network, for example, authenticated the report that Press Secretary James Brady had died by accepting its correspondent's eyewitness account that presidential aides were "dissolved in tears." Indeed, they were. But not because they *knew* Brady had died, but because they had *heard* he had died on another network. Thus, a network authenticated a false report by taking as evidence the behavior of people acting on the basis of that false report. Noted correspondent Marvin Kalb (not involved in the incident) said of Brady's aides and TV reporters, "They had no information of their own. They turn to us, we turn to them and we both keep missing. It's a very peculiar arrangement."[2]

It is to that peculiar arrangement that we turn in this chapter. More specifically our focus is on how television news covers the unexpected, that is, the fantasies created as TV news mediates our political realities in crises.

TV NEWS AS FANTASYLAND

Since 1959 the Roper Organization, Inc., a nationwide polling firm, has been conducting surveys of the public's opinion of TV news. Beginning in 1963 a higher proportion of Americans named television as a news source than they did newspapers, radio, magazines, or other people. By 1980 Roper found that 64 percent named TV among the media they rely on for news and 40 percent cited TV as their sole source of news (almost twice that for any other medium). Moreover, Americans regard television as the most believable news medium; TV news has a two-to-one advantage over newspapers as the most credible news medium.[3] Citing TV news as most believable, however, need not imply Americans actually believe everything in the medium. A nationwide Harris Survey in 1981 revealed that only about one in four Americans trust "very much" the national news on TV, the world news, or the news from Washington, D.C. (newspapers receive even lower ratings for trust).[4]

So we have an anomaly, that is, the medium on which most Americans rely and the medium that is the most believable source of news for them, television, is not trusted very much by most of these same people. Why do people rely on what they do not trust very much? To explore that question we need, first, to review briefly why people rely on the mass media for information generally and, second, to explore the characteristics of TV news that make it the major and most believable source.

Media Dependency

In the book's introduction we noted that people are increasingly dependent on the mass media for their versions of reality. We can succintly review that notion by examining what is known as the dependency theory of mass communication.[5] Proponents of this theory argue that in simple societies people's realities stem from their life histories, personal experiences, and social connections. But as society grows more complex, opportunities for firsthand experiences with social and political institutions decrease; moreover, resources for direct involvement are scarce. People have little direct awareness of what happens outside their immediate surroundings. As the mass media become the chief source of information about society at large, people are increasingly dependent on mass communication for visions of what is real and unreal. Under such conditions of media dependence, it follows that (1) the more dependent people are on mass media for information, the more likely they will change their opinions as a result of that information; (2) the more mass-mediated information meets people's needs, the more dependent they are on it and, hence, the more influential the media; and (3) the more developed a society's media, the more people rely on it during periods of social conflict, crisis, and change.

Certainly, television has developed rapidly in the last three decades. There are many consequences of that development. Two are especially noteworthy. The first we have already alluded to, that is, people have grown increasingly dependent on TV as an information source. Second, the logic of television has increasingly become the logic of all the mass media. But what is television's logic? Recall that we designated the logic of mediated realities as essentially a dramatic logic. Within that context each medium possesses a logic of its own, that is, a format for "how material is organized, the style in which it is presented, the focus or emphasis of particular characteristics of behavior, and the grammar of media communication . . . a perspective that is used to present as well as interpret phenomena."[6] For television generally we can readily see that its logic, or format, conforms to the melodramatic imperative described in the book's introduction. That logic also pervades more and more of newspaper and newsmagazine design. Think, for example, of the tendencies of newspapers to adopt more open designs—layouts that appeal to the eye, a clean look, color photographs, compact articles. Or consider content. The logic of *People* magazine is largely that of television. The political men and women of *People*, like so many of the political figures covered by television, are celebrities, people not known necessarily for achievements but "known for well-knownness."[7]

Granted that the logic of television generally is melodramatic, does this apply to news programming as well as TV's entertainment programming? Is not TV news informative and true, TV entertainment fanciful and fiction? Our view is that the logic of TV news is every bit as melodramatic as that of television entertainment programming. It is that melodramatic logic of TV news that attracts audiences. It makes TV the major source of news for most Americans, the sole source for a plurality and the most believable to a majority—even though only one in four trusts TV news very much. What line of reasoning leads to such an argument?

News and Truth

In the same classic work, *Public Opinion*, in which he remarked on the mediated realities of Miss Sherwin of Gopher Prairie, journalist Walter Lippmann took great pains to distinguish between news and truth. They are "not the same thing." Wrote Lippmann, "The function of news is to signalize an event, the function of truth is to bring to light the hidden facts, to set them into relation with each other, and make a picture of reality on which men can act."[8] Hence, "journalism is not a first hand report of raw material, . . . [but a] report of that material *after it has been stylized*."[9] And unless it can be clearly demonstrated that news deals with "accomplished fact, news does not separate itself from the ocean of possible truth."[10]

If news is not truth, what is it? The American philosopher George Herbert Mead provided one answer. He argued that journalism reports "situations through which one can enter into the attitude and experiences of other people." In that respect news is like drama. It can pick "out characters which lie in men's minds," then express "through these characters situations of their own time but which carry the individuals beyond the actual fixed walls which have arisen between them."[11] For Mead most journalism was not *information* journalism, which deals with facts and truth, but *story* journalism, which gives us accounts of things that we find emotionally exciting, aesthetically gratifying, and personally meaningful in our daily lives.[12]

If Mead was correct that most journalism was story journalism, then TV news is certainly so. It is storytelling. Television news employs the logic of dramatic narrative through verbal and nonverbal symbols, sound and visual imagery. Reuven Frank, producer of "NBC Nightly News," once commented:

Every news story should, without any sacrifice of probity or responsibility, display the attributes of fiction, of drama. It should have structure and conflict, problem and denouement, rising action and falling action, a beginning, a middle and an end. These are not only the essentials of drama; they are the essentials of narrative.[13]

Television news thus imposes on reported events a thematic unity consistent with the demands of dramatic logic, a unity that makes those events real-fictions. Real-fictions are compositions of sound and sight that select and organize facts in ways that yield a sense of purpose that might not otherwise exist without the thematic unity imposed by the TV story.[14] The resulting real-fiction is at the same time an entertaining, larger-than-life drama that sparks people's interests, yet one that permits them to relate the larger than life to their everyday lives. Television news thus performs the task Mead assigned journalism, that of giving people the opportunity to soar "beyond the actual fixed walls which have arisen between them."

In this sense TV reporting is a literary act,[15] a continuous search for story lines. Such story lines may incorporate the metaphors and plots of novels, folk traditions, and myths. Indeed, a few scholars argue that TV news stories appeal to broadcasters and viewers alike because of mythic adequacy, that is, the degree that stories are deeply rooted in cultural mythology and exploit appealing aesthetic qualities.[16] Conformity to the requirements imposed by the melodramatic imperative is a key way that producers of TV news, anchors, and correspondents achieve mythic adequacy. The same melodramatic formats available to entertainment programmers are options for producers of TV news: adventure, mystery, romance, pathos, nightmare, comedy, and the like pervade children's programs, sports coverage, soap operas, situation comedies, and docudramas. When faced with an event that requires prolonged storytelling—say a presidential campaign, the seizure of hostages in a foreign country, a threat of war, and so on—a variety of melodramatic formats may be adapted to news coverage, thus imposing a thematic unity (a story) on what might otherwise seem unrelated events.

There is evidence that TV news contains mythic elements. In 1978 a communication scholar, Robert Rutherford Smith, analyzed the weekday evening newscasts of ABC, NBC, a public broadcast station, and a local TV station. The one-week period aired a total of twenty thirty-minute broadcasts. Smith discovered marked patterns that constituted mythical narratives. Among them were:

1. TV reports social reality by creating stories with men as the key actors; in most instances these men are government officials.
2. Government, more frequently than any other group, is the actor in TV narratives.
3. Government is also the group most frequently acted on.

4. Women are treated as members of a mythical chorus, neither acting nor acted on.
5. The actors are portrayed as making decisions, suffering through discomfort, and sometimes catching villains.
6. The emphasis in the stories is on injustice, corruption, and the testing of strength—all common mythical themes.

Concluded Smith:

In the place of sirens, demons, sensations of flying or falling, we have a new narrative: political leaders as an omnipotent elite, beyond both marketplace and law, struggling with each other to determine the rules under which the rest of us must live. The Greek gods on Mount Olympus were no less remote and only slightly more powerful.[17]

Different TV news networks may, of course, adopt different melodramatic formats. Hence, different news organizations may cover identical events, yet tell different stories. For one it may be a tale of pathos, for another a heroic victory over great odds, for yet another a mystery to be unraveled. Regardless of content, however, each melodrama is a fantasy—a symbolic reality created and transmitted through the newsmaking process—that receives different melodramatic presentations by TV news networks offering diverse fantasies for nightly consumption. Hence, to the question, To what can news be likened if not to truth?, one answer is fantasy, the captivating melodramatic creations of the news media that submerge events in an ocean of possible truth. To see how such storytelling, and fantasy chaining, occurs through TV news, we turn to four cases of how TV mediated the realities of critical events.

WHO IS THE ENEMY? COVERAGE OF FOREIGN CRISES

As Doris G. Graber has noted:

Public crises are natural or manmade events that pose an immediate and serious threat to the lives and property or to the peace of mind of large numbers of citizens. . . . They trouble the public's peace of mind even when they threaten no personal harm to most observers.[18]

Long before Miss Sherwin of Gopher Prairie found it impossible to conceive of a war in France without the aid of news stories and photographs, news organizations mediated the realities of foreign crises for the public. In some instances they not only mediated such crises but they also helped produce them. Consider the perhaps apocryphal example of publisher William Randolph Hearst's role in starting the Spanish-American War. Hearst's *New York Journal* and Joseph Pulitzer's

New York World were waging a circulation war. Hearst needed a good story to boost sales. So, he sent artist, Frederic Remington, to Cuba to provide visual accounts of the insurrection against the Spanish. Remington arrived in Cuba, looked around, then wired Hearst: "Everything is quiet. There is no trouble here. There will be no war. I wish to return." Hearst fired back a reply: "Please remain. You furnish pictures. I will furnish war." Shortly thereafter the battleship Maine blew up in Havana harbor. The Spanish said it was an accident. With no evidence, Hearst laid the blame on the "enemy's secret infernal machine," trumpeted for war, and finally got it.[19]

Hearst's coverage of Cuba was but one of many melodramatic scenarios news organizations have used to report foreign crises. During World War II electronic journalism joined print reporting: the legendary CBS correspondent Edward R. Murrow recounted the Battle of Britain each night. Americans viewed melodramatic accounts of major battles through *March of Time* and the *Movietone News*, staples of movie houses in that era. What all of these melodramas had in common was a clear depiction of good guys and bad guys, enemies and friends. In the finest tradition of the melodramatic art, crisis reporting blamed the villains, praised the victims, cheered the heroic. But things grew more complicated after World War II. By the time of America's first televised war in Vietnam (as it has often been called), a new scenario for crisis coverage unfolded, that of "Who's the enemy?"

Vietnam: A Case of Body Counts

In an insightful analysis of news coverage of the Vietnam War, reporter and media critic Edwin Diamond identifies distinct phases.[20] Each might be likened to the sequence of dramatic logic described earlier (p. 14) in our discussion. The phases play out a plot line of "Who's the enemy?"—a plot unified by a daily measurement of enemy casualties. Phase one for Diamond consisted of the "benign ignorance" of the press with respect to Southeast Asia. From the close of World War II until the early 1960s, American journalists rarely visited the Indochinese Peninsula, thought it important, or bothered to link it to U.S. national interests. The scenario that journalists were later to fashion still lay outside the imagination. Diamond's second phase extends from 1961 to 1965. It consisted of a gradual military buildup, one very similar to the rising action of an unfolding drama. News organizations began to regard Vietnam as an American story. Journalists reported favorably on the U.S. commitment to contain communism, prevent a takeover of all of Southeast Asia, and avoid a dominolike fall of nation after nation to the enemy. Between 1965 and 1968 the war intensified to large-scale conflict. As it did, there was a third phase of news coverage, one paralleling the transition from rising action to turning point in drama. Nightly network TV news programs provided viewers with a "living room war" of swooping gunships, firefights, bomb strikes, thatched-roof huts aflame, and displaced families of haggard old people, crying babies, and maimed mothers and fathers. The turning point of coverage came with a fourth phase, the Tet offensive of January–March 1968. Enemy attacks hit each city, town, hamlet, and military installation in South Vietnam. Militarily the thrust resulted in heavy losses to enemy forces. The mediated reality, however, was a "psychological blow" to Americans, one that intensified pressures in the United States to end involvement. The drama's action began to fall as a fifth phase of news coverage began, one extending from 1969 into 1975. Its character was heralded in a telex message from the executive producer of "ABC Evening News," Av Westin, to his Saigon bureau:

I think the time has come to shift some of our focus from the battlefield, or more specifically American military involvement with the enemy, to themes and stories under the general heading: We Are On Our Way Out of Vietnam.[21]

The denouement to the Vietnam melodrama came on April 19, 1975, as TV carried pictures of the last Americans being evacuated by helicopter from the roof of the U.S. embassy in Saigon. President Gerald Ford supplied the tidy resolution by noting we had "closed a chapter in the American experience."

As noted, the content around which the acts and scenes in the melodramatic coverage revolved was a plot of "Who's the enemy?" The melodramatic imperative demands sharp distinctions between "us" and "them." The "us" in the Vietnam War was clear enough, that is, the U.S. forces and the South Vietnamese allies it was our Manifest Destiny to save. What was at issue in the news mediation of Vietnam realities with respect to "us" was not the identity but the motives of that group. During the reporting phase of the gradual military buildup and through a good portion of the phase covering intensified conflict, news coverage was supportive of the "us" in Vietnam. Around the time of the Tet offensive, news coverage of the "us" grew increasingly critical, but there was little confusion regarding who "us" included. The watershed in reporting of U.S. motives in Vietnam was symbolized in 1968 following the Tet offensive when CBS's Walter Cronkite visited Vietnam. From U.S. military officials he received assurances that Tet had been a victory for "us." From his CBS colleagues in the field he heard otherwise, that is, that American involvement had been a mistake from the start, that U.S. officials were deceitful in claiming the war was being won. Cronkite returned to New York to broadcast that the war was a stalemate, victory was not in sight nor would it be, and that it was time to negotiate a settlement "not as victors, but as an honorable people who lived up to their pledge to defend democracy, and did the best they could."[22] "Us" had been wrong, "us" had not won, but "us" remained honorable. Reputedly President Lyndon Johnson took heed of the newly mediated political reality of the "us" espoused by Cronkite and told his press secretary that if he had lost Walter Cronkite he had lost Mr. Average Citizen. That it "was the first time in American history a war had been declared over by an anchorman,"[23] however, is probably as melodramatic a claim as Hearst's wire to Remington.

"Them" was another matter. Diamond points out that in the 1950s and 1960s South Vietnam was teeming with all kinds of groups—northerners, southerners, Communists, resistance fighters, Socialists, religious factions, nationalists, and others. The early term that was applied to these diverse—often conflicting—groups was Vietcong or the Cong, a shortened form of Cong-san (Communist). Although antigovernment forces in South Vietnam called themselves the National Liberation Front (NLF) and rejected the label Vietcong because it identified antigovernment forces as Communist, the name Vietcong stuck. As the military buildup by U.S. forces began, the mediated reality for Americans was simple enough: the enemy consisted of Communists. News stories carried phrases labeling the NLF as the "political arm of the Vietcong," as the "Communist National Liberation Front," and as "Communist" insurgents or guerrillas. By the mid-1960s, as Diamond remarks, Vietcong and NLF (or the Front) vanished as designations for the enemy altogether. "Them" were called Communists, Reds, or received some similar label.

By 1966–1967, however, the enemy was taking on a new mediated reality. The term Vietcong made a comeback and the phrase North Vietnamese troops made an entrance. Both supplanted Communists and Reds. The shift came in part because it was apparent that North Vietnamese troops were indeed in South Vietnam. Moreover, journalists began to recognize that non-Communist elements comprised portions of the Vietcong and that one must account for them. R. W. Apple, Jr., Saigon bureau chief of the *New York Times*, forbade use of the term Communist in any *Times* story on Vietnam, an edict not lost on producers of network TV news as well. As the 1970s began there was another twist, that is, increasingly the enemy was simply called the enemy. However, things came full circle in May 1970 when President Richard Nixon ordered combat forces into Cambodia. His purpose, he announced, was to "drive the Communists from staging areas." Soon the mediated reality repeated itself—the term Communists yielded to Vietcong or North Vietnamese, then, the term enemy made a comeback.

Does it matter who the enemy was in Vietnam? It does. What people call things influences how they act toward those things. A word for something carries with it an image, an iconography. Diamond admits that, "the inability to find a proper name for the enemy was not . . . one of the 'big' themes of the Vietnam War." But, he says, it was not a minor matter either. For that war, he asserts, was one of words and images: "The *iconography* of Vietnam—how it was pictured—helped determine the direction of American policy."[24] And just as "the nature and direction of 'the enemy' remained 'elusive' and 'enigmatic' until the end,"[25] so did the shifting fortunes of American involvement and resolve. Militarily, then, perhaps the inability to label the enemy was not one of the big themes of the war, but melodramatically it was a key aspect of the crisis coverage.

In the Vietnam news melodrama support for "us" shifted and the identity of "them" was never clear. Yet, one theme was repeated in nightly newscasts, one that served to tie the continuing story together night after night no matter what the confusion over winning or losing, involvement or disengagement, friends and enemies. Throughout the war TV news reminded us daily of the number of casualties among "us" and "them." The daily body count was a reminder that some melodramas have no happy endings. It was also an example of another feature of the melodramatic imperative in TV news, the demand for keeping score. The imperative surfaced again in 1979–1980 on another stage, Iran. But it was days of captivity not body count that provided an overriding theme.

Iran: Days of Captivity

On November 4, 1979, U.S. staff and personnel stationed at the American embassy in Iran were taken hostage. For the next 444 days network television news narrated a story unprecedented in its melodramatic proportions. Like the mediated realities of the Vietnam War, those of the Iranian hostage crisis (as it came to be known on nightly news programs) unfolded in several acts, portrayed the good and the bad, and employed melodramatic language.

The hostage crisis received more televised news coverage than any single event since the medium came of age. For the first 43 days after the hostage seizure, the event was the lead story on all three TV news networks' evening broadcasts. Approximately two-thirds of each network's evening newscast involved the hostage story. In addition each network's morning news/information/entertainment show (ABC's "Good Morning America," NBC's "Today," and CBS's "Morning") devoted ample air time to the crisis. There were TV specials and documentaries. PBS's "The MacNeil/Lehrer Report" devoted numerous programs to the topic. And ABC expanded its news coverage with a late-night series "The Iran Crisis: America Held Hostage" that challenged NBC's venerable "Tonight Show" (with Johnny Carson as host) for top spot in viewing ratings. The hostage crisis provided a remarkable opportunity for TV news to mediate the political realities of Americans: "The seizure of the American embassy was tailormade for the American networks. Drama, conflict, international tension rising and falling, open and behind-the-scenes negotiations, American hostages, foreign mobs, oil production, hostage families, a stark and simple confrontation between two sides."[26]

As with the Vietnam War, the phases of coverage of the crisis ebbed and flowed in dramatic pattern.[27] Again, there was a phase of "benign ignorance," one extending from the end of World War II to the 1970s. As with Southeast Asia, press coverage of Iran was sparse. Then came the prerevolutionary phase of 1972–1977. Journalists wrote stories of Iran's drive for modernization, its role in oil production, its international position, and—slowly increasing after 1974—the shortcomings of the Shah's regime and of internal problems. Iran received increased news coverage in 1978–1979 as internal conflict intensified, revolution broke out, the Shah went into exile, and the regime of Ayatollah Khomeini came to power. The hostage seizure in November 1979 suddenly turned the Iranian story into an American crisis melodrama. Subsequent phases of coverage involved saturation accounts of rising and falling hopes for the hostages' freedom in the winter and early spring of 1979–1980, the abortive military rescue attempt in April 1980, the virtual disappearance of the story from TV screens during the presidential election campaign of 1980 (except for rumors of a last-minute preelection possibility of the hostages' release), and—finally—renewed saturation accounts of efforts to secure the hostages' release prior to the inauguration of Ronald Reagan. The denouement of the melodrama came at last on inauguration day, January 20, 1981.

A former U.S. Undersecretary of State, George Ball, commented more than twelve months after the hostage seizure that "Television played it like a soap opera, and made it the greatest soap opera of the year."[28] As any TV viewer knows a soap opera often has many subplots. Television's melodramatic news coverage of the hostage crisis was no exception. The subplots combined to support a general scenario very much like that played out in Vietnam, that is, "Who's the enemy?"

One such subplot can be labeled "Who rules Iran?" At the time of the Iranian revolution in 1978–1979, the American news media described the opposition to the Shah in unflattering terms—"leftist mobs," "black-robed mullahs," and "religious fanatics" engaged in riots, anarchy, and rampage. When the downfall of the Shah disproved press reports that he was "firmly in control," the media quest for the realities of Iranian political power began. The hostage seizure in November 1979 sharpened the question of "Who rules Iran?" Television news offered a variety of candidates—the Ayatollah Khomeini, his Revolutionary Council, the militants, Foreign Minister Bani-Sadr (later President Bani-Sadr), Foreign Minister Ghotbzadeh, the Parliament, Khomeini's opposition, and religious fundamentalists.[29] Finally, not being able to identify (and personify) a specific source of political power in Iran, the news media hit on a simple solution. If no single power ruled, the nation must be in anarchy. Thus, during the five months prior to the April 1980 military rescue effort (a period of negotiations for the hostages' release) when hopes for an end to the crisis intensified only to be disappointed time after time, the mediated reality was that the Iranians could not be trusted because no one was in control.

A second subplot revolved about the question, "Who are the militants?" The word militants was the standard tag given by TV journalists to the group that seized the American embassy. Variations on the theme included activists, student militants, and Leftist militants. But who were they? Marvin Kalb, then diplomatic correspondent for CBS News, supplied an answer, one that had previously surfaced in newspaper accounts as well. Quoting "diplomatic and intelligence experts," Kalb identified the militants as a coalition of Palestinian guerrillas, Iranian extremists, and Islamic fundamentalists. In a TV interview George Ball asserted that the hostage seizure was "orchestrated by well-trained Marxists."

Paralleling the subplots of Iranian political power and the character of militancy was yet another subplot, "What is Islam?" The mediated reality of Islam provided by TV news yielded a negative assessment: Islam was militant, fanatical, dangerous, and anti-American. As Edward W. Said has noted, the iconography of Islam in the news media was one of a combination of oil suppliers, terrorists, and mobs bent on driving out the "great Satan America," chanting "death to Carter," and releasing darkness to engulf light.[30] Commented ABC correspondent Bob Dyk from Iran the day following the takeover of the embassy, a "smouldering anti-American passion" was loose in the Islamic nation.

In relating such subplots in the hostage melodrama, TV news had no trouble labeling heroes, villains, and fools. The heroes were the hostages enduring unknown agonies at the hands of their captors. The villains were the militants acting, said ABC's Sam Donaldson on November 4, with the "blessing of Khomeini," a blessing that ABC's Ted Koppel in the same report found "ominous." The fool, and a pathetic one at that, was the deposed Shah who roved from Mexico to the United States to Panama to Egypt in search of safe haven for exiles. The very label of Shah carried melodramatic implications. He had been an ex-Shah since early 1979. That he retained his title by virtue of the news media carried the implication that the Iranian revolution was either illegitimate or had never really taken place. In addition to heroes, villains, and a fool, there were victims. These were the families of the hostages who, back in the United States, were portrayed endlessly in TV news as "bracing for trouble," having "hopes dashed," and "bearing up under the long ordeal."

In addition to plots, subplots, and a cast of characters, the hostage melodrama on TV news used devices stirring emotions, creating suspense, and heightening expectations. Journalistic language evoked images consistent with melodramatic plot lines. For example, following the failure of the rescue effort in the Iranian desert on April 25, 1980 (the "175th day of captivity"), ABC anchor Max Robinson spoke of how the failed mission was "hardest on the relatives" of the hostages, who were riding an "emotional roller coaster." The next day ABC confirmed the "fears" of the hostages' families by reporting that "militants . . . [had] moved the hostages" from the American embassy, speculating that the captives might be tried before a "hanging judge."

Visual symbols also evoked melodramatic themes. ABC, for example, incorporated a logo of a blindfolded hostage into virtually every account of the hostage crisis. Juxtaposition of visual symbols helped chain out the fantasies created about Iran to wider areas. In typical reports TV news would first depict the chanting crowds outside the American embassy in Teheran, allegedly yelling anti-American slogans. (On one report ABC's Frank Reynolds related the crowd was chanting its "hatred of America," his interpretation of their yelling "God is great.") This was followed by a filmed report of Iranian students in the United States chanting support for the Iranian revolution and clashing with anti-Iranian Americans. Such visuals left several impressions—that the enemy was in the United States as well as in Iran, that all Iranian students in the United States agreed with the hostage seizure, and that America was rife with violent, anti-Iranian sentiment.[31]

Television coverage of the hostage crisis had its critics. Some argued that TV news had overplayed the story, focusing too much attention on it. George Ball, for instance, opined that TV had played the situation up so that it became the central issue of American foreign policy to the exclusion of more pressing concerns. Other critics noted the one-sided character of news coverage; it was largely anti-Iranian, anti-Khomeini, anti-Islamic, and antirevolutionary. Moreover, it tended to be pro-Shah, pro-U.S. Government's point of view, and (in the early stages) pro-Carter administration. Critics also noted that the visual emphasis largely excluded a thorough analysis of the background and context of America's earlier involvement in Iran, the *politics* of Iranian rule, the diversified and conflicting factions in Iran and Islam, and the viewpoint of the revolutionaries. Finally, critics argued that television journalism had been gullible and manipulated.

Although the televised demonstrations outside the American embassy were staged nonevents, TV reported them anyway. When the bodies of those Americans killed in the aborted rescue attempt were displayed by the Iranians for purposes of achieving television exposure, American networks carried the film. Mediated realities were orchestrated realities.

Whatever the criticism, the soap opera played out the full scenario. And, unlike Vietnam, there was a happy ending. The television networks exploited the final act, the release of the hostages and their return, to the fullest extent that dramatic license would allow. In the last week of the "444 days of captivity," nightly network news programming focused heavily on the hostage release. In addition the three major networks added thirty-seven hours of special coverage. The new kid on the block, the twenty-four hour Cable News Network, dealt almost exclusively with the hostage story during that period. All this emphasis on the denouement provided three subplots. First, there was the suspense over whether the hostages would *really* be set free this time or would there be a snag and the Iranians renege? Second, if released, would the hostages be victims of the Stockholm syndrome, an alleged emotional malady characterized by depression, strong dependency needs, and exhaustion when captives are freed from their captors. Third, after their release, TV news made much of alleged cruel and brutal treatment of the hostages by their captors. As it turned out there was no snag, no Stockholm syndrome, and stories over barbarous treatment vanished quickly. For TV news the crisis was over and stories about Iran, just as after 1975 stories about Vietnam, were as hard to see on the nation's TV screens as the celluloid images in movie houses once the film projector is turned off.

THE HORRORS TONIGHT:
TV NEWS AND DOMESTIC CRISES

We said earlier that in adapting to the melodramatic imperative different television news networks might use different melodramatic formats to achieve mythic adequacy. Such diversity is particularly apparent in TV coverage of domestic crises. Two cases suffice to illustrate such differences.

Technological Fables

It was 4:00 A.M. on the morning of Wednesday, March 28, 1979. Ten miles southeast of Harrisburg, Pennsylvania, sat Three Mile Island (TMI), locale of two nuclear power plants designated TM–1 and TM–2. The TM–2 plant was operating at 97 percent capacity. Suddenly a series of pumps that feed water through the steam generators of the plant, producing electricity and cooling the nuclear fuel core, shut off. Thus began the incident that became "the accident" that resulted in a major news story of domestic crisis. In the next month the three major TV networks devoted almost six and one-half hours of all their nightly news programs to coverage of TMI, just one and one-half hours less time than they had devoted to coverage of all nuclear energy stories in the previous decade.

The accident at TMI certainly had the elements of a major news story. It was a story that abounded in rumors, conflicting statements from officials of government and the nuclear industry, uncertainty and fear about radiation releases, the likelihood of a mass evacuation, the threat of explosion from an alleged hydrogen bubble trapped in the reactor, and the possibility of a nuclear meltdown. The film *The China Syndrome* (about an accident at a nuclear facility) released earlier in the year was no more gripping in its fictional suspense than the events at TMI. Life it seemed was imitating art. The provost of a university located near TMI captured the flavor of the event:

Never before have people been asked to live with such ambiguity. The TMI accident—an accident we cannot see or taste or smell—is an accident that is invisible. I think the fact that it is invisible creates a sense of uncertainty and fright on the part of people that may well go beyond the reality of the accident itself.[32]

There are various ways to examine TV news coverage of TMI. For example, the Media Institute analyzed the content of nightly TV news coverage of the accident from March 28 to April 20, 1979. The study classified all reports on TMI in one of five ways:

1. News reports covered the who, what, where, when, and why facts of the event.
2. Peripheral reports dealt with insignificant background, color, or opinion material that was not necessary for understanding the event.
3. Perspective reports included factual explanatory information contributing to understanding.
4. News/peripheral combinations.
5. News/perspective.

Using this scheme, 67 percent of all TV news reports on TMI were news, 7 percent news/peripheral, 11 percent peripheral, 12 percent news/perspective, and 4 percent perspective.[33]

Such findings tell us that news dominated TV reports on the accident, but they say nothing about the format of such mediated realities nor if all three major television networks reported the same realities. A study undertaken by a task force of a presidential commission appointed to investigate the accident at TMI is more helpful in this respect. That study analyzed the content of TV news reports for the first week of the accident and classified statements in those reports as either "reassuring" or "alarming" to viewers. It found that for all networks reassuring statements outweighed alarming ones by a 59 to 41 ratio. There were slight network differences. CBS and NBC reports each contained 62 percent reassuring statements, ABC's ratio was 55 to 45 reassuring over alarming.[34]

But how reassuring or alarming are the overall visions of reality presented by the networks and do those visions differ? Yet, another study yields an understanding of those matters. It analyzed the content of all nightly network TV coverage between March 28 and April 30, 1979.[35] Its purpose was to contrast the various story lines, or melodramas, contained in reports on TMI. A variety of rhetorical traditions characterize American journalism. At least four of these are aesthetic in tone, contain melodramatic elements, and evoke certain types of fantasies. Basically these are:

The informative tradition. Stories in the informative tradition emphasize factual information. They stem from a long tradition of wire service journalism that reports the objective facts of who, what, when, where, and how. The information is verified either through documentation (on TV this often means showing copies of "official reports") or quotations from "reliable sources." The facts are reported in a calm, dispassionate, reassuring way. The vision evoked is of events that are awesome, yet understandable and manageable. The managers are an elite of officials, scientists, technocrats, and experts who can be trusted to do the right things.

The sensationalist tradition. Some stories alarm, frighten, threaten, provoke, anger, and sadden. In the tradition of fear and pathos they tug at the heartstrings. The human interest story that emphasizes conflict, suffering, and personal loss is but one example. The vision evoked is one of troubled times, the good intentions of the populace face the menace of untrustworthy rulers victimizing the ruled.

The feature story tradition. Feature stories focus on context and the relationship between news events and larger issues. They narrate in a style that is calming and reassuring, not threatening and alarming. They invite people to see that a variety of forces, some good and some bad, shape destinies. They offer a vision not so much of being able to manage affairs (as do informative stories) or being victimized (as do sensationalist accounts) but as being resigned to take what comes along and make the most of it.

The didactic tradition. Didactic accounts stress explanation and education. They tell how things work, how they are built, how they can be used. The style is of the elementary school teacher breaking down complexities into simplified parts. Mysterious human contrivances and motives can be grasped, diagrammed, memorized. Once the magic is gone people can survive.

These four traditions offer categories for classifying the manifest content of TV reports about TMI. Overall the three networks devoted about equal time to accounts that informed, sensationalized, featured, or explained TMI events. But there were marked differences among the TV networks in coverage. Each reported a different reality of TMI: CBS was informative, ABC sensationalist, and NBC instructive.

Of the air time devoted to reports on TMI by "CBS Evening News," 44 percent stressed factual information, whereas 22 percent was sensationalist, 23 percent feature, and 11 percent didactic. The CBS reports typically consisted of interviews with energy officials, scientists, and technicians. Visuals evoked the imagery of government offices, scientific laboratories, and technicians hard at work coping with problems. A vision of professional competence emerged, a fable of experts acting as responsible members of the community to bring technological dangers under control. Implicit was a reaffirmation of faith in trustworthy elites, beneficial technology, and orderly society and, thus, a manageable reality.

The CBS vision was implicit not only in the individual reports of anchors and correspondents but also even more so in the juxtaposition of those accounts. Night after night the scenario was one of anchor Walter Cronkite saying, in effect, "Gee whiz! Things are bad." CBS correspondents would then follow with painstaking factual reports that said, "Yes, things are bad but don't panic for the experts can manage. Here's why." A much reassured Cronkite would then close with a comforting, "And that's the way it is." For example, when the TMI crisis reached its most intense period on March 30 there were reports of a possible meltdown, a mass evacuation. An alarmed Cronkite came on the air:

The world has never known a day quite like today. It faced the considerable uncertainties and dangers of the worst nuclear power plant accident of the atomic age. And the horror tonight is that it could get much worse. It is not an atomic explosion that is feared. The experts say that is impossible. But the spectre was raised of perhaps the next most serious kind of nuclear catastrophe —a massive release of radioactivity. The Nuclear Regulatory Commission cited that possibility with an announcement that, while it is not likely, the potential is there for the ultimate risk of a meltdown at the Three Mile Island atomic power plant outside Harrisburg, Pennsylvania.

CBS correspondents, however, followed Cronkite's alarming lead-in by emphasizing what the experts said about a meltdown, concluding that, indeed, "it is not likely"; things would improve. Coverage ended with a calm, less strident Cronkite in a picture of bemused repose.

For ABC the accident at TMI was a sensational story. Almost two-thirds of their air time devoted to TMI reports was sensationalist, about one-fourth was informative. ABC combined metaphors, images, analogies, and verbal/nonverbal messages into an intense melodrama much like the fable of Frankenstein's monster. Whereas CBS trusted experts, ABC went instead to the townspeople, villagers, and schoolchildren. Human reaction to the event rather than the event itself was the story. Typical reports pictured an on-the-scene correspondent facing the camera with the nuclear plant's cooling towers in the background. Visuals of empty schoolyards, residents leaving the area, milk cows grazing in the plant's shadow (for a story about possible milk contamination) evoked images of trouble. For ABC there was much to fear —radioactivity, toxic gases, poisoned milk, polluted water, hydrogen explosions, core meltdown, evacuations over clogged highways, and threatening wind currents. Reports of official reassurances carried skeptical overtones. Uncertainty, ambiguity, and fear arousal constituted the leading motif of ABC accounts.

Again the juxtaposition of anchor/correspondent reports reinforced the story line. Anchor Frank Reynolds of ABC would lead with a message of "Good grief! Things are bad and could get worse." ABC correspondents would follow with a series of reports showing things indeed getting worse. On March 30 Reynolds opened with:

The news from Harrisburg, Pennsylvania, nuclear energy plant is worse tonight. For the first time an official of the Nuclear Regulatory Commission said today there is the possibility, though *not yet* the probability, of a meltdown of the reactor core. In plain language, that would be a catastrophe!

Follow-up reports evoked the not-yet and impending-catastrophe themes to portray an overall drama of fright, panic, and disaster.

For NBC the TMI story was part feature, part education. NBC air time devoted 54 percent of its coverage to features, 29 percent to didactic reports. There was a division of emphasis between anchors and correspondents. For instance, 60 percent of correspondent reports employed the feature motif to 28 percent for anchors, whereas 70 percent of anchor time was didactic compared with 20 percent of correspondent coverage. NBC features emphasized lengthy interviews with groups of people—both experts and men-in-the-street. But people talked less to reporters than to one another. There was minimum editing of videotaped conversations. Talking heads (persons speaking directly to the camera in a rambling, uninterrupted fashion) were typical of NBC features. The didactic reporting by NBC anchors had two key characteristics. First, the anchors employed casual, measured speaking voices paced in low-key tones, punctuated with numerous pauses, and yielding an impression of detachment. Second, anchors strained to make complexities clear, combining professorial calm with colloquial expressions. John Chancellor, for instance, took great pains—and much air time—to explain with visuals how a nuclear power plant was like a teakettle.

The combination of didactic anchors and feature-oriented correspondents made for an assuring, nonthreatening series of accounts about TMI. "Ah shucks," say the NBC anchors, "things are bad but maybe not too bad if we learn how things work." To which NBC correspondents chorus, "Ho hum, yes things are bad but life goes on." Thus, on March 30 while Cronkite spoke of "the horror tonight" and Reynolds of "catastrophe," Chancellor in a dry, detached delivery almost without inflection said:

There was serious trouble today at the Three Mile Island nuclear plant in Pennsylvania, trouble serious enough to cause the evacuation of small children and pregnant women from a five-mile area around the endangered plant. The problem is that it is more difficult than had been thought to cool the radioactive fuel inside the power plant, and until it is cooled, it is very dangerous. The situation was described this afternoon as stable, but the experts are going to have to decide in the next day or so just how to cool the nuclear material, and there's no option they have that's guaranteed to be safe.

Three networks, three styles, three visions, three realities: CBS's world of trustworthy elites, ABC's world of beleaguered masses, and NBC's world of the calm, resigned educated. Those visions are not confined to TMI. Consider another crisis, one of actual rather than potential catastrophe.

The Crash of Flight 191

On Friday, May 25, 1979, an American Airlines DC–10, Flight 191 from Chicago to Los Angeles, crashed on takeoff, killing all passengers and crew members. It was the worst air crash in U.S. aviation history. And, for the next seven weeks, the crash of Flight 191 and its aftermath was to unfold as yet another opportunity for TV news to mediate the realities of crisis.

First, the essentials. As Flight 191 made its ascent from Chicago's O'Hare International Airport, an engine fell off. Why? That question was to vex investigators for weeks, force repeated groundings of all DC–10s in the United States and other nations, inconvenience thousands of airline travelers, breed conflict among government officials, yield financial losses to airlines, provoke actions from a variety of interest groups, and raise doubts about air safety. In short, the crash of Flight 191 had ingredients of a good news story—conflict, ambiguity, widespread concern, action and reaction. As in the case of TMI, however, there was not one story but three—informative, sensationalist, educational. Again, CBS recounted the tale of technological expertise solving a puzzle: what caused the DC–10 crash and how could the problem be corrected. On the other hand ABC reported the confusion and bungling of government and industry officials; once again the populace was at the mercy of technocrats. And NBC told the story of the DC–10—its history, design, construction, financial prospects—and of the plurality of groups concerned with its future.

Of the total air time (a little over three hours) devoted to the DC-10 story from May 25 to July 13, 1979, by the news networks, 44 percent was informative, 32 percent sensationalist, 19 percent feature, and 5 percent didactic. As with TMI, the bulk of informative coverage was with CBS, fully three-fourths of story time classified as informative. The factual information emphasized technology. For example, on the date of the crash CBS superimposed upon the television screen a running transcript of the dialogue contained in taped recordings made while the aircraft was in flight, and within the aircraft itself. The picture on the screen at the time of the superimposing was of a running tape recorder—the equivalent of documentation on which informative stories depend. Later reports quoted from "authoritative directives." Experts emerged as "reliable sources"—government officials, flight data technicians, Federal Aviation Administration (FAA) investigators, FAA inspectors, the words of a federal judge. Correspondents reported from the steps of a score of government office buildings. When the fleet of DC–10s was grounded for inspection and modification, CBS provided factual details of the number and type of air craft involved, the grounding procedure, and the clearance procedures. The search for—and the correction of—DC–10 defects was for CBS conducted in congressional hearings, meetings of the National Transportation Safety Board, laboratory wind tunnels, countless government and industry documents. Fittingly, the crisis ended for CBS when FAA head Langhorne Bond announced he had "resolved all safety questions" regarding the DC–10. Reported CBS anchor Roger Mudd, experts had "unleashed the DC–10."

For ABC human interest was the focus of the story. Seventy percent of ABC coverage was in the sensationalist category, most of the remainder informative. It was a "holiday crowded" airplane that crashed. ABC covered Memorial Day services "for the victims" and pictured "neighbors still in shock." Anchor Max Robinson recounted the tale of a "collie named Charlie" whose owners had died in the crash; as Robinson related the tale, the camera panned from Charlie to the empty swings and playground where Charlie's young friends had once been. As with TMI, technology and technocrats were the villains of the ABC melodrama. "DC–10s have had problems all along," reported ABC science editor Jules Bergman. Small wonder that the technical design of the crashed plane had failed—a "missing bolt," "the fitting where disaster began," "faulty phylon mountings," "sheared hydraulic lines." And, when efforts were made to correct problems of grounded DC–10s, said Bergman, new problems were "caused by inspections." Reports of conflicts between, and confusion among, officials and engineers appeared nightly, scarcely the picture of cool technocratic competence witnessed by viewers of CBS. The grounding of the DC–10s was for ABC a story of distressed passengers with serious doubts about their safety, not a story of efforts to get the fleet back in the air. Finally, when the grounding order was lifted on July 13, ABC emphasized that on the first DC–10 flight only "100 were on board" and, then, closed with an interview with one man who refused to take the flight.

For NBC the crash of Flight 191 was a feature story. Forty-two percent of the network's coverage could be so classified, another one-fourth informative. NBC covered the technical side of the story by detailed visual closeups of engine mountings, phylon assemblies, wing retractors, and mechanical linkages. Government action was depicted in coverage of lengthy presentations by witnesses at hearings—again, in the talking-head motif. Passenger inconvenience was portrayed not by interviews with passengers but by picturing passengers talking with one another. As DC–10s were inspected, John Chancellor reported with professorial detachment the number that had "passed examinations" and that had "flunked the exams." Frequently reports of the day's news were framed in a fashion to summarize historically the context of all that had preceded it, not only since the crash on May 25 but also with respect to the design and manufacture of the DC–10s, their location throughout the world, the role of the FAA, the part played by congressional hearings, and the nature of federal judicial intervention. And when on July 13 the first DC–10 to fly after grounding took off, NBC had a camera crew not merely at the air terminal (ABC did, CBS did not) but also took the crew aboard the flight and showed passengers conversing with one another during the flight.

Fuel pumps did fail at TM–2. Flight 191 did crash. However, what people learn of such "horrors tonight" depends less on the happenings themselves than how TV news networks tell their stories. What people know, then, depends on where they turn their TV dials. Or, is it possible they actually know nothing?

CONCLUSION: ACQUAINTANCE WITH,
NOT KNOWLEDGE ABOUT

Seeing is believing, or so the adage goes. The adage makes as much sense with TV news as with direct personal experience. Television news offers credible visions of reality even though they are mediated rather than firsthand accounts. In some ways they are even more believable. Experience, after all, often produces insoluble problems, complex solutions, a sense of confusion. The good, bad, and beautiful overlap; heroes, villains, and fools are not easily sorted out; what seems to make sense today may not do so tomorrow. Not so with TV news. The dictates of the melodramatic imperative call for a clear plot line, sharply delineated characters, simply defined problems, no confusion over causes, and tailor-made solutions.

Seeing is believing in TV news, but it is not knowing. Four decades ago sociologist Robert E. Park wrote about the nature of news and of knowledge.[36] Park had been a journalist before taking up a teaching career so that he had both a practical and theoretical grasp on things. What news does, he said, is give people an "acquaintance with" events. It does not provide a "knowledge about" them. A person is acquainted with something or someone when it is called to one's attention. It is a superficial relationship, as when one might be acquainted with the fact that Springfield is the capital of Illinois or with the checkout clerk at the supermarket. The acquaintance may be even more detailed than that, but it scarcely can be likened to an intimate understanding of events or persons. Knowledge, however, does imply a depth of understanding. To know a person is to be far more than merely an acquaintance. Knowledge implies familiarity with backgrounds, origins, implications, and consequences of things. Knowledge is not simply a glimpse of things but a theoretical grasp as well, a grasp of complexities as well as simplicities, of patterns and contradictions, of alternatives rather than single explanations.

There was no TV news when Park wrote. His distinctions, however, are even more valid today. Television news is an acquaintance medium not a source of knowledge. The headline service that is nightly network news calls things to viewers' attention and tells a neatly packaged tale about them. One can expect about as much knowledge from TV news as from any twicetold tale. Consider the four cases described in this chapter—Vietnam, Iran, TMI, and the DC-10. The unfolding melodramas captured viewers' interests, gave them a version or versions of what was happening, and a tidy resolution of problems. Thus, in Vietnam came the "end of an era," in Iran "day 1 of freedom after 444 days of captivity," at TMI the "all clear" for residents to return, and the "unleashing of the DC–10." Thereafter, each item all but vanished from the news. Each crisis had served its melodramatic purposes and, because no longer a crisis, no longer news. But just as one would scarcely claim knowledge of home construction after hearing the fable of the "Three Little Pigs," one would hardly claim knowledge of the four crises from TV coverage.

Television news provides single pieces of information on a nightly basis. It unifies that fragmentary communication, not by building a body of understanding based on a testable theory that explains events, but by weaving bits and pieces into an appealing story. Unlike a scientific explanation that must account for diversified, even contradictory, facts, TV news is selective. What fits the plot line best receives emphasis; what does not, receives less coverage or is ignored. The appeal is not to understanding but to imagination.[37] We have seen this to be the case in crisis coverage; in the following chapter we explore how it works with more routine political coverage as well.

NOTES

1. Doris A. Graber, *Mass Media and American Politics* (Washington, D.C.: Congressional Quarterly, 1980), chap. 8.

2. Harry F. Waters, "TV News Under the Gun," *Newsweek* (April 13, 1981): 104, 107. The Kalb quotation appears on p. 107.

3. "The Public's Opinion of TV," *Broadcasting* (April 13, 1981): 84–89.

4. The Harris Survey, "Trust of Media Shows Decline," *Knoxville Journal* (July 2, 1981): p. A–5.

5. S. J. Ball-Rokeach and M. L. DeFleur, "A Dependency Model of Mass Media Effects," *Communication Research*, 3 (January 1976): 3–21.

6. David L. Altheide and Robert P. Snow, *Media Logic* (Beverly Hills, Calif.: Sage Publications, 1979), p. 10.

7. Daniel J. Boorstin, *The Image: a Guide to Pseudo-Events in America* (New York: Harper & Row, 1964), p. 57. (Colophon Books). See also William S. Maddox and Robert Robins, "How *People* Magazine Covers Political Figures," *Journalism Quarterly*, 58 (Spring 1981): 113–115.

8. Walter Lippmann, *Public Opinion* (New York: Macmillan, 1922), p. 358.

9. Ibid., p. 347.

10. Ibid., p. 340.

11. George Herbert Mead, *Mind, Self, and Society* (Chicago: University of Chicago Press, 1934), p. 257.

12. See Edwin Diamond, "Disco News," *Washington Journalism Review*, 1 (September/October 1979): 26–28.

13. Quoted in Edward Jay Epstein, *News from Nowhere* (New York: Random House, 1974), pp. 4–5. (Vintage Books)

14. Walter R. Fisher, "A Motive Theory of Communication," *Quarterly Journal of Speech*, 56 (April 1970): 132. See also David M. Berg, "Rhetoric, Reality, and Mass Media," *Quarterly Journal of Speech*, 58 (April 1972): 255–263 and Robert Darnton, "Writing News and Telling Stories," *Daedalus*, 104 (Spring 1975): 175–194.

15. David L. Eason, "Telling Stories and Making Sense," *Journal of Popular Culture*, 15:2 (Fall 1981): 125–129.

16. John Shelton Lawrence and Bernard Timberg, "News and Mythic Selectivity: Mayaguez, Entebbe, Mogadishu," *Journal of American Culture*, 2 (Summer 1979): 328.

17. Robert Rutherford Smith, "Mythic Elements in Television News," *Journal of Communication*, 29 (Winter 1979): 82.

18. Graber, *Mass Media and American Politics*, op. cit., p. 225.

19. The story is recounted in Phillip Knightley, *The First Casualty* (New York: Harcourt Brace Jovanovich, 1975), pp. 55–56.

20. Edwin Diamond, *The Tin Kazoo* (Cambridge: M.I.T. Press, 1975), pp. 113–129.

21. Quoted in Diamond, Ibid., p. 126.

22. Quoted in Gary Paul Gates, *Air Time: The Inside Story of CBS News* (New York: Berkley Publishing Corp., 1978), p. 221.

23. David Halberstam, *The Powers That Be* (New York: Alfred A. Knopf, 1979), p. 514.

24. Diamond, *The Tin Kazoo*, op. cit., p. 123.

25. Ibid., p. 129.

26. Frederic B. Hill, "Crisis Management with an Eye on the TV Screen," *Washington Journalism Review*, 3 (May 1981): 27.

27. On the phases of news coverage see Barry Rubin, "Iran," *Washington Journalism Review*, 2 (April 1980): 35–39; and Edward W. Said, *Covering Islam* (New York: Pantheon Books, 1981).

28. *Newsweek* (November 17, 1980): 57.

29. Edward W. Said, "Iran," *Columbia Journalism Review*, 18 (March/April 1980): 23–33.

30. Said, *Covering Islam*, op. cit., chap. 2.

31. David Altheide, "Network News: Oversimplified and Underexplained," *Washington Journalism Review*, 3 (May 1981): 28–29.

32. Quoted in "The Need for Change: The Legacy of TMI," *Report of the President's Commission on the Accident at Three Mile Island* (Washington, D.C.: U.S. Government Printing Office, 1979), p. 81.

33. Media Institute, "Television Evening News Covers Nuclear Energy: A Ten Year Perspective" (Washington, D.C.: Media Institute, 1979).

34. "Report of the Public's Right to Information Task Force," *Staff Report to the President's Commission on the Accident at Three Mile Island* (Washington, D.C.: U.S. Government Printing Office, 1979).

35. The material reported here on TV news coverage of TMI and in the next section on TV news coverage of the DC–10 crash are based on a study conducted by the authors in 1980–1981. Details of the analysis appear in Dan Nimmo and James E. Combs, "'The Horror Tonight:' Network Television News and Three Mile Island," *Journal of Broadcasting*, 25 (Summer 1981): 289–293; Dan Nimmo and James E. Combs, "Fantasies and Melodramas in Television Network News," *Western Journal of Speech Communication*, 46 (Winter 1982): 45–55; and James Combs and Dan Nimmo, "The Return of Frankenstein: The Aesthetic of Three Mile Island Coverage by ABC Evening News," *Studies in Popular Culture*, 4 (Spring 1981): 38–48.

36. Robert E. Park, "News as a Form of Knowledge," *American Journal of Sociology*, 45 (March 1940): 669–686.

37. Robert Petrognani, "Politics as Imagination," *Communication*, 5 (April 1980): 239–243. See also two selections in Elie Abel, ed., *What's News* (San Francisco: Institute for Comparative Studies, 1981): Edward Jay Epstein, "The Selection of Reality," pp. 119–132; and William A. Henry III, "News as Entertainment: The Search for Dramatic Unity," pp. 133–158.

A Man for all Seasons

The Mediated World of Election Campaigns

It is a five-minute biographical film, one that many Americans viewed on their TVs early in the 1980 presidential campaign. It opens with Ronald Reagan accepting his party's nomination. A flashback takes the viewer to pictures of the candidate's youth in "America's heartland, small-town Illinois," to Hollywood where Ronald Reagan attracted audiences because he was "so clearly one of them," to his World War II military record, to Reagan's work as a "dedicated union man," and, then, to his success as California's governor after taking over "a state in crisis." The overall message: "Governor Reagan dealt with California's problems. He will do as much for the nation."

There was nothing particularly unusual about the Reagan TV ad. Candidates for public office routinely employ a variety of spot advertising, minidocumentaries, lengthy biographical sketches, televised town meetings, call-in radio shows, and other electronic devices to campaign. Other propaganda pops up in brochures, newspaper advertising, billboards, yard signs, lapel buttons, bumper stickers, even— would you believe?—on toilet paper. Considerable time, money, and artistic talent is expended on convincing voters that each candidate is a man or woman for all seasons, capable of anything the times, situation, and constituents demand.

Not only have candidates' propagandistic appeals become routine but so also has the coverage of election campaigns by the news media. Thus, for example, studies of recent presidential campaigns repeat what is becoming an old refrain: the news media devote more coverage to the horserace (who is winning, who is losing) than to the substance of the campaign, to the personas of the candidates than the issues that divide them, to outcomes than process, and to the day-by-day events of the campaign than enduring trends.[1] One political scientist argues that news coverage is so routine that there is a twelve-year cycle in presidential elections.[2] First, the news media portray a campaign (say, 1936, 1948, 1960, 1972) as one of conflict—a raw struggle for power dividing the nation. Four years later (1940, 1952, 1964, 1976) there is a campaign of conscience; principle dominates over politics, candidates appeal to the nation's moral fiber and rectitude while promising the people to restore decency to government. Four more years pass and the media presentation of the presidential campaign shifts to an emphasis on conciliation; the stress is binding the nation's wounds, bringing Americans together—tolerance, comfort, good will, and confidence in the future (1944, 1956, 1968, 1980).

Like fantasies, cyclical descriptions of how things happen simplify complexities; it is tempting to force campaigns into the conflict-conscience-conciliation cycle if the electoral year rather than the substance of the campaign so demands. The point, however, is not that a cyclical pattern exists to presidential elections (it probably does not), but that campaigns are so ritualized that one could suspect it did.

CAMPAIGNS AS RITUAL DRAMA

Whether mediated through campaign propaganda emanating from the candidates or the news stories of journalists, or some combination of both, election campaigns are ritual dramas. A ritual is simply a series of acts that, for the most part, are regularly and faithfully performed time and time again. Religious ceremonies, administering the oath of office to public officials, playing the national anthem prior to sporting events, the salute to the flag—all exemplify public rituals. When the elements of a drama repeatedly relate to one another in a ritualistic fashion, we have a ritual drama.

Oriental theater is a good example of ritual drama. The drama not only entertains but repeats myths, legends, and stories of why things are as they are, why people and gods do as they do. The dramas sometimes feature people, sometimes puppets. In either case they are ritualistic, conforming to the audience's demand that the same stories be retold over and over in precisely the same ways. One form of ritual drama is the seasonal ritual. Just as the rotation of spring, summer, fall, and winter seasons brings a sense of continuing renewal of nature, dramas of seasonal ritual give a sense that the nation is reborn. The drama brings together the ideals, principles, and aspirations of a people, recalling for them that for which they stand and what they can achieve. The seasonal ritual revives the vitality of a population, reminding them anew of their greatness.

Students of archaic societies have argued that government might have originated in ritual, that the first kings were skilled in ritualism and magic.[3] Be that as it may, there is certainly a ritualistic quality about much of our politics. Election campaigns can be likened in America to seasonal rituals that seek "periodically to renew" America's "vitality and thus ensure its continuance."[4] Consider presidential elections. They consist of dramas about an ideal community that we have either lost and must regain (recall Ronald Reagan's nostalgic calls in 1980 for the return of America's greatness) or have yet to find. By renewing the belief that the story has a happy ending, that is, that greatness can be found or regained, the seasonal ritual of the presidential campaign plays out its quadrennial scheduling. We explore three aspects of that seasonal drama—campaign fantasy themes, melodramas, and scenarios.

THE 1,000 PERCENT MISUNDERSTANDING: A CAMPAIGN FANTASY

We begin by going back to 1972. The contest was between the incumbent team of President Richard Nixon and Vice President Spiro Agnew for the Republicans and Senators George McGovern, seeking the presidency, and Thomas Eagleton, running for the vice presidency, for the Democrats. Or so it started out. But before the contending tickets had even squared off in earnest, events overwhelmed the Democrats and a mediated fantasy overwhelmed events. Vice presidential candidate Thomas Eagleton resigned from the Democratic ticket in what came to be called the Eagleton Affair. Analysis of that affair, as Ernest Bormann notes, "reveals the awesome power of the electronic media to provide, in the form of breaking news, the dramatizations that cause fantasies to chain through large sections of the American electorate and that thus provide the attitude reinforcement or change that results in voting behavior which elects a president and a vice president."[5]

We have noted earlier that mediated political realities are symbolic, that is, they consist of a set of symbols purporting to represent the way things are, symbols that people take for granted *are* real. A political party seeking power forges an identity and makes propagandistic appeals accordingly. Those symbolic statements constitute the rhetorical vision of the party. Bormann points out that one element frequently appearing in such party visions is the term new. Democrats have a long history of identifying themselves as new—the New Freedom of Woodrow Wilson, New Deal of Franklin Roosevelt, and so on. In the 1972 campaign the McGovern forces spoke much of a New Politics. As a rhetorical vision, the New Politics stood for a movement of good against evil. The vision foresaw 1972 as a last chance to bring honesty, decency, ethics, and moral superiority back to American politics. McGovern was the life-force of the movement, the hero of the drama his supporters saw unfolding. His rhetoric clearly labeled the villains— not only Richard Nixon, but Lyndon Johnson, Hubert Humphrey, Richard Daley, and any other politician who had allegedly turned America into a militarist, racist, closed society. Americans must be liberated from their old politics. That would be accomplished first by liberating the Democratic party, that is, by delivering it to the New Politics. So McGovern appealed to the young, blacks, Chicanos, Indians, women, poor, and elderly for support, turning his back on party and labor bosses. Clean, Virginal, Visionary—that was the New Politics.

Politicians planning a presidential campaign can move in several directions. They can, as Bormann recognizes, emphasize the setting of the upcoming drama—the goodness or badness of the times, the greatness of America, the greatness and compassion of Americans, and so on. Or action can be the theme—what the candidate will do in office, positions, proposals, concrete details, and so on. Again, the stress could be on motives, for example, a call to arms, sacrifice for principles and ideals, the launching of a crusade, and so on. McGovern strategists could have selected any of these, but instead focused on his persona. Persona, for Bormann, is the character a person plays in a drama. In a public drama, such as a presidential campaign, the way a candidate dramatizes himself cloaks him with a general character that is a key symbol in the campaign's rhetorical vision.

In the 1972 Democratic campaign the emphasis on the McGovern persona—as moral, clean, decent, fair, visionary, and *new* instead of just another politician—would symbolize the New Politics. Although the New Politics might win a party's nomination, there was no assurance that it alone could defeat Richard Nixon. The money, contacts, organizational efforts, and endorsements from the old politics could not be ignored. Hence, some rhetorical strategy, or symbol, must bridge the gap between new and old. The vice presidential slot on the ticket was suited for this symbol. First Senator Edward Kennedy was approached. He said no. Other overtures were considered. Finally, Thomas Eagleton, U.S. Senator from Missouri, entered the picture. He was young, attractive, a new face, yet with strong ties to party regulars, organized labor, and other key groups. Eagleton it was.

With the close of the Democratic convention, McGovern went off to the Black Hills of South Dakota to vacation, plan for the upcoming campaign, and—because he was followed by an army of reporters and TV cameras—orchestrate some good news for his candidacy. But that was not to be. Within days after their arrival at the vacation retreat, McGovern and Eagleton called a news conference. The subject was Eagleton's mental health problems, that is, three times in the past he had voluntarily entered hospitals for treatment of nervous exhaustion. Eagleton read a statement, reporters asked questions, the candidates responded. At one point McGovern restated the wisdom in his judgment in selecting Eagleton and stressed he would not hesitate to place the government in Eagleton's hands.

Millions of Americans, however, did not see the press conference. What they did see and read about were edited, interpreted, and mediated versions of what took place. For example, they heard CBS anchor Roger Mudd that evening refer to Eagleton as obviously "nervous" at the press conference, to a "major crisis" in the McGovern camp, and to "persistent rumors" of Eagleton's "possible drinking problem." Or, if NBC was their preference, TV viewers heard David Brinkley mention electric "shock therapy."

Once uncorked, the fantasy genie in the Eagleton Affair bottle moved rapidly. *The* story of TV network news was the Eagleton story. The evening after the first press conference McGovern appeared in an interview with ABC's Harry Reasoner and Barbara Walters, seated at a picnic table near the vacation hideaway. Again he expressed his support for Eagleton. He would discourage any effort on Eagleton's part to leave the ticket. In his commentary on the same newscast ABC's Howard K. Smith reported that McGovern had said he was "1,000 percent resolved to keep Eagleton as a running mate." But the same evening other journalists hinted not all was well in the McGovern camp. NBC reported that "off the record" a number of Democrats thought the Eagleton disclosure had hurt the ticket. The next night NBC noted that a "top" McGovern aide called the affair a blow to McGovern's chances. The next evening ABC spoke of McGovern's men as "deeply worried," in part because the presidential candidate was so "defensive." Two nights after the story broke CBS devoted a major portion of its evening newscast air time to the Eagleton Affair: Roger Mudd listed all newspapers coming out for Eagleton's withdrawal; a McGovern fundraiser responded in an interview that the disclosures were hurting the campaign's finances and that the election might still be won if Eagleton withdrew; a Democratic leader in New York asserted that people were "scared" about giving power to a man who might buckle under the presidency's pressures. The Eagleton fantasy intensified even more when columnist Jack Anderson claimed that Eagleton had a record of arrests for drunken driving. Eagleton faced the cameras for ABC News, said Anderson's assertion was a "damnable lie," denied any such arrests, and vowed not to let a lie drive him from the ticket. The next evening Eagleton repeated again for TV news cameras that he would not leave the race, "never."

Thus, *the issue* of the Eagleton Affair had boiled down to whether or not he should stay on the ticket. Despite Eagleton's resolve (and McGovern's public assertions to the contrary), pressures were building for withdrawal. The news media contributed their share. CBS showed film of Eagleton, in shirt sleeves, on the phone trying to drum up support. The Democratic national chairwoman was reported urging Eagleton to resign. ABC reported Democratic state chairmen deeply split on the issue. NBC News' John Chancellor pondered why McGovern had let the affair go on so long (less than a week at that point!). CBS reported McGovern would soon announce a final decision. Finally, seven days after it began the fantasy of the Eagleton Affair ended. Eagleton resigned. (Coincidentally, later the same day Jack Anderson reported that his earlier charges about Eagleton were unsubstantiated.)

But the fantasy had done its damage. It struck to the core of the New Politics's rhetorical vision. Portrayed first as stoutly supportive of Eagleton, the hero of the New Politics, McGovern, was soon labeled indecisive, wishy-washy; then, as yielding to pressure; finally, as just another inept, inconstant, faithless, self-serving, expedient politician. As Bormann concludes, subsequent news of the McGovern campaign was more likely to be interpreted along the lines of McGovern the politician than in keeping with the New Politics's rhetorical vision.

SOAP OPERAS OF 1976 AND 1980: CAMPAIGN MELODRAMAS

Most political discussion and campaign speeches, writes political scientist Murray Edelman, "consist of the exchange of cliches among people who agree with each other. The talk, therefore, serves to dull the critical faculties rather than to arouse them. Participation of this sort in an emotionally compelling act in which each participant underlines its reality and seriousness for every other is the most potent form of political persuasion."[6] Consider Edelman's view, then reflect on the content of any TV soap opera. Note the similarities. In soap operas the characters exchange cliches, often in agreement with one another; the viewer's critical faculties dull; a facade of reality and seriousness prevails; and, yet, it is all emotionally compelling. And, to add to Edelman's thoughts, presidential campaigns bear another likeness to soap opera, that is, they go on forever. No sooner does election day end than the next contest for the presidency begins, if in fact it did not already start during the previous campaign! Hence, we are not surprised to find pollster Louis Harris telling us, in a nationwide poll of Democrats and independents conducted scarcely four months after Ronald Reagan's inauguration, that Senator Edward Kennedy leads former Vice President Walter Mondale for the 1984 Democratic nomination by 31 to 22 percent.

As a recurring, emotionally compelling, seasonal ritual, the presidential campaign possesses all of the requirements of melodrama. No wonder, then, that the news media (especially television news) adapt coverage of campaign events to the requirements of the melodramatic imperative. Sensing this, as we shall see later in this chapter, candidates adjust their persuasive appeals to melodramatic requirements.

But we begin with the news media. The presidential campaign coverage by the principal media—TV, radio, newspapers, and newsmagazines—is programmed as a continuing story (much as a soap opera continues over one or more TV seasons). A continuing news story consists of running coverage of separate events, piecing them together within the context of a unifying theme, perhaps with a catchy gimmick to remind audiences of that thematic unity—the body count in Vietnam, days of captivity for U.S. hostages in Iran, the horror-tonight theme of Three Mile Island (TMI), or Campaign 1980. Continuing news of events as ritualized as what occurs in a presidential campaign is particularly suited to a dramatic format: introduction, rising action, turning point, falling action, denouement. Each phase of the presidential election coverage, from preprimaries to postelection analysis, is a minidrama along the lines of the five-part structure. The overall scenario is roughly preprimary introduction (beginning at least a year before the presidential election), caucus and primary rising action, a turning point with selection of party candidates, falling action (but with varied intensity levels) during the general election campaign, and resolution on election day.

Setting the Stage

The presidential campaign coverage in both 1976 and 1980 adhered to dramatic structure. As 1975 came to a close, the news media introduced the plot line for each party. The Republican contest would pit incumbent President Gerald Ford against the unlikely challenge of Ronald Reagan, that is, moderate against conservative Republicans. The Democrats would sort themselves out between a liberal standardbearer, perhaps Senator Birch Bayh because Edward Kennedy was unavailable (but would he accept a draft?) and a conservative leader, undoubtedly Senator Henry Jackson. The introduction to the 1980 melodrama also began well before the election year. For the Republicans the plot line would, we were told, unfold as a contest between Ronald Reagan on the right (if his health held up) and a gaggle of potential moderates, some viable contenders and others not. The burning question among Democrats in mid-1979 was "Will Teddy run?" By early fall it was "When will Teddy announce?" The plot of the upcoming melodrama was clear, that is, the restoration of Camelot.

In the introductory scenes of the news media melodrama two

things occur. Both are essentials of the melodramatic imperative. One
is that the news attaches labels to candidates that characterize heroes,
villains, and fools. Such characterizations inform readers and viewers
how to think about the dramatis personae of the seasonal ritual. Critic
Kenneth Burke has noted that all journalism, including objective reporting, is a creative and imaginative work that sizes up situations,
names their elements, structure, and outstanding ingredients, and
"names them in a way that contains an attitude toward them."[7] With
that thought in mind, recall the fantasy characters created by the news
media for the Democratic contest in 1976: "a tall and witty former professional basketball player," "earthy, barrel-chested new radical with a
folksy populist pitch and quick mind," "the freshest of new faces,
preaching the politics of skepticism and diminishing expectations,"
"soft-talking, evangelist-sounding peanut farmer," "crippled, confined
to a wheelchair, hard of hearing." Because fame is fleeting, readers may
not recall the names connected with these 1976 stereotypes. They
were, respectively, Morris Udall, Fred Harris, Jerry Brown, Jimmy Carter, and George Wallace.[8] Consider a second example, this time from
the preprimary phase of the 1980 Democratic campaign. *Time* and
Newsweek sized up the situation for incumbent Jimmy Carter in the early fall as gloomy. His presidency was "weakened" and "vulnerable,"
"enfeebled" to the point of hopelessness; "nearly everywhere he went
the shadow of the phantom of Ted Kennedy's candidacy seemed to
follow."[9]

Such characterizations relate to a second aspect of the melodramatic imperative of campaign news coverage. The introductory phase of
the news melodrama unveils expectations. It decrees who are serious
contenders, who are not; who is leading, who is trailing; who can win,
who will lose. Because a melodrama is a simplification of complexities,
the imperative demands that, if there are a large number of candidates
entering the contest for a party's nomination, they must be narrowed,
or winnowed, down quickly. Lead and supporting players must be
established quickly. Otherwise the plot line is confusing; audiences
may be lost. To anticipate how the winnowing will go, the news media
rely on a number of indicators—opinion polls, assessments by experienced politicians and observers, the status of each candidate's campaign organization, who is supporting whom, the size of the contenders' financial war chests, even the amount of coverage the media
themselves are giving respective candidates. In 1976 the news media
revealed that it was unlikely that the Republican party could mount a
serious challenge against a sitting president; among Democrats the serious candidates would be Henry Jackson, Birch Bayh, and perhaps—
but probably not—George Wallace, whereas a host of faceless un-
knowns, such as "Jimmy Who?", would fall by the wayside.

Many Are Called, Few Are Chosen

With the preliminaries out of the way, the stage is set for the rising action of the seasonal melodrama of a presidential campaign. Of course,
as any viewer of soap operas knows, it is the nature of melodrama that
things do not go as expected. Outside forces intervene, peril besets the
characters, some hopes are dashed and others raised, contradictions
emerge between what is and what was to be. So it is with the news
media's melodramatic coverage of presidential campaigns.[10]

For Democrats in 1976 the principal contradiction came early, for
Republicans it took a little time. To a large extent the gulf between unfolding and expected Democratic plots derived from the joint actions of
the news media and the forces of "Jimmy Who?" Always fearful of the
unexpected, of missing early trends, people in the news media try to
anticipate contradictions. In the process they help produce them. In
1976 unprecedented coverage focused on the earliest formal competition between Democratic candidates, the January delegate caucuses in
Iowa. Largely ignored in 1972, the Iowa caucuses in 1976 were touted
as "psychologically crucial," a "test" to establish a "highly prized"
sense, that is, "momentum."[11] Carter's campaign recognized an opportunity and seized it. Said Carter adviser Tim Kraft, "We knew the thing
was going to be covered. Politics is theater. We planned for that."[12]
When the smoke cleared, Carter had received but 13 of 47 delegates;
more delegates remained uncommitted to any candidate than Carter
had won. Yet the news media's melodramatic imperative demands
clear-cut winners and losers; having blown a heretofore minor campaign event out of proportion, journalists, then, had to say, "What
happened?" CBS correspondent Roger Mudd provided the theme that
was to resound throughout the remaining weeks of the rising action of
the prenomination ritual: "He was the clear winner in this psychologically crucial test. . . . So the candidate with that highly prized political
momentum tonight is Jimmy Carter."[13]

So the unexpected had happened. Melodramatic requirements reconciled the contradiction:

1. That there be an early test of strength between combatants.
2. That there be a clear-cut winner.
3. That momentum be bestowed on that winner.
4. That future campaign events conform to the newly emergent
   scenario.

What Weaver notes about TV news probably applies more broadly:
"The entire melodramatic apparatus of TV news is designed to single
out one politician and lift him up to the heights of power and glory.
Television loves a winner, a man of the people, the hero of its story."[14]

Despite close "victories" and later faltering, Carter played the lead in the remainder of the Democratic melodrama. With but a 28 percent plurality in the New Hampshire primary, he yet became the "front runner," the "man to beat." Paletz and Entman sum up the melodramatic theme well:

Carter, an unknown, was sweeping his party by storm, addressing the voters' new "conservative mood," ministering to their *angst* and alienation. Because this theme was so firmly established in the early primaries—and because so little attention was given the later contests—strong showings by Udall, Jackson, and Jerry Brown in large industrial states did much less for their hopes than Carter's early "victories" in bucolic Iowa and New Hampshire.[15]

In sum, then, the period of rising action in the Democratic melodrama of 1976 was relatively brief, culminating in the turning point of the early primaries. Not so for the Republicans. The turning point came much later, virtually not until the early sessions of the Republican nominating convention. The unifying theme was "incumbents don't lose party nominations." Early Gerald Ford primary victories, regardless of narrowness (only fifteen hundred votes in New Hampshire), resounded the theme. Challenger Ronald Reagan was quickly boxed in by yet another requirement of the melodramatic imperative, that is, candidates run not only against one another but against a phantom candidate named "Expected."[16] "Expected" is the percentage of the primary vote the news media anticipate and report a candidate will receive. "Expected" serves as a standard against which to measure the candidate's success or failure, victory or defeat. If the candidate gets a higher proportion of the vote, the media reports the candidate "exceeded expectations;" if a lower percentage, the candidate's performance was "disappointing." Recognizing this, candidates try to manipulate "Expected," usually poor-mouthing chances, much like a football coach contending for the national championship agonizes in the press over all his problems. Reagan's forces, however, were not pessimistic in 1976 and, so, press accounts hinted at victory in early key primaries. When Reagan lost in those primaries (for example, 49 to 48 percent in New Hampshire), the mediated reality was one of a loss to "Expected" as much as to Gerald Ford.

Reagan's failure to live up to expectations in the early primaries contributed to the building rhetorical vision of presidential invincibility. Reagan's victories in southern primaries in mid-spring provided the opportunity to heighten the conflict. Indeed, by mid-May Ford trailed in the delegate count, but regained "momentum" in his home state of Michigan on May 18. From that point on the rising action of the melodrama unfolded in news accounts of Ford's "closing in on the nomination." Yet, as in any good soap opera, there remained a tantalizing doubt. Uncommitted delegates, read the news, would decide the nomination. The turning point coincided with the Republican convention. Prior to it, Reagan announced his choice for a vice presidential running mate, Senator Richard Schweiker of Pennsylvania. In the media melodrama this served as the required crisis. The "make or break gamble" failed in a twofold way. For one, noted press accounts, conservative delegates as yet uncommitted to either candidate gravitated to Ford out of dismay over the selection of the liberal Schweiker. Second, the gamble forced the issue, that is, a convention vote on a proposal by Reagan forces to require Ford to name his running mate prior to balloting on presidential candidates. Ford's 112-vote victory provided the required dramatic climax.

Campaign 1980 is relatively fresh in people's minds. Extensive re-counting is unnecessary here. The melodrama for Democrats that had been introduced in 1979 was the Kennedy challenge. The plot that unfolded was of Kennedy: collapse, revival, resurrection. For the news media the fact that the preprimary form chart was phony was stark. In the fall of 1979 polls showed Democrats favoring Edward Kennedy over Jimmy Carter about 2 to 1; by the next spring the proportions were reversed. What melodramatic imperative could reconcile the contradiction? Weaver notes that a key characteristic of melodrama is that the lead characters face "intensified peril" as they engage in their all-out struggle. One peril is the "intervention of outside forces." One such voice is "the people" speaking at the polls.[17] But another voice is that of events, what the Italian political philosopher Machiavelli called *fortuna*. In the media melodrama of Campaign 1980 *fortuna* smiled on Jimmy Carter, frowned on Edward Kennedy. The smile came in the opportunity for Carter to rally support by coping with the hostage crisis in Iran and the Soviet Union's invasion of Afghanistan.

Political scientist Murray Edelman theorizes that people in a world they perceive as cold, complex, bewildering, and crisis-ridden seek reassurance. Like children, they want to be told things will be all right. Or at least they want to get such an impression. "And what symbol can be more reassuring than the incumbent of a high position who knows what to do and is willing to act when others are bewildered and alone?" asks Edelman. To leave the impression of being able to cope, an incumbent needs two things: (1) a crisis providing the opportunity and (2) a "dramaturgical performance emphasizing the traits popularly associated with leadership: forcefulness, responsibility, courage, decency, and so on."[18] Iran and Afghanistan provided the opportunity; Carter's Rose Garden strategy was the performance.

The frown on Fortuna's face looking at Kennedy, as viewed in press fantasies, was creased with many lines. These included Kennedy's awkward campaigning style, slips of the lip, poor campaign organization, and the ever-present Chappaquiddick fantasy. At one and the same time media accounts chained out the Chappaquiddick fantasy, then used it to explain Kennedy's losses to "Expected." Investigative pieces in *Reader's Digest* and the *New York Times* delved into Kennedy's involvement in the 1969 automobile accident at Chappaquiddick in which a woman staff member was killed. In a CBS–TV interview, correspondent Roger Mudd focused on Chappaquiddick in questioning Kennedy while on the screen visuals portrayed the driver's side of a car moving in the dark toward the now-famous bridge. The fantasy obviously raised serious questions about Kennedy's crisis-coping abilities. The questions were not lost on Jimmy Carter who implied Chappaquiddick when he noted that he had "never panicked in a crisis." Even when the fantasy seemed to have run its course, by the March primaries, media accounts breathed new life into it. Week after week candidates competed in statewide primaries each Tuesday. Each Tuesday night TV news networks reported winners and losers, interpreted outcomes, adjusted and reoutfitted "Expected." The Tuesday night primaries became as routine as "Monday Night Football," especially on ABC. And each Tuesday night ABC reporter Lynn Sherr provided results of ABC's exit polls, opinion samplings of those leaving the voting booths. With ritualistic consistency she noted that, when asked reasons for not voting for Kennedy, doubts about his trustworthiness and steadiness surfaced.

But the vale of the Kennedy challenge continued and as the primary season wore on he won not just "expected victories" but suffered "upsets." Dogged determinism and revival, however, did not produce victory at the nominating convention. The media query was repeated endlessly, "Why does Kennedy stay in the race?" The rhetorical vision evoked as an answer was *motive-talk*, that is, discourse about why people do what they do. Again the melodramatic imperative prevailed. As Weaver notes, press coverage of campaigns seldom attributes laudable motives to politicians unless such coverage has already awarded them heroic status. There were too many chinks in the armor of the princely heir of Camelot, consequently, the news melodrama could not portray Kennedy's motives as altruistic. Melodramatic logic dictated ulterior aims—ambition, personal pique with Jimmy Carter, anguish over early defeats, a calculated look ahead to 1984, and, as Weaver notes, a likening to the media image of any politician who is seen as "driven by deep passions and uncontrollable compulsions that he himself scarcely understands."[19]

The turning point had passed, however. The incumbent had stood off the Kennedy challenge. Yet, there was more to come. There had to be a final reconciliation of the contradictions unfolded in the Kennedy challenge. It came with media coverage, instant analysis, and interpretations of Kennedy's "rousing" speech before the Democratic national convention. Although the cause had been lost, the fight had been valorous. Democrats would contest the general election with a knight of lesser luster after all.

If the media melodrama surrounding Democrats in 1980 was the Kennedy challenge, that for Republicans was the Reagan vulnerability. The preprimary news scenario depicted Reagan against the field. It implied two things. One was that a single contender would emerge "from the pack" to challenge Reagan for the nomination. The other was that Reagan probably did not have staying power and would not survive the nomination struggle. In a perceptive little essay entitled "The Press Was the Last to Know,"[20] media observer Edwin Diamond critiques press coverage of the Reagan campaign from November 1979 through May 1980. The basic theme was that Reagan could not win. Why? One reason, repeated often in early press accounts, was age. He was too old. By mid-March the age factor faded and another emerged, that is, Reagan was too extreme. Electable candidates occupy the political middle of the road, said the fantasy; Reagan is on the right; hence, he is not electable. Yet, age and ideological positions notwithstanding, Reagan continued winning primaries. A new reason for Reagan's vulnerability arose, that is, he was too dumb to be president. Stories told of Reagan's lack of familiarity with issues, superficial understanding of problems, misstatements of facts.

The fantasy that Reagan could not win was imposed on campaign events that seemed to explain why things were going as they were. A hardworking, energetic, youthful George Bush captured "momentum" by a slim victory in the Iowa caucuses. Implicit was the view that age was a factor. Yet, Reagan defeated Bush and others in New Hampshire. Why? New Hampshire Republicans are conservative, said the mediated reality, hence, Reagan's appeal. Moreover, by seeming not to be "forceful" in a televised forum with other candidates, Bush's image of energy and firmness was "weakened." Primaries rolled on. Suddenly John B. Anderson registered "a strong showing," one "better than expected" (but not winning) in Vermont and Massachusetts. CBS's Walter Cronkite was moved to declare Anderson a serious contender. What was the explanation of the "Anderson appeal?" Anderson fit the melodramatic imperative: unlike Reagan he was a new face, unlike Reagan he was moderate, unlike Reagan he was electable. But "The Anderson Difference" proved no more long lasting among primary voters than "The Anacin Difference" among migraine sufferers. As Reagan's nomination seemed more and more assured, the fantasy of a Gerald Ford candidacy chained out. That too soon vanished, the nomination was secured, the turning point reached. The Reagan vulnerability went the way of the Kennedy challenge.

Democrats Versus Republicans: An Anticlimax

In any melodrama the unveiling of the mystery proves more absorbing than discovering that the butler did it, rising action seems more intriguing than falling. In the mediated realities of presidential campaigns, the news portrayal of nomination politics is of such intensity that the general election seems almost an anticlimax. There is small wonder. The Who-Will-Win?, How-Did-He-Win?, Where-Does-He-Stand? stories of the nomination minidrama set the stage, rhetorical visions, and fantasies for much of what is to follow. The preformed stereotypes afford the basis for the What-Is-He-Really Like?, Who-Is-Ahead?, What-Difference-Does-It-Make? stories on the general election campaign.

But falling action is only relatively less intense than rising. Ritualistic though postnomination politics may be, it still can have its exciting moments, or at least they can be seized on as such and dramatized to draw and entertain an audience. Here the melodramatic imperative dictates a focus on the unusual, the novel, the extraordinary. Frequently this is the campaign gaffe—the error of fact or judgment, the injudicious remark, the off-color joke, or other faux pas. Such items are trivial on reflection, but they are a godsend to journalists striving to convert the daily humdrum of a campaign into appealing fare. What were some of the "big" stories of 1976? Born-again Jimmy Carter's confessing lust in his heart in a *Playboy* interview and Gerald Ford's questioning Soviet domination of Eastern Europe in a televised debate. And of 1980? Consider as possibilities Ronald Reagan's misstatement about the birthplace of the Ku Klux Klan and Jimmy Carter's evoking his daughter Amy's opinions in a presidential debate.

This is not to say that such gaffes are insignificant or unimportant to many voters. Perhaps they are. Rather, it is to say that the general election campaign denouement in recent mediated melodrama has stressed two fantasies. One fantasy is that the heroes emergent from the crowd during the nominating season are heroes no more. They are idols with feet of clay, mere mortals perhaps not qualified to be president. The fantasy of rags to riches yields to a ship of fools. The second fantasy is that such a focus obeys one final requirement of the melodramatic imperative of campaign coverage—it characterizes the overall plot of the general election, labels it, and criticizes it. Thus, the 1976 focus became: two nice, well-meaning, largely unknown and faceless men, average in achievement and vision, seeking the presidency. What difference does it make? Ho hum, how dull. And in 1980 it became: Carter lacks the strength and vision, to make a difference; Reagan's positions, although tenable, will never clear Congress anyway; Anderson cannot win. What difference does it make? Ho hum, how dull.

Thus entertained for more than a year by the soap opera of presidential politics, the audience gets to take part in the play's outcome on election day and thereby provides the final resolution. One-half exit the theater (do not vote), others half-heartedly wander on stage (vote aimlessly), a minority are avid performers (they care who wins).

Paul H. Weaver sums up the overall impact of the news media on those of us who are "captives of melodrama." He writes that, "At its best, journalism is a kind of window on the world, one that offers an inevitably limited but useful view of what is going on." But, he goes on, "At something less than its best, journalism is a screen on which deceptive images dance—today's seeming truths, tomorrow's undoubted foolishness." (Recall Plato's anecdote about the prisoners in the cave.) "The problem," he notes, with TV news (and we believe with other media as well) is that, "in its enthusiasm to expand its viewers' sense of the world, it has tended to transform its window into a screen, preventing the people and their representatives from seeing each other unvarnished and unmediated."[21] That may trouble Weaver, but not presidential candidates. They accept the screen, indeed preen for it. Thus, they mediate a few realities of their own.

A LITTLE BIT OF STAR QUALITY: ORCHESTRATING THE SEASONAL DRAMA

To what degree do fantasies, rhetorical visions, and melodramatic portrayals make a difference in how people vote? We do not know the answer to that question. Studies of voting either do not address that question or, if they do, address it in ways that provide little help. For example, a major study of the 1972 presidential election dismisses the Eagleton Affair as an important vote factor. Few people voted for or against George McGovern on the basis of his handling of that episode.[22] But that says little. What we do not know is how the course of the campaign might have developed had the New Politics's rhetorical vision not been destroyed so soon after McGovern's nomination. Indeed, one could assert that precisely because that vision faded few persons were influenced by the Eagleton Affair one way or another. Had the vision expanded, the symbolic environment of the campaign—and the manner in which subsequent Watergate revelations were interpreted—might have been different.

Regardless of how voters respond to such visions, however, politicians deem them vital and, hence, endeavor to orchestrate them. A popular Broadway musical, *Evita*, glorifies the life of Evita Peron—singer and actress, then, mistress and wife of a former Argentine dictator—who achieved considerable political influence in her own right. Asked in one scene what people can expect of her, she responds with

the song, "Just a Little Bit of Star Quality." To give voters a little bit of
star quality is what all campaigners seek. Let us see how.

Campaign Propaganda as Fantastic Art

In the Introduction of this book we noted that some fantasies chain out
so widely, become so durable, and are so believable that they become
part of a nation's culture. They are myths. One such political myth in
America is the presidential myth. That myth endows the office with
greatness and power. Who holds the office is "president of all the people." And regardless of the problems facing a sitting president and the
failures of the incumbent in dealing with them, every four years hope
springs eternal that a "new face" or the "right man" will restore the
office and make it again the nation's salvation—as with Washington,
Jefferson, Lincoln, Wilson, Franklin Roosevelt, or any other member of
the presidential pantheon.

We said that myths can lend legitimacy to fantasies that conform to
them. They can also give rise to fantasies. Such is the case of the presidential myth. It inspires among the people the fantasy that it does
make a difference who wins, who loses. Among journalists it yields
fantasies that issues should divide candidates, candidates should campaign on issues. But they do not. Hence, there is no real difference.
People and press are not alone in having fantasies. For the presidential
myth inspires fantasies among candidates about being president—that
they are "presidential timber," that they project a "presidential image," that they are "presidential" and will solve the nation's woes.
After all, did not Jimmy Carter in 1976 entitle his campaign biography
Why Not the Best?

Candidates, of course, are in a position to act out their fantasies.
They dramatize their fantasies by creating rhetorical visions. These visions appear over and over again in each candidate's propaganda. Each
speech, brochure, position paper, slogan, TV and radio advertisement,
and so on, is a carefully crafted effort to portray the candidate's rhetorical vision. Such crafting is an artistic enterprise. Hence, campaign
propaganda can be regarded as an example of fantastic art, that is, the
use of artistic devices to promote a candidate's rhetorical vision of his
presidency. If successful, the candidate's fantasy chains out to become
the news media's and the voters' fantasy as well.

Campaign propaganda aims at mediating two closely related, overlapping fantasies. First, propaganda constructs fantasies about the
candidate, his qualities, qualifications, program, and destiny. Second,
propaganda mediates realities about the nature of the world, the array
of forces, dangers, threats, and enemies that must be confronted and
vanquished. The linkage of the two fantasies is essential, that is, the
destiny of the candidate becomes the destiny of the political world.

An entire industry now exists to construct such fantasies, craft appropriate propagandistic artifacts for them, and espouse each candidate's rhetorical vision. This industry of "propartists"[23] consists of specialists with a variety of skills. There are, for instance, organizers, fund raisers, pollsters, TV producers, filmmakers, advertisers, public relations personnel, press secretaries, hairstylists, and all manner of other consultants. The industry has developed an aesthetic style consistent with the artistry of modern advertising. Two devices in that artistry are particularly key mechanisms, positioning the candidate and fashioning the image.

In commercial advertising *positioning* places a product at a particular point or with a particular stance as a means of distinguishing it from competing products that, in substance, are strikingly similar to the product being huckstered. The attempt is to carve out a share of the market. But it is not the unique traits or qualities inherent in the product that are stressed. Rather, advertisers mold a picture of the product as distinct because of the people who buy or consume it. Consider beers. Many are indistinguishable in taste, but TV ads alert us that Miller Lite is favored by former athletes, Schlitz is the cool and tough brew of macho James Coburn, and Natural Light is the favorite of discerning women. Now consider candidates, specifically Jimmy Carter in 1976. Remember the precampaign scenario of the news media: the 1976 Democratic nomination fight would boil down to liberals buying Morris Udall, conservatives purchasing Henry Jackson. Jimmy Carter's pollster, Pat Caddell, advised against Carter's positioning himself on the liberal/conservative continuum. Caddell noted that his polls indicated a large portion of Americans were disenchanted with government and with the failure of politicians, liberal or conservative, to solve problems. He advised Carter to position himself as the anti-Washington candidate. Carter did, carved out a whole new market, and ended up with the nomination.[24]

Positioning puts a candidate in a place to run *from* in the campaign. *Image making* is what the candidate runs *as*. The process is not one-way. Voters' impressions of candidates' qualities derive only in part from campaign propaganda; how voters contrast the candidate's fantasies with their own makes a difference. A household cleanser or trash bag may position itself to carve out a market segment, but if "Big Wally" or the "Man from Glad" does not conform to what the pop song calls "dreams of the everyday housewife," the desired image may not follow. Fashioning image themes that strike responsive chords requires skill, resources, and luck. In 1980, with varying degrees of success, the process gave us George Bush jogging while he waved and talked, to remind voters he was not like the older Reagan; John B. Anderson telling us that he was a "candidate with ideas," to mark himself off from the Republican pack; and Jimmy Carter dramatizing himself as "moral" and "a good family man," to denote he was no Kennedy.

Following Ronald Reagan's successful 1980 campaign against Jimmy Carter, his key advisers revealed the scenario they had conceived to bring a Reagan victory.[25] Their account reveals considerable concern with both positioning and image making. In a memo entitled "Seven Conditions of Victory" the advisers speak explicitly of positioning Reagan to win support among Independents, supporters of John B. Anderson, disaffected Democrats, urban ethnics, and Hispanics. Such positioning was achieved not by emphasizing any new issues but by hammering away at inflation, unemployment, economic growth, and the ills of the federal government—all fantasy themes carefully crafted by the Reagan campaigners. Insofar as image was concerned, the focus was on leadership. In June of 1979 Reagan's pollsters conducted a nationwide survey in which they "tested six scenarios for the future." These scenarios ranged from a future wherein "less is better" to "America can do." The "can do" scenario emerged as the one Americans believed in, emphasizing that America could be strong again if it but selected good leaders. Thus, the presidential myth, once again verified, became the touchstone of image making for the Reagan forces. Postelection polls confirmed that of voters who ranked strong leadership high among attributes a president should have, two out of every three bought the Reagan fantasy and voted for him.

The No Theater of Campaign Debates

Capitalizing on enduring aspects of the presidential election's seasonal ritual, such as on the presidential myth, is a key task for each candidate's staff of prop artists. In recent presidential elections a new dimension has been added to the ritual, namely, debates between presidential candidates. These take a variety of forms. In three elections they have consisted of one or more debates between the contenders of the two major parties—in 1960 between Richard Nixon and John Kennedy, in 1976 between Gerald Ford and Jimmy Carter, and in 1980 between Ronald Reagan and Jimmy Carter. In 1980 Ronald Reagan also debated independent candidate John B. Anderson. During the prenomination acts of the election melodrama, there have also been forums in which candidates seeking their party's nomination have come together to respond to questions from a panel of interrogators.

A key rationale for these debates is to give voters an opportunity to size up the candidates, their qualities, and their positions on issues and, thus, make a more informed choice than if they had to rely solely on news-mediated or candidate-mediated fare. Watching candidates go at one another ("let's you and him fight"), however, has become a mediating ritual in its own right, one providing yet another means of fantasy creation and chaining. In fact, presidential debates provide an ideal forum for candidates to espouse their rhetorical visions.

For one thing, presidential debates are scarcely spontaneous, un-rehearsed confrontations. Instead, they are what Daniel J. Boorstin calls pseudo-events.[26] In fact, debates join most other campaign events in that respect. A pseudo-event is one that is planned for the immediate purpose of being reported, yet what actually happens is never clear, even though the event itself was intended to have a self-fulfilling char-acter. In sum, a pseudo-event is a media event. Consider the planning of presidential debates. Considerable thought goes into deciding whether to challenge an opposing candidate to debate or whether to accept a challenge. Thus, a predebate between candidates' advisers takes place in the news media over whether to debate at all. Once that is resolved, elaborate negotiations between candidates' advisers work out details of attire, rostrum sizes, makeup, lighting and camera angles for TV, the format of the debate, who will participate, location, time, and so on. Indeed, as little as possible is left to spontaneity.

Nor are presidential debates debates. The common understanding of a debate is a conflict or argument over a clearly defined proposition. Each side speaks to that proposition for an alloted time, has an oppor-tunity to rebut and interrogate the opposition, and sums up its posi-tion. Presidential debates never involve clearly defined propositions for argument. At best, the point at issue is vague. It boils down to "there should be a change." The ins should be replaced by the outs. In each presidential debate thus far that implicit proposition has favored the challenger—Kennedy challenging the Eisenhower-Nixon administra-tion in 1960, Carter challenging the Ford administration in 1976, Reagan challenging Carter in 1980. Nor is there an exchange over the implicit proposition. Instead, the basic format has consisted, with variations, of questions asked of each candidate by a panel of journa-lists, each candidate responding or counterresponding, but rarely con-fronting one another. Although follow-up questions by panelists or fol-low-up comments by the candidates have been worked into the debate format, the candidates are able to sidestep them. What comes from the candidates' lips are "grooved responses."[27] Grooved refers to what one would get if a phonograph needle were placed in a recording groove, that is, a pat, predictable response generally borrowed from the candi-date's standard speech made throughout the campaign. In sum, the grooved response is a rerun of the candidate's rhetorical vision.

The alleged debates are not always informative either. When they end it is not always clear just what happened. The thirst to determine immediately "what happened" is, however, considerable. The quench-ing takes several forms. First, there is the question, Who won? Within minutes after the debate (sometimes even during it) pollsters man their phones in efforts to conduct surveys of who people think won or lost. It may be that most people do not know, but once told that a nationwide poll said that candidate *A* won, people buy that fantasy. As later polls are taken, the candidate early surveys labeled the victor increases that candidate's victory margin. So important a part of the process of presidential debates have postdebate polls become that one TV network, ABC, added a new wrinkle in 1980. Following the Reagan-Carter debate, Ted Koppel, ABC correspondent, invited viewers to dial special telephone numbers (at a "small cost") to register their verdicts of winner and loser. Koppel admitted the survey was "not scientific," but was "random" (which it was not because random means everyone having an equal chance of being counted, whereas the procedure instead was one of self-selection). ABC was widely criticized for the stunt because it violated both scientific and journalistic standards for conducting and reporting systematic opinion surveys. Be that as it may, the ABC survey stands as one of the best examples of instant fantasy chaining on record.

Along with the "Who won?" question arises the issue question. Debate postmortems, however, dwell less on points of substantive differences between the candidates than on gaffes. As noted earlier, a gaffe is inconsistent with the rhetorical vision of the candidate making it. When President Ford in a 1976 debate said, and later reaffirmed, that, "There is no Soviet domination of Eastern Europe and there never will be under a Ford administration," he scarcely evoked the image of an informed leader. Yet, precisely because such gaffes are unexpected, unrehearsed, ungrooved, they make news. Being remarks that lie outside what is expected of the ritual, they seem to contradict the very myth that spawns the ritualistic campaigning itself, namely, the presidential myth. The candidate not comporting himself according to the rituals of that myth is in deep trouble. For, as with any pseudo-event, the end is supposed to be self-fulfilling, that is, to demonstrate that it does make a difference who is president. The mediated reality is that a gaffe serves to underscore such a difference.

One other aspect of the debate ritual requires emphasis. The presidential debates are media events, solely TV events. Recall the first debate in 1976 between Ford and Carter. As Carter commenced his final rejoinder of the debate, the TV audio went off. For twenty-eight minutes, it remained off. There was no debate. Ford remained riveted at the podium, Carter remained at the podium, sitting briefly. When the trouble was corrected, the debate renewed. The lesson was clear: no media, no debate. A study of the 1980 presidential debates by Berquist and Golden emphasizes the role played by the news media in their staging. The authors argue persuasively that in 1980 media personnel led the call for televised debates between candidates. Then, once there were debates, media accounts of them (especially criticism of candidates' performances and of formats) shaped how viewers perceived the debates. Specifically, media criticism concluded that issues of substance were less important than matters of delivery, appearance, and style and that debate formats favored the candidates' rather than the public's interest.

One version of Asian ritualistic theater is called No theater. It is so ritualistic, so repetitive, that there is no room for improvisation, character development, or plot change in even the slightest form. Presidential debates are the No theater of the mediated reality of presidential elections.

IT'S THE REAL THING

We suspect there will be readers who disagree with our rendition of presidential campaigns as seasonal rituals of fantasies, rhetorical visions, and melodramas. Surely behind these shadows are real candidates dividing on really important issues that make a substantial difference in who is elected president. Perhaps. But we contend that it is more likely that there are several realities to each real candidate, several realities to each candidate's stands, and several realities implied in the difference it makes as to who wins and loses. But for most of us that multiplicity of overlapping and contradictory realities is simplified, shrunken to a mediated reality for each presidential campaign. That mediation follows a logic that consists of the constraints placed on candidates, journalists, and voters by the melodramatic imperative and the fantasies and rhetorical visions that parallel it. It is not a choice between a mediated, melodramatic election and a real election. As the soft drink commercial says, the melodrama is the real thing.

Other critics observe that it is "trivially obvious and thoroughly misguided" to regard elections as melodrama. It is obvious, presumably, because elections have always been thought to be, and criticized as, melodramatic. (The horserace metaphor, for example, dates back to the elections of Andrew Jackson). And it is misguided, for it fails to take seriously the myth-enhancing rituals of elections; "the real characteristics of elections *are* the recurring themes, the banal appeals, the dramatic incidents, and the personal images" rather than dispassionate, reasoned discussions of policy alternatives.[29] To such an overall criticism we respond yes and no. Yes, the melodramatic character of elections has long been noted and criticized, but that has not prevented generations of Americans from believing that a given melodrama was "the only act in town" and being misled accordingly. And, yes, the myth-enhancing features of melodramatic elections are indeed the "real characteristics" of those contests. Granted that elections are not, could not, and perhaps should not be policy-making exercises in America. But if policy choices are not at issue, as they are not, then, other choices are: Which fantasies, rhetorical visions, melodramas, and myths are voters to accept? Which political destiny is their destiny? Which candidate envisions it?

If this line of reasoning merits consideration, then perhaps the required skills for citizenship are not those taught in civics texts—being interested and motivated to political discussion and activity, acquiring political knowledge, being principled, and reaching choices by rational thinking. Perhaps instead citizens must become critics—drama critics, rhetorical critics, speech critics. Thus prepared they can undertake the crucial task of conducting critiques of dramatic performances, fantasy themes, rhetorical visions, and melodramatic rituals. Thereby they might not only demand more of candidates, campaigners, and journalists in the election melodrama but also of their own acting performances as well.

NOTES

1. For the 1972 campaign see Thomas E. Patterson and Robert D. McClure, *The Unseeing Eye* (New York: G. P. Putnam's Sons, 1976); for the 1976 campaign see James David Barber, ed., *Race for the Presidency* (Englewood Cliffs, N.J.: Prentice-Hall, 1978). (Spectrum Books); and Thomas E. Patterson, *The Mass Media Election* (New York: Praeger Publishers, 1980); for the 1980 campaign see Michael Robinson and Margaret Sheehan, "How the Networks Learned to Love the Issues," *Washington Journalism Review*, 2 (December 1980): 15–17

2. James David Barber, *The Pulse of Politics* (New York: W. W. Norton & Co., 1980).

3. A. M. Hocart, *Kings and Councillors* (Chicago: University of Chicago Press, 1970); Sir James Frazer, *The Magical Origins of Kings* (London: Dawson of Pall Mall, 1968).

4. Theodor H. Gaster, *Thespis: Ritual, Myth, and Drama in the Ancient Near East* (New York: Henry Schuman, 1950), p. 3.

5. Ernest G. Bormann, "The Eagleton Affair: A Fantasy Theme Analysis," *Quarterly Journal of Speech*, 59 (April 1973): 143–159. The discussion in this section relies on this provocative analysis. See also Charles R. Bantz, "The Critic and the Computer: A Multiple Technique Analysis of the ABC Evening News," *Communications Monographs*, 46 (March 1979): 27–39.

6. Murray Edelman, *The Symbolic Uses of Politics* (Urbana: University of Illinois Press, 1964), p. 18.

7. As paraphrased by James W. Carey, "The Communications Revolution and the Professional Communicator," in Paul Halmos, ed., *The Sociology of Mass Media Communication* (Staffordshire, England: University of Keele, 1969), p. 36.

8. Barber, *Race for the Presidency*, op. cit., p. 115.

9. See Dan Nimmo and Karen S. Johnson, "Positions and Images in Campaign Communication: Newsmagazine Labeling in the 1980 Pre-Primary

Presidential Contests," in Joseph P. McKerns, ed., *Third Annual Communication Research Symposium: A Proceedings* (Knoxville: College of Communications, University of Tennessee, 1980), pp. 36–54.

10. See Paul H. Weaver, "Captives of Melodrama," *New York Times Magazine*, August 29, 1976, pp. 6, 48, 50–51, 54, 56–57; and David L. Swanson, "And That's the Way It Was? Television Covers the 1976 Presidential Campaign," *Quarterly Journal of Speech*, 63 (October 1977): 239–248.

11. David L. Paletz and Robert M. Entman, *Media Power Politics* (New York: Free Press, 1981), p. 35.

12. Quoted in Jules Witcover, *Marathon* (New York: Viking Press, 1977), p. 202.

13. Quoted in Paletz and Entman, *Media Power Politics*, op. cit., p. 35.

14. Weaver, "Captives of Melodrama," op. cit., 51.

15. Paletz and Entman, *Media Power Politics*, op. cit., p. 37.

16. A. Schardt, "Rating Campaign Coverage," *Newsweek* (March 24, 1980), pp. 89–90.

17. Weaver, "Captives of Melodrama," op. cit., p. 6.

18. Edelman, *The Symbolic Uses of Politics*, op. cit., p. 81.

19. Weaver, "Captives of Melodrama," op. cit., p. 48.

20. Edwin Diamond, "The Press Was the Last to Know," *Washington Journalism Review*, 2 (July/August 1980): 14–15.

21. Weaver, "Captives of Melodrama," op. cit., p. 57.

22. Arthur H. Miller, Warren E. Miller, Alden S. Raine, and Thad A. Brown, "A Majority Party in Disarray: Policy Polarization in the 1972 Election." Paper delivered at the annual meeting of the American Political Science Association, New Orleans, September 1973.

23. See Gary Yanker, *Prop Art* (New York: Darien House, 1972).

24. Nicholas von Hoffman, "The President's Analyst," *Inquiry* (May 29, 1978): 6–8.

25. Richard Wirthlin, Vincent Breglio, and Richard Beal, "Campaign Chronicle," *Public Opinion*, 4 (February/March 1981): 43–49.

26. Daniel J. Boorstin, *The Image: A Guide to Pseudo-Events in America* (New York: Harper & Row, 1964). (Colophon Books)

27. See *Carter vs. Ford: The Counterfeit Debates of 1976* (Madison: University of Wisconsin Press, 1980).

28. Goodwin F. Berquist and James J. Golden, "Media Rhetoric, Criticism, and the Public Perception of the 1980 Presidential Debates," *Quarterly Journal of Speech*, 67 (May 1981): 125–137.

29. W. Lance Bennett, "Myth, Ritual, and Political Control," *Journal of Communication*, 30 (August 1980): 178.

3

The Re-presentation of History in Popular Culture

Media Melodramas and Popular Images of Politics

"History," said industrial genius and political crackpot Henry Ford, "is bunk." What Ford had in mind about history is not clear. But if he were alive today, he might be thinking of the overabundance of media melodramas about the past. Television, films, and other media constantly dramatize the past for us. We seem never to tire of melodramas set in historical settings, be they the Old Testament or last year's big news stories. The movie industry long ago learned that people love to see adventures, mysteries, and romances placed in past settings. The television industry sets both specials and serials in historical times and places. The publishing industry merchandises popular books with plots located in every conceivable historical period. In this chapter we explore some of these mediated historical realities, pointing to what such re-presentations of past events and personages imply. The point of this inquiry is simply that much of what we "know" about the past—and indeed by extension the political present—is mediated and shaped by popular depictions. Thus, our political knowledge of the past and present is partially formed by the dramatic fantasies of popular media. By pointing to the fantastic aspects of such depictions, perhaps we can—Mr. Ford to the contrary—debunk such popular fare and remind the reader that historical truth is not as easily arrived at as media melodramas might suggest.

THE MELODRAMATIC USES OF THE PAST

In his book, *The Uses of the Past*, historian Herbert J. Muller wrote: "The past has no meaningful existence except as it exists for us, as it is given meaning by us. . . . Our task is to create a 'usable past,' for our own living purposes."[1] It is a paradoxical fact that the past both occurred and *is occurring*. The past occurred, to be sure, but it is a past that is vast, complex, and perhaps even ultimately unknowable. Complete knowledge sufficient to describe and explain the past would require omniscience. Even in our memories of our own lives, what we can and do remember is limited, patchy, and selective. Some of our past we have forgotten, other parts we want to forget, still others we reconstruct. We give meaning to our pasts, meaning useful in the present. We may have hated growing up in a small town or on a farm at the time, but we remember it fondly later when living in an impersonal big city. We may even idealize our pasts. If we use, reuse, misuse, and abuse our own personal pasts, why should we expect anything different from the historical past, the pasts of groups, nations, and civilizations? Societies, like individuals, live in time, develop a history, and reconstruct and use the past for present purposes.[2]

Like individuals and small groups, nations develop shared myths and fantasies about their past. These pass down between generations through folklore, that sophisticated folklore known as academic history, official celebrations, and the mass media. Folklore about Andy Jackson or Harry Truman passes on by word of mouth, perpetuating a dramatic fantasy about heroism. Public officials use rhetorical visions to celebrate a version of the past they want people to remember and emulate. They thereby place themselves within the heritage of a mythical past. Professional historians constantly "revise" the past, interpret, and even incorporate "new" histories (e.g., black history, women's history, the history of communications) to accommodate present purposes and interests.

Our focus here is on how the mass media use the political past for various purposes. The chief motive is to merchandise entertainment. Media industries, such as film production companies in Hollywood and television networks, discovered long ago that history sells. But it is not the history of the schoolroom, that is, the laborious reconstruction of verifiable facts and competing interpretations. Rather, media history is the history of popular myth and fantasy that mediated versions both reflect and shape. Media reflect popular images of the American past (or the past of groups and institutions) through efforts to sell familiar and acceptable dramatizations that appeal to what people want to believe about the past. At the same time mediated realities also shape what people think about the past by reminding them of what they already think and by perpetuating, and sometimes revising, what people of new generations will believe about history. The popular media are thus important teachers of the past, providing audiences with rhetorical visions of what happened in history, old or new.

A few examples illustrate the point. Hollywood moguls discovered decades ago that dramatizing biblical stories attracted mass audiences. Cecil B. De Mille and other directors worked out a successful formula for such fables: tell a well-known biblical story and include plenty of gory battles, dancing girls, evil tyrants, sumptuous palaces, chariot races, beautiful Christian girls tortured in dungeons, and other titillating fare. The faithful get to see "the Bible come alive" and those of lesser faith get sensational entertainment. The Romans and Philistines make perfect villains, the Christians are good victims, and the biblical setting is exotic. It is no secret that Hollywood took great liberties with these stories. Our knowledge of the Bible has probably been shaped by these popular depictions. Similarly, American images of the Civil War have been affected by such films as *Birth of a Nation* and *Gone with the Wind*. Our belief in the Western myth has been given impetus by Hollywood's eternal retelling of that important cultural tale.

So it is that our fantasies about the past are provided technicolor, widescreen, quadraphonic imagery by the dream factory of Hollywood. Even though "political" films were usually avoided by the studios, Hollywood nevertheless influenced the popular imagination of the American political past. Abe Lincoln was always a good audience draw; Hollywood paid homage to, and thus perpetuated, the Lincoln legend. Most popular films of the golden age of Hollywood were affirmative in their image of government and politics, a point discussed in detail in Chapter 4. In more recent decades, Hollywood has taken a different view of the American past and politics. In the Western, for example, a fantasy has been reversed: the Indians have become the good guys and the cavalry the bad guys. Similarly, political films have begun to include themes of corruption, conspiracy, and irresponsibility at the top without the saving grace of a cleansing political hero.

The advent of television brought dramatization of popular fantasies about the American past into the living room. Television quickly adapted the popular formulas of Hollywood, including use of the mythological past. Walt Disney gave us a new Davy Crockett; Warner Brothers and other studios created a rash of new Western heroes, such as Matt Dillon of "Gunsmoke." As television developed, it adapted old formulas to the new medium. Fears that TV would destroy Hollywood vanished as it enriched the dream factory as never before.

Television producers did discover they could do things with history that Hollywood had avoided or abandoned. The TV networks had brought from radio a tradition of electronic journalism. Armed with the visual power of television, producers developed the news documentary—a combination of journalistic and art forms that slowly began to appeal to ever larger audiences. One of the first big successes of the genre was "Victory at Sea," a retrospective series on the World War II naval story. Edward R. Murrow pioneered news documentaries with "See It Now," including a now famous broadcast on the Communist-hunting tactics of Senator Joseph McCarthy. "CBS Reports" did controversial documentaries on the plight of migratory workers and on Pentagon propaganda techniques. "60 Minutes" became a top-rated show. Growing success aside, however, the extent that news documentaries faithfully re-present past events or contemporary processes has been debatable. Because their producers often share many of the entertainment motives, values, and media practices of those who make biblical epics, Westerns, and situation comedies, it is not always easy to sort fiction from fact in what passes for historical programming on television.[3] As with television journalism generally (recall the discussions in Chapters 1 and 2), the melodramatic imperative plays a large role.

Whether the format for presenting the past is news, documentary, or fictional entertainment, the theatrical canons of melodrama are the rule. Melodrama is the mode of entertainment for popular audiences and can easily accommodate and enact mass fantasies. Melodrama simplifies and dramatizes a complex historical world, includes thrilling events and the element of chance, and reflects the topical fantasies that mass audiences envision at a particular time. Melodramatic plot formulas include adventure, mystery, romance, and nightmare, or combinations of these. Melodramas are either fantasies of reassurance or fantasies of fright, telling us that "things are OK, do not worry" or that "things are not OK, do worry." These melodramatic characteristics, to which we alluded earlier, make popular fantasies about the past especially suited to melodramatic portrayal. The constraint of time, the viewing habits of mass audiences, and the normal impulse of creators to transform reality into drama all conspire to produce an endless procession of popular melodramas about the past. History is re-presented as a melodramatic struggle of heroes, villains, and fools, all of whom represent some moral or cultural symbol.[4]

YOU WERE THERE: VARIETIES OF HISTORICAL MELODRAMA

The televised depiction of the popular past involves different subjects from either the remote or recent past that are placed in a melodramatic plot and setting. There are at least four varieties of historical fantasy on

TV: the instant history, the historical biography, the historical panorama, and the fiction fantasy.

Instant History

Frequently contemporary newsworthy events achieve immediate historical significance through quick reconstruction in televised specials or miniseries. In 1976, for instance, terrorists hijacked an airplane filled with Jewish passengers. The highjacker forced the aircraft to be flown to Entebbe, Uganda. After negotiations for the passengers' release broke down, Israeli troops staged a successful raid on the Entebbe airport, killing the terrorists and spiriting the hostages away. Such an event has—one can almost hear a TV writer urging a television executive—great dramatic possibilities. Immediately after the event, *eight* different Entebbe projects were conceived for production. The first produced had an around-the-clock filming schedule. It premiered only nine days after shooting. A paperback book on Entebbe appeared twenty-two days after the raid. Two TV networks ran competing versions of the Entebbe incident. In effect, note Lawrence and Timberg, "the epic docudrama became a secondary news source for many Americans."[5]

The term docudrama, of course, combines documentary with drama and is often used to describe all historically oriented popular TV productions. The docudrama joins two traditions in television, the news documentary with the melodramatic fictional story. The docudrama formula is admirably suited to instant history because the televised portrayal gives palpable life to what people more or less know as a news document (a recent event in the news) and, therefore, a fact of contemporary history. Moreover, because both television nightly news and televised documentaries frequently adapt melodramatic attributes, the logical leap of TV to creating instantaneous documentary histories with a dramatic plot, characters, and a setting based on the real-life event is but another acceptance of the melodramatic imperative. Although a bastardized form, instant history is rooted in television tradition.

Instant histories yield the illusion that viewers are participating in a re-creation of the real event. The real participants at Entebbe received fictional characterization in the drama: the Israelis appeared heroic and disciplined in the execution of the raid; the terrorists came across as fanatical and dangerous villains; the passengers acted as either pitiful victims or defiant heroes; an Israeli officer died a martyr; and Idi Amin, ruler of Uganda, was a mad fool. By casting actual participants into role types, the TV show transformed reality into summary labels, giving melodramatic shape to fantasies of the event; a show sympathetic to the Ugandans and the terrorists would create a markedly different fantasy. Too, the confusions and different perspectives such an event entails receive coherent dramatic unity through the docudrama. The rough edges of realities are smoothed into a logical plot, given order to fit a fantasy about what happened and why. The docudrama of instant history interprets events for audiences, giving a meaning things did not necessarily possess when they happened. Drama, thus, interprets life, but as a mediated interpretation of a raw event.

Thus, to claim (as promotional spots for TV docudramas so often do) that an instant history is a "true story" is misleading. The purpose of the program is not historical authenticity or accuracy but entertainment. Such tales are exploitative, utilizing an emotionally charged event to attract viewers and sponsors, and hyping the sensational aspects of the event in the story. Indeed, whether a news event is selected at all as the subject of TV treatment relates to its mythic adequacy or "the degree to which the features of an event conform to the pre-existing features of a mythic paradigm."[6] In the case of Entebbe the story included the captivity of innocent victims by savage hostage takers and innocents dramatically rescued by the intervention of a heroic force. Like the cavalry galloping to the aid of the wagon train besieged by Indians, the Israeli raid conformed to imperatives that appeal to deeply rooted fantasies in a potential audience. This criterion of popular adequacy influenced the production and broadcast in 1981 by ABC of "Miracle on Ice," a reenactment a year later of the U.S. Olympic hockey team's victory over the Soviet Union, and subsequently winning the gold medal, at the Winter Olympics (see Chapter 6). The victory occurred in the wake of the seizure of the American embassy in Iran, the Soviet invasion of Afghanistan, the heightening of international tensions and, in reaction, an outburst of American patriotic fervor. The Olympic hockey victory had mythic adequacy: not only did the U.S. team win but also the victory came over a hated and threatening enemy. Given Soviet hockey supremacy, it was a David and Goliath match. "Miracle on Ice" combined original sports footage with a behind-the-scenes look at how solid American virtues—hard work, teamwork, and never say die—paid off against the "enemy." But, although instant history related a fantasy about political victory in the hockey match, the Soviets (we may rudely remind ourselves) are still very much in Afghanistan!

Most instant histories do not deal directly with political themes, although they often have political implications. "Raid on Entebbe" told a political story of Israeli heroism versus Arab terrorism, perpetuating a fantasy of heroes and villains in the Middle East struggle. The Olympic hockey story, less overtly political, appealed to patriotic pride and implied Soviet villainy. Two docudramas with even more avowedly political content portrayed, in fictional form, the events surrounding the Watergate era of American politics in the early 1970s. After the resignation of President Richard Nixon in 1974, many of the persons connected with the Watergate scandal wrote books about their experience. Watergate turned out to be one of the most financially rewarding literary events of our time! The two most important TV histories of the scandal were based on two such books, one by John Ehrlichman, the other by John Dean. The Ehrlichman-based Watergate docudrama entitled "Washington: Behind Closed Doors," starred Jason Robards as President Monckton. In 1977 it attracted over 50 million viewers for a twelve-hour miniseries. Robards-Nixon-Monckton, cast as the villain of the drama, is mean, neurotic, and maudlin, consistent with the public fantasy about Nixon's character. Around President Monckton revolve the key personages and big events of the time, beginning long before Watergate but evolving into that event. The story mixed fact and fiction, including political tidbits, such as the allegation that former President John Kennedy had foreign enemies assassinated and that the CIA director kept a mistress.[7] The Dean story, "Blind Ambition," centers more on his private life and how it deteriorates because of Watergate. Nixon, Bob Haldeman, and others are duplicious and calculating, whereas Dean is a young man gone astray by falling in with the wrong crowd. One critic dubbed the program a "docusoap opera."[8] Both productions, indeed, took a major and complex political event and transformed it into melodrama, complete with family crises, beautiful women, palace intrigues, an array of familiar characters, gossip, and personal problems of alcoholism and nervous breakdowns.

In an essay on the docudrama formula, author Mark Harris argues that the docudrama neither dramatizes nor documents history. Audiences see not what happened but themselves. Docudramas create and feed popular fantasies of life in high places. "We think we are seeing the insides of things—Washington behind closed doors."[9] The Watergate melodramas appealed to mass voyeurism, the fantasies people have about the misdeeds, political and personal, of the mighty. The stories did not dramatize the constitutional, political, or moral questions raised. Indeed, those persons Nixon's foes thought the real heroes of the scandal—Judge John Sirica, Leon Jaworski, even Deep Throat—were barely mentioned, much less depicted, in the two TV productions. Instant history is a fantasy of the emperor with no clothes, of the struggles of courtiers and courtesans, who, like the rest of us, have personal and business problems. The glimpse behind closed doors into the Oval Office exposed a president and his associates as petty and ordinary people, just as a glimpse into bedrooms reveals the same relational problems that beset all star-crossed lovers. The Watergate instant histories provided the pleasurable fantasy of watching all the president's men struggle and fall. The tradition of melodrama, writes one observer, included such features as the "audience's sentimental faith in poetic justice" and "its mistrust of the wealthy and the socially elite."[10] The voyeuristic peek at the Watergate melodrama let audiences enjoy fantasies about poetic justice being visited on those in the palace.

Historical Biography

A second use of the past for television fantasy is the historical biography.[11] Here the TV production focuses on a historical personage. The melodrama centers around his or her heroic character and deeds. Sometimes the historical biography has as its subject one who is relatively unknown, but who does great things or who might have been great but, tragically, died young. The range of great things can vary from Caryl Chessman's long but eventually unsuccessful effort to avoid execution by the state of California to Wilma Rudolph overcoming childhood disease to become an Olympic star. It is noteworthy how many televised historical biographies involve a person who dies young —Babe Didrikson Zaharias, Mary White, Lou Gehrig, Brian Piccolo, Joseph Kennedy, Jr., and on and on. This fascination with young and untimely death among talented people is perhaps the ultimate cultural voyeurism. One can only wonder if such productions are popular because people enjoy watching such a tale. If so, in this realm of the psychodynamics of culture, one can ask but not answer the speculative question, What deep mass fantasy is involved in such a macabre voyeurism?

Most historical biographies are about well-known great men and women. Sometimes, as with the case of "Franklin and Eleanor" (Roosevelt), they involve both. But most focus on a great man—a general, a senator, a president. They trace his participation in "big" events as well as aspects of his personal life. The formula for the historical biography evolved during the decade of the 1970s. In that decade these were productions of the careers of a wide variety of relatively recent American public figures—Franklin Roosevelt, Truman, Eisenhower, and John Kennedy as presidents; Patton, MacArthur, and Eisenhower as military leaders; even depictions of people who were, at least for some, villainous, such as Huey Long and Joe McCarthy.

The appearance of all these TV biographies tapped a mass fascination with past and present American leaders. The 1970s was an unheroic age in the wake of Vietnam and Watergate and the consequent disillusionment with presidential heroism. Just as many people came to distrust and dislike contemporary presidents—Nixon, Ford, and Carter— they also seemed willing to venerate past presidents (and other leaders) as heroic. If people seemed willing to believe the worst about present leaders, they also seemed receptive to believing that past leaders were not only better leaders but also more "human." This fantasy drew melodramatic shape from the TV historical biography.

Televised biographical dramas in the 1970s emphasized personal leadership wherein the decisiveness and human qualities of the leader made a key difference in the historical circumstances of the time. Indeed, the plot line often suggested that the depicted leader triumphed *because* of his personal qualities. Thus, the genre devoted a great deal of time to the backstage private lives of the great. Again voyeurism offered glimpses into how great men lived—including their vices. Viewers saw President Truman cursing, drinking bourbon and branch water, and playing poker with his cronies; General Eisenhower smoking heavily and involved in an affair with his pretty English driver, Kay Sommersby, in London; Franklin Roosevelt making martinis and consorting with his old flame, Lucy Mercer, at Warm Springs. The vicarious insights into the private peccadillos of the great may humanize them, even elevate them in some viewers' esteem! Personal charisma and even failings, the biographical formula hints, are sources of a leader's political success. Leaders have common sense that stands them in good stead in political situations because they have a common touch and common habits. Thus, a TV biography had Martin Luther King, Jr., eating chitterlings in his kitchen and delivering great speeches; FDR poring over his stamp collection and fighting the Great Depression; Harry Truman interspersing cards and booze with negotiations with Stalin.

The historical biography, by treating both the public and private lives of historical celebrities, conforms to and promotes two mass fantasies. First, it reassures that there were great men who guided America through great times, thus perpetuating the myth that heroes are the nation's salvation in times of trouble and that they will emerge again in future crises. The confusions of the 1970s impelled this nostalgic yearning for heroes and, indeed, for clear purpose and moral rectitude. Second, by including the private life of the great figure, historical biography restores not only faith in heroic public men but also in public faith in "true" and "honest" relations. The melodramatic depiction of Eisenhower's love affair with the English driver is not sordid but sweetly romantic. The fantasy thrives that great men are charmingly domestic and down to earth. That common quality is, thus, what we must seek in leaders again. The historical biography is a formula depiction of men who are a combination of public and private power, the former flowing from the latter. Wives, mistresses, aides, and servants all see the power of the man. The historical biography denies the old saw, "no man is great to his valet." Rather, he is great because he is domesticated, kind to his team of aides-de-camp, secretaries, and pets. The historical biography creates the illusion that the White House, the European Theater in World War II, and international conferences are run like a family business.

One of the most provocative of TV biodramas was the six-hour 1979 miniseries "Ike." Dwight Eisenhower is depicted as Ike, the Kansas farm boy, who rose to lead the Allies "to victory over Nazi Germany in the greatest war in the history of mankind." But Ike also was "the human being who found tenderness and compassion in the British girl, Kay Sommersby, he made the first female Five Star Aide in the annals of warfare." Ike is a hero who succeeds because he displays common traits in both public and private life. He is a man of simple virtue who appeals to both the attractive driver and Prime Minister Winston Churchill because of his simplicity and character. He is a democratic "man of the soil" who can inspire loyalty because of his moral fiber. Further, he is a man of decision who sees the right course and guides the reluctant or shortsighted into seeing the wisdom of what should be done. He is always persuasive and prescient because what he wants done turns out to be the correct path. Too, Ike is a man of responsibility, courageously taking the blame for mistakes, agonizing over decisions involving many lives, and remaining humble in victory. Finally, he is charismatic, a man whom the great, his camp followers, and ordinary soldiers see as a natural leader. The affair with the driver gives him sexual charisma. Kay is irresistibly drawn to him and senses both his public and personal power; she feels she "belongs to him" but knows that he has a larger destiny to fulfill and that she is not a part of that.

"Ike" is an example of the melodramatic imperative at work in TV historical biography: elements of domestic family setting, sanitized and bittersweet wartime romance, a background of intensified peril, character tested by suffering, and a denouement when the hero experiences both public triumph and private loss. It also says volumes about mass fantasies of leadership. Popular interest in the private lives of the great goes far beyond historical biographies; people judge leaders not only by their public proposals and issues but how they live their private lives as well. This is the *domestication of politics*. It puts politicians and their families in a constant spotlight of popular attention. The activities of President Jimmy Carter's brother or President Ronald Reagan's offspring can be an embarrassment and a political liability. Jerry Brown and Ted Kennedy experiences difficulty in presidential politics because of well-publicized private lives. In a larger sense, historical biographies make life difficult for contemporary politicians because they cannot always live up to the heroic standards of the giants of the past. As long as people fantasize about the lives of past leaders, they can apply those heroic standards to contemporary leaders; present-day officials always suffer by comparison. Although historical biographies may offer, like much of melodrama, a fantasy of reassurance, that very reassurance subverts the reputations and, thus, the political support of contemporary leaders. Nostalgic fantasy, after all, is romantic, set in a much more pleasant, reassuring, and exciting time than the present, which by comparison is a confusing and inchoate reality with leaders who are less than heroic and who must, then, cope not only with the fortunes of contemporary politics but also with romanticized and larger-than-life predecessors. What we see in the romanticized leaders of the historical biography we admire and forgive, but we admire and forgive little in the actual leaders of the here-and-now.

Historical Panorama

Historical panorama is an all-encompassing re-presentation of the past. It tells the story of a major historical process through sweeping melodrama. The historical panorama uses a variety of characters interacting in the context of an ongoing historical event. Using familiar melodramatic touches, it traces the impact of the event on "real" characters. The characters are stereotypes, composite figures who represent a social-type characteristic of the melodrama. The panoramic fantasy reduces complex historical processes to the interplay of heroes, villains, and fools in an exciting backdrop of action and change. By doing so, this TV formula narrates a tale of both the characters and the process. It captures the vastness of historical development by relating it to a cast of identifiable characters.

The two most successful TV historical panoramas to date have been "Roots" and "Holocaust." The original "Roots," broadcast in 1977, attracted an estimated 130 million viewers. All eight "Roots" episodes had audiences in the top fifty programs ever shown on TV; one episode was at that time the largest single TV audience ever (51 percent), topped since only by the "Who Shot J. R.?" episode on "Dallas" (53 percent). [12] "Roots" not only attracted large audiences but also stimulated widespread responses. Survey research indicates that large segments of the "Roots" audience became emotionally involved in the show, responding to the saga of slavery with sadness and anger and being moved by such memorable scenes as the capture of Kunta Kinte and the sale of Kizzy away from her family.[13] Much of the show's success can be attributed to its fantastic quality, dramatizing a vast historical process through the experiences of one family. In particular, it offers blacks a myth of Eden, models of courage, the eventual triumph of the family, and clear stereotypes of villainy in the white characters who commit evil deeds. It narrates to both blacks and whites a parable of hope, that is, that the progress of blacks will continue into the future and that eventually racial intolerance will end. Indeed, white respondents in surveys believed "Roots" would make them respond to blacks with increased sympathy and tolerance. "Roots" fleshed out for American blacks their own myth of origins (the African Dream) and it also incorporated them into the pageant of America. The panoramic scope of the teledrama gave blacks a part of the American Dream, namely, oppression and poverty can be overcome by individual heroism and perseverance. One observer noted that "Roots" is in the tradition of "progressive history . . . [that] viewed history in the simple terms of a conflict between the forces of good and evil, freedom and oppression, democracy and aristocracy, and so forth." "Roots," he points out, is based on progressive themes: "Its heroes and villains were unambiguous and the program reaffirmed basic American values and ideals."[14] By depicting that racial intolerance was, and is, the fault of individual villains and not the system and by showing the triumph of an American family, "Roots" assuaged white guilt feelings and promised hope for progress through the saga of an American family. "Roots," then, is a melodramatic fantasy that humanizes the roots not only of black Americans but also the blight of slavery and racial oppression that has plagued American life and politics from its inception. ("King," the televised historical biography of Martin Luther King, Jr., by comparison was a dismal ratings failure, probably because, unlike "Roots," it did not have a happy ending: King is assassinated, and the program says that the racial problem is *not* solved.)

"Roots" I and II, wrote one observer, were

in essence television equivalents of the medieval morality play. . . . The productions are neither fact nor fiction, but rather didactic popular entertainments in which the characters behave less like individuals than as personifications of good and evil, of caste and class. What gives the dramas their peculiar power is their evocation of a satanic reality that haunts our past as much as Adam's fall haunted the medieval Everyman.[15]

"Roots" was the re-presentation of a past that was successful because it had mythic adequacy. It created for Americans a usable past about an era and a people rarely treated in popular culture. For the first time in a major popular TV production, the victims of slavery were the heroes. As an "epic of origin and destiny," "Roots" was a popular historical panorama that provided Americans with a memorable rhetorical vision that may shape racial consciousness for a long time to come. If the political and social effect of "Roots" is to increase racial understanding and tolerance, then, the maudlin melodramatic structure to the show and its historical inadequacies will be forgiven.[16]

"Holocaust," first broadcast in 1978, was a four-part dramatization of the systematic destruction of European Jews by the Nazis. It attracted an audience of 120 million. Like "Roots," it traced the history of members of one large family, their adventures and travails during the rise and fall of Nazi Germany. It included villainous characters (most in the Nazi SS) and a fool drawn into the Nazi order, a Lieutenant Dorf. Like "Roots," "Holocaust" was attacked for turning one of the most amazing and horrible events of modern times into melodrama. Jewish writer Elie Wiesel, himself a survivor of the Holocaust, attacked the show as transforming "an ontological event into soap opera." The characters are stereotyped composites, the situations are "typical," and the show aims at being panoramic. Wiesel was afraid the show was misleading, again reviving the myth that the Jews were passively led to slaughter without resistance.[17] Because, like "Roots," it was most people's only "look" at the Holocaust, their rhetorical vision of it derived in part from the telecast. And, again like "Roots," the drama ends on a note of hope: the Nazis meet defeat, and even though most of the Weiss family die at the hands of the Nazis, the son and his girlfriend escape to start a new life in Israel.

It is difficult to establish the effect "Holocaust" will have on the political consciousness of Americans. By offering a mediated reality of the Holocaust, the drama simplifies the horror as stereotypic characters and episodes. By humanizing systematic murder so vast that it is difficult to comprehend, perhaps the drama taught something (although partially fictional) about an almost unimaginable event. It should be noted that "Holocaust" had direct political effects when broadcast in West Germany. The Holocaust had not been emphasized in German history and was a virtual taboo in conversation. When it was proposed in 1979 to show "Holocaust," directors of West Germany's largest television network did not broadcast it on the main channel but on a group of regional stations. This, they thought, would effectively bury the event. But the telecast attracted far larger audiences than anticipated. Chancellor Helmut Schmidt praised the series in the Bundestag as encouraging "critical reflection." The widespread popular discussion the show generated revived feelings of outrage and guilt. Indeed the broadcast was the first treatment of, or talk about, the Holocaust many young Germans had ever experienced. "Holocaust" was later broadcast before the German Parliament, then deliberating the extension of the statute of limitations for prosecuting capital offenses committed in World War II beyond its expiration date of 1979. The political fantasies revived or created played a role in the Parliament voting to extend the deadline. The show also aired in East Germany and evoked reactions in other countries, such as The Netherlands and Austria.[18]

Historical Fiction

Historical fiction is a fictional/factual fantasy based on a "What if?" It combines historical individuals who, in fact, lived with events that happened, but it fictionalizes them by inventing historical scenes and dramatizations. Two examples of this televised fantasy are "The Trial of George Armstrong Custer" and "The Trial of Lee Harvey Oswald." Custer's Last Stand in 1876 is one of the most mythologized events in the romance of the West, and Custer is one of the most mythologized figures. In popular culture Custer emerges as a romantic and dashing hero and as an Indian-slaughtering villain. The trial speaks to that ambivalence and to uncertainties about a central myth, The West.[19] Was the conquest of the West a heroic drama conducted by fearless men, such as Custer, or was it a brutal savaging of an indigenous peoples for purposes of greed conducted by raging villains, such as Custer? Equally, curiosity prevails about the guilt of Lee Harvey Oswald. By creating a TV fantasy about his surviving to be tried, the teledrama played on lingering doubts about what *really* happened in Dallas. Did Oswald act alone in the assassination of President John Kennedy? Was he part of a conspiracy? Or was he a fall guy? As you might expect, both shows leave us hanging because the audience is divided: Custer is acquitted, but ambiguously, and we are still left in doubt about his character. Oswald is duly tried but reveals nothing, and he is shot before the verdict is read! Such TV plays are not mythically adequate because they do not resolve the troubling situation. We still do not know how to think about either the Western adventure or who actually shot Kennedy. But it may be, as one observer notes, that such fantasies "may offer a way of vicariously fulfilling needs and resolving anxieties by carrying through with something that was cut short by history."[20]

These different types of historical fantasies get on TV for a wide variety of reasons. The logic of both the medium and of the particular formula dictates that it be melodramatic, reducing history to a personal drama understandable in human terms. It appeals to the vicarious in us, to our desire for inside dope about the great, for romantic leaders, for hopeful interpretations of history. TV historical fantasies are exploitative in the sense that they take liberties with history for entertainment purposes. The ones that are widely watched may affect fantasies about the past and by extension the present and the future.

THE PEOPLE'S TEMPLE:
A CASE OF MIXED RE-PRESENTATION

Occasionally things happen that are so fantastic, involve remarkable characters, are vastly panoramic in scope, and prove so interesting to audiences that their mediation through news and docudramas requires a mixture of melodramatic formats to provide them poetic justice. Such were the events surrounding the bizarre case of a religious cult in Jonestown, Guyana. In November 1978 virtually all of the members of an agricultural community founded by a church called the People's Temple located in Guyana, South America, committed suicide. Over nine hundred people—the estimates vary—either took poison or were shot, many of them apparently voluntarily. This relatively unknown group immediately became grist for various mass-media mills—television news and documentaries, newsmagazine and newspaper accounts, editorial page handwringing, radio and TV talk shows, instant books, a television instant history, and a movie.

Beginning on November 19, 1978, the Guyana story surfaced. Soon it became a major news fantasy that chained out in the media. The network news program that took the lead in reporting the story—and indeed in the long run devoted much more time to it than the other networks—was NBC, for very emotional reasons. The weekend NBC news of November 19 showed a severe and excited anchor Jessica Savitch recounting the first sensational aspects of the story, the murder of Congressman Leo Ryan and others at an airstrip close to Jonestown. NBC had vivid videotapes of the incident. Then, it became clear that NBC reporter Don Harris and others had also been murdered. In the days to come NBC capitalized on the tapes of the shootings, interviews with Jim Jones, shots of Jonestown and the aftermath. The language that characterized the rhetorical vision emerged quickly on NBC as well as the other networks—"mass suicide and murder," "cultists," "death camp," "socialist utopian empire," "assassination and terror squads," "brainwashing and mind control," and of course "tragedy." The exotic setting added to the intrigue: on November 22, with countless members of the Guyana settlement still allegedly and mysteriously missing, Walter Cronkite of CBS speculated that they could be in the forest around the camp, one of the "densest and deadliest jungles" in the world, replete with "poisonous viper snakes, man-eating pirana fish, malarial mosquitos, and quicksand" but with the saving grace of "friendly Indians." On the next night, with the leader of the People's Temple, Reverend Jim Jones, still apparently unaccounted for, Max Robinson of ABC noted that the mystery "has deepened," and "the question remains, Is cult leader Jim Jones still alive?" Jones, like Hitler, "used doubles"; his followers "are quoted as saying they don't believe he's dead"; a boat is "missing from the river which he might have used to flee." In the days to come the networks followed the story through the escalating figures of the number who died, the return of the bodies home (including that of Jones), the disposition of the People's Temple in San Francisco, and the prosecution of killers.

The Guyana story was a natural for the mass media. It had the essential melodramatic ingredients for a popular news story. It involved the adventure of news heroes cut down by fanatics; the mystery of how such a terrible thing could happen; the romance and pathos of lovers and families parted by the suicide; and the nightmare of apparently sane people poisoning themselves and their children on command. Jim Jones became for the media a demonic figure, whose organizational, sexual, and personal power over his followers was both fascinating and frightening. In more general terms the story condensed a rhetorical vision that represented for mass audiences the *cult fantasy*, the fear of new and bizarre religions (e.g., the Moonies, Hare Krishna) that ordinary people—especially America's children—may be lured into joining. Jim Jones's cult represented to many in the media audience the ultimate danger and fate of such groups: that they turn people into zombies, exploit members sexually and financially, expect complete obedience to a dictatorial leader, pervert religion into fanatical submission, and for some even prove that racially integrated groups or collectivist societies cannot work.

The cult fantasy is a lurid one, and the alleged activities of Jones and his followers became a *paradigm fantasy*, one that represented for many people in the mass-mediated audience the consequences of cultism. In other words, media re-creation of the Guyana settlement and the events of November 1978 was a melodrama of what cults are like or, at least, the potential they have for evil. The fantasy themes that chained out among the public through various media after the Jonestown suicide likely constitute the rhetorical vision many people wish to entertain of the world of cults, which of course may include many religious groups that do not even consider themselves cults and do not do the things Jones did. But a paradigm fantasy, communicated to a mass public, may stick as *the* fantastic reality of all such religious groups.

In any case, as the Guyana story developed rapidly through eyewitness accounts, interpretive background stories, and visual images, the melodramatic possibilities became clearer. Guyana was a fantasy of fright in which a nightmare world was created and headed by a figure of demonic power who dominated the group through evil means. Jones and his intimates became villains, Congressman Ryan and reporter Don Harris heroes, and the "inmates" of Jonestown fools and finally victims. A newspaper picture showing only Jones's tinted-glasses covered eyes was captioned, "Are these the eyes of a madman?"

The first "instant history" of Guyana appeared in book form—the *Washington Post's Guyana Massacre: The Eyewitness Account*, by "the reporter who saw it all," Charles A. Krause.[21] The rhetorical vision of nightmare is implicit in the language of the book: "nightmare days of terror and tragedy"; "paranoid messiah of a terrorized but devoted congregation"; "frenzied dramatic ritualism"; "how the madness of one man could converge with the spirit of an age in upheaval to weave a doomed nexus out of strands ranging from the most ancient of human instincts and customs to the physiology of the mammalian brain."[22] Krause's book, published a month after the Jonestown suicide, pieced together—through Krause's own experiences, interviews with survivors, and other sources—the beginnings of a rhetorical vision of the story that was to form the basis eventually of the CBS–TV instant history. Within the range and canons of melodrama, the quality of dramatic productions—including the degree of sensationalism—can vary greatly. Melodrama typically involves a moral tale of the struggle of morality versus immorality and satisfies mass-audience desire for both thrilling and sensational fare combined with some sort of affirmation that evil is punished and that morality is vindicated. We might term a melodramatic nightmare fantasy an immorality play in which ordinary "moral" life is disrupted by some immoral [or sometimes amoral, as the Three Mile Island (TMI) accident] force that threatens us. Because the immoral force is satanic or demonic, the nightmare fantasy must establish evil intent, that is, the motives of the villain must be portrayed as immoral. The demonic leader is charismatic, but his personal charm is used to dominate, manipulate, and exploit those who fall under his spell. This avoids overtly sociological or political explanations of an event like Jonestown, making it stem from the demonic power of the leader who misleads and ultimately destroys his followers. Audiences do not want the guilt for such awful events pinned on amorphous social causes, which are difficult to identify and might even include themselves as the culprits; rather, they prefer a flesh-and-blood villain whose fault it all is.

Even given the dramatic logic implicit in such mass-mediated fantasies, production values of a nightmare tale can either exploit the sensationalistic aspect to the point of ludicrousness or use it more responsibly in the context of the larger story. The former is evident in the quickie movie that emerged on Jonestown, entitled *Guyana: Cult of the Damned*. With a cast of players whose days of film stardom were well behind them—Stuart Whitman, Joseph Cotten, Gene Barry, Yvonne DeCarlo, and many, many more—the film portrayed the tragedy in fictional form. Fictional names were substituted for the leading figures—for Jones, Ryan, and so on. The locales were the same as the news event, but the names of the religious cult, the agricultural community, and other groups and locals were changed. The film accented pure sensationalism of the type seen in afterhours drive-in theaters, where, incidentally, the film had many of its showings. Torture, beatings, rape, incest, drug abuse, medical malpractice—every conceivable titillating aspect of the original People's Temple news stories commanded emphasis. The film combined instant history and historical fiction in lurid, almost soft porn fashion.

A higher quality version was the CBS made-for-TV production broadcast entitled "Guyana Tragedy: The Story of Jim Jones." This production illustrated that, within the framework of melodramatic instant history, the rhetorical vision created can enrich for viewers the background and development of Jones and his cult and how the members eventually wound up committing suicide in Guyana. As historical biography, the story revolves around the character of Jim Jones, tracing him from his origins in smalltown Indiana to success as a charismatic preacher and church leader and to the establishment of the utopian settlement in Guyana. As a child, he "plays" preacher and thinks himself "called"; he is sincerely concerned about racial prejudice; and he successfully begins an interracial church in Indianapolis. But his leadership ability and organizational success pale beside (as it must be in tragedy) flaws in his character: he a believer, then a charlatan who becomes a demon. The social good he seeks falls before egomania, the lusts of the flesh, drugs, and the intoxication of power. A key scene is when Jones talks with Father Divine, a well-known black minister who claimed to be God. Divine suggests to Jones that to "produce God" for his flock he use their worldly possessions and give them a whole new life, even if he does not really believe in it all. Jones's charlatanism thus established, he proceeds to descend into demonic megalomania and eventual disaster.

In subsequent scenes, Jones takes amphetamines and then harder drugs. He makes love to adoring women in his congregation. He conducts fraudulent faith healings, justified as reinforcing faith. The People's Temple gains political influence, acquires a great deal of money ("I didn't know I had Machiavelli working in the accounting office," he remarks to a female accountant who informs him of her financial jugglings, then makes love to her). With his immorality established, Jones's demonic domination of the group grows with his self-image, with such self-references as "I am the chosen one," "Follow me," "I am the Father. I am God." His demonic spell over his followers grows with stern discipline, public humiliation, and physical intimidation of cult members. As the group moves to San Francisco and then to Jonestown, Jones's megalomania deteriorates into paranoia and brooding self-absorption. He sees traitors everywhere and CIA plots to destroy him and his dream. He demands loyalty tests, such as mock suicide rituals. After the murder of Congressman Ryan, his family gathers, and most members docilely take the cyanide-laced Kool-Aid. Jones rants on while most all are dead; he is finally shot in the closing scene.

The mediated political reality of this particular show is suggestive.

At root is a *Hitler fantasy*, which holds that groups of people can fall under the spell of a demonic figure and do his bidding unto death.[23] Jones is a bush-league Führer, running a little Fascist empire in Guyana and destroying his group by his own madness. The mad genius— Frankenstein, Caligari, Rasputin—is a familiar character in popular melodrama, and the characterization of Jones here is much in that mold. The will to power of the mad genius violates the ordinary values and habits of bourgeois decency and looses the furies of sexual license and unbridled sadistic power. Jones's Guyana creation violates the canons of American social and political life, that is, individualism, property ownership, marriage, racial separation, and freedom. It thus falls into the political demonics that mass audiences often associate with totalitarianism: a popular perception is that totalitarian leaders are demons who enslave their people and turn them into robots, with no souls or will, to do their evil bidding. The Jonestown story is a fantasy, then, not only of the consequences of cultism but also as a paradigm case of the demonics of totalitarian societies.

It must be said that CBS's instant history of Jones and Jonestown is one of the best of the genre. While meeting audience expectations, the show likely gave viewers a better picture of what happened at Jonestown than the more piecemeal and immediate stories of the evening news. The docudrama format of a multihour telecast permits considerably more background material, character development, and historical re-creation than is possible in straight news formats. Even though some scenes in the show were fictional and others were condensed, even though characters were flat composites, even though sensational elements were included for their lurid quality, and so forth, CBS's Guyana story illustrates the uses of instant history to give some story sense for popular consumption. But it should always be remembered that such stories give us a media truth and not a historical truth. The instant history re-presents a past in a more retrospective way than the evening news coverage can, but it remains fantasy—not to be confused with truth. The truth, as in so many historical events, may have died with those wretched folk at Jonestown, quickly lost in the mists of time.

NOTES

1. Herbert J. Muller, *The Uses of the Past* (New York: Oxford University Press, 1957), p. 33.

2. See George Herbert Mead, *The Philosophy of the Present* (LaSalle, Ill.: Open Court Publishing Co., 1959).

3. A more extensive treatment of the relationships between popular culture and politics is James Combs, *Polpop: Politics and Popular Culture in America* (Brunswick, Ohio: King's Court Communication, 1982).

4. See Earl F. Bargainnier, "'Hissing the Villain, Cheering the Hero: The Social Function of Melodrama," *Studies in Popular Culture*, 3 (Spring 1980): 48–56.

5. John Shelton Lawrence and Bernard Timberg, "News and Mythic Selectivity: Mayaguez, Entebbe, Mogadishu," *Journal of American Culture*, 2 (Summer 1979): 324.

6. Ibid., p. 328.

7. Michael Arlen, "Getting the Goods on President Monckton," in Horace Newcomb, ed., *Television: The Critical View* (New York: Oxford University Press, 1979), pp. 160–169.

8. Arthur Unger, "John Dean's Version," *Christian Science Monitor*, May 17, 1979, p. 14.

9. Mark Harris, "Docudramas Unmasked," *TV Guide* (March 4, 1978); reprinted in the *Chicago Tribune*, March 8, 1978, sec. 3, p. 12.

10. Bargainnier, "Hissing the Villain," op. cit., p. 50.

11. Much of the material in this section is adapted from James Combs, "Television Aesthetics and the Depiction of Heroism: The Case of the TV Historical Biography," *Journal of Popular Film and Television*, 8 (June 1980): 9–18; see also William H. Cohn, "History for the Masses: Television Portrays the Past," *Journal of Popular Culture*, 10 (Fall 1976): 280–289; Erich Foner, "The Televised Past," *Nation* (June 16, 1979): 724–726; Bill Davidson, "Docudrama: Fact or Fiction," in James Monaco, ed., *Celebrity* (New York: Dell Publishing Co., 1978), pp. 55–62; N. Swallow, "Television: The Integrity of Fact and Fiction," *Sight and Sound*, 45 (Summer 1976): 183–186; "Do TV Docu-dramas Distort History?" *U.S. News & World Report* (May 21, 1979): 51–52; and Joseph P. McKerns, "Television Docudramas: The Image as History," *Journalism History*, 7 (Spring 1980): 24–25, 40.

12. Lawrence W. Lichty, "Success Story," *Wilson Quarterly*, 5 (Winter 1981): 63.

13. Kathy La Tour, "'Roots' Postlude: Survey Charts Viewer Response," *National Observer* (June 20, 1977): 2. The data were drawn from a national survey by the Center for Policy Research, New York.

14. McKerns, "Television Docudramas," op. cit., p. 25.

15. Karl E. Meyer, "Rootless Mini-series," *Saturday Review* (January 20, 1979): 52–53.

16. See Phillip Wander, "On the Meaning of 'Roots,'" *Journal of Communication*, 27 (Autumn 1977): 64–69; Kenneth K. Hur and John P. Robinson, "The Social Impact of 'Roots,'" *Journalism Quarterly*, 55 (Spring 1978): 19–24; Howard F. Stein, "In Search of Roots: An Epic of Origin and Destiny," *Journal of Popular Culture*, 11 (Summer 1977): 11–17.

17. Elie Wiesel, "Trivializing the Holocaust: Semifact and Semifiction," *Chicago Tribune*, April 30, 1978, sec. 2, p. 1.

18. John Vinocur, "'Holocaust' TV Series, Criticized, Is Sidelined by West Germans," *New York Times*, July 2, 1978; "'Holocaust' Audience Far Bigger Than West Germans Anticipated," *New York Times*, January 23, 1979, p.; John Vinocur, "Germans Are Caught Up by 'Holocaust' Telecasts," *New York Times*, January 23, 1979; "39% of German TV Viewers Watch 'Holocaust' Episode," *New York Times*, January 26, 1979; "Widow of Heydrich Says 'Holocaust' Ignores Facts," *New York Times*, February 5, 1979; see too Harold de Bock and Jan van Lil, "'Holocaust' in The Netherlands," and Peter Diem, "'Holocaust' and the Austrian Viewer," in G. Cleveland Wilhoit and Harold de Bock, eds., *Mass Communication Review Yearbook*, vol. 2 (Beverly Hills, Calif.: Sage Publications, 1981).

19. Paul A. Hutton, "Custer's Last Stand," *TV Guide*, November 26, 1977; reprinted in the *Chicago Tribune*, November 28, 1977, sec. 5, p. 12.

20. McKerns, "Television Docudramas," op. cit., pp. 24, 40.

21. Charles A. Krause, *Guyana Massacre: The Eyewitness Account* (New York: Berkley Publishing Corp., 1978).

22. Ibid., pp. 2–4.

23. Donald M. McKale, "Hitler's Children: A Study of Postwar Mythology." *Journal of Popular Culture*, 15:1 (Summer 1981): 46–55.

4

Political Celebrity in Popular Magazines

On May 20–21, 1927, an unknown flyer named Charles Lindbergh flew a small airplane across the Atlantic, landing at Le Bourget near Paris. Much to his surprise and eventually chagrin, Lindbergh was immediately transformed into a famous personage, what we now call a celebrity. His flight was hailed as a stupendous event worthy of national celebration. He was celebrated in newspaper editorials and stories, in tickertape parades, and in speeches by politicians. Lindbergh's flight was transformed into a heroic drama representative of the American Dream. He was likened to a lone pioneer achieving something on his own in the new technological age. He received many proposals of marriage from strangers. The press hounded his every step and covered in detail his marriage to the beautiful debutante, Anne Morrow. Later, the celebrated kidnapping and murder of his infant son became sensationalist media fare. Lindbergh was a very private man who disliked publicity and, so, spent the rest of his life almost as a recluse. Yet, he remained a celebrity whose very mystery intrigued the mass media to continue to report his activities.[1]

Lindbergh was one of the original cases of someone caught up in the nexus of celebrity who neither wanted nor understood it. But most people who become celebrities are not so reluctant. Nietzsche long ago wrote of the "will to power;" nowadays we might write of the will to fame. Since the 1920s, we have been attracted more and more to the private lives of public figures from sports, entertainment, cafe society, and other forums. Figures such as Lindbergh, Babe Ruth, and Douglas Fairbanks, Sr. were celebrated by the public no matter what. People read and talked about the off-field antics of Ruth as well as his on-field exploits. People followed the scandalous behavior of movie stars; consequently, a whole gossip industry of fanzines (fan magazines) and new columns devoted to Hollywood arose around the movie studios. Publicists and agents used propaganda skills to groom the "image" of the famous or the soon-to-be-famous. Today Americans can identify literally hundreds of celebrities, and they feel that they "know" them somehow.

The *celebrity* has its own logic. A celebrity is a "human pseudo-event," people "known for their well-knownness."[2] The relationship between the celebrity and the public is vicarious. The fan fantasizes the celebrity who occupies a world more interesting and exciting than that in which ordinary mortals live. Celebrities are more talented, beautiful, richer, sophisticated, moral or immoral, heroic or villainous than ourselves. They live in a play world of drama—of adventure, mystery, romance, pathos, and nightmare. Celebrity logic casts public figures as a social type in public dramas. They are a public representation of a popular need for identifiable, if fantastic, types. It is no accident that Hollywood developed typecasting, wherein actors and actresses played the same character types in movie after movie. We identify John Wayne, Marilyn Monroe, or Humphrey Bogart as archetypical representations of social types both on and off the screen. Celebrities exist as much because we need them as they need us.

In his book on Douglas Fairbanks, Sr., Richard Schickel meditated on the phenomenon of celebrity. Beginning with the 1920s the mass communication revolution meant that more and more Americans would live with two realities, the reality of everyday life and the fantastic reality occupied by celebrities. He argues that "the people who existed in this separate reality—the stars and celebrities—were as familiar to us, in some ways, as our friends and neighbors. In many respects we were—and are—more profoundly involved with their fates than we are with those of most of the people we know personally." He notes that political issues, among other things, do not have "real status . . . until they have been taken up, dramatized, in the celebrity world." The politician can only "exert genuine influence on the general public" to the extent that he or she becomes a celebrity. He concludes that, "it is in this surreal world that all significant national questions are personified and thus dramatized."[3]

Perhaps it should not surprise us that many people "live" so much in the fantastic world of the celebrity. After all, we spend much of our time watching TV and movies, reading papers and magazines, and listening to radio. We "know" dozens, even hundreds, of celebrity figures from the world of mass-mediated sports, religion, television, movies, publishing, politics, and other forms of entertainment. Indeed, it is likely that "most Americans probably spend more time in artificial interactions than they do in real ones."[4] Such artificial social interactions (parasocial interactions) mean that we have a vicarious experience with a fantasy figure, a celebrity who lives in the fantastic world of the media.[5] Celebrities are the dramatis personae of our vicarious mass-mediated melodramas. The logic of celebrity is related to the psychologic of individual experience and the logic of media melodrama.

NEWS THEATER

The logic of celebrity, then, involves a collaborative process of mass public, mass media, and mass celebrity. The relationship is symbiotic: the psychologic of the mass includes a desire for fantasy figures; the mass media discover and cater to this need; and celebrities play the roles that make them the fantasy figures the mass public desires. For example, mass-mediated news spends much time and effort reporting the activities of newsworthy media figures. Apparently there is an inexhaustible interest in such figures among the mass public. Too, those who would become public figures seek out media that communicate celebrity.

For news media this process has been called *news theater*.[6] Celebrities and the mass media mutually exploit each other in the presentation of staged performances by celebrities in conjunction with mass media for the entertainment of mass audiences. The news media make potential celebrities famous and celebrities, in turn, make news. Indeed celebrities are "symbolic leaders" who perform key roles in public drama.[7] Our rhetorical vision of the worlds of entertainment, news, and politics is peopled by show biz, news, and political celebrities on whom we depend to sustain a public drama that we attend. Celebrity fantasy figures, such as Johnny Carson and Reggie Jackson, are familiar to us from the dramatic worlds of late-night and sports entertainment, respectively. Figures such as Walter Cronkite and Tom Brokaw are media celebrities from the world of news. And, of course, politicians are celebrities. In public drama these categories merge: news celebrities are news themselves; entertainers get involved in the public drama of politics; newspeople are urged to run for office; politicians become entertainers. Our rhetorical vision is transformed by news theater into a gigantic and unending global public drama in which celebrities overlap traditional institutional and social categories. If news theater threatens to make all the mass-mediated world a stage, it also makes traditional distinctions among types of celebrity players obsolete.

POLITICAL CELEBRITY

Recall Schickel's remark that politicians have become celebrities. Politics is part of the public drama of news theater, bending to the logic of celebrity. Politicians are fantasy figures in the blending rhetorical vision of the celebrity world. They are the dramatis personae of our vicarious mass-mediated political melodrama. They serve the same vicarious psychological functions as other celebrities. The better-known ones represent for us some variation of political types that we expect to act in the political drama. Politicians seek, and are expected to appear in, nonpolitical media forums as part of the public drama, performances that "prove" their celebrity status. A new political figure, say John B. Anderson, immediately becomes a celebrity. To the extent that one hopes to remain a national figure and, as Schickel says, exert genuine influence on the general public, one must cultivate celebrity status. In this respect Anderson's celebrity was short lived.

In a Machiavellian sense, then, celebrity has its political uses. Political celebrities exploit news theater in the same way as other celebrities, only for political purposes. To a very large extent, contemporary American politics is government by publicity. Publicity is derived from news theater. Becoming a political celebrity—indeed, almost any kind of celebrity—yields political power. To the extent that one achieves media publicity and a celebrity reputation, that celebrity is a political advantage. It is almost a prerequisite to political success nowadays to become a celebrity first. Politicians, thus, study the arts of self-promotion and recruit assistance from professionals skilled in publicity.

Politicians seek to control their celebrity image through adroit presentation of their celebrity self in mediated political life. They seek access to celebrity-oriented media—talk shows, gossip magazines, Sunday newspaper supplements, and other forums—as much as do movie stars or rock singers. They differ from some other celebrities in that they do not want bad publicity, such as exposés of their private lives that cast them as villain or fool. Other celebrities may thrive on notoriety, but the political celebrity very largely cannot survive a bad press. People's moral and political expectations change over time, however, and politicians can now do many of the things common to other celebrities—divorce, date beautiful jetsetters, have problems with family members on drugs, marry movie stars, and so forth. Because we expect politicians to consort with other celebrities, we learn to evaluate them accordingly. When the Governor of California, Jerry Brown, went on an African safari with a famous rock singer, Linda Ronstadt, and became the cover story in *Newsweek*, we witnessed but one example of the celebritization of politics.

Politicians are, thus, fantasy figures as much as are other celebrities. As symbolic leaders they represent not only politics per se, but also values, lifestyle, and glamor. We celebrate them for a complex of reasons and expect them to act in the public drama in a way consistent with our assessment of what they are. Our rhetorical vision of politics includes political celebrities playing both political and nonpolitical roles —members of families, fathers and mothers, churchgoers, amateur athletes, football fans, hunters and fishermen, and so on. Americans fantasize about politicians' entire lives, including aspects about which they know little or nothing in fact.

This process reaches its most ludicrous proportions in recurrent rumors that famous politicians who died long ago are not really dead but alive and in hiding. This kind of fantastic rumor appeared after the death of many historical personages. Hitler, for example, allegedly survived World War II and was in hiding (in Argentina or the South Seas) awaiting the proper moment to return. Franklin Roosevelt, Ché Guevara, Emiliano Zapata, and Joseph Stalin also supposedly survived demise. More recently, rumors that John Kennedy was alive, although a vegetable, have circulated persistently. Kennedy is variously thought to be on an upper floor of Bethesda Naval Hospital, at Parkland Memorial Hospital in Dallas, at the Quantico Marine base, or on Aristotle Onassis's island in Greece.[8] A celebrity figure may thus be of such importance that followers accept the fantasy of everlasting life.

POLITICAL SUBPLOTS OF THE NATIONAL SOAP OPERA

The political celebrity, then, seeks and finds mass-mediated forms that exhibit admired traits for mass audiences. As with the Hollywood star and other forms of celebrity, an industry has developed to communicate political celebrity. Like the gossip magazines and columns of Hollywood, this industry rests on collaboration rather than on adversity between media and the celebrity. The focus of an article, book, photo essay, or interview is usually sympathetic and unhostile, indeed, staged in cooperation with the celebrity and his publicists. Typically, the content of the mediated forum is about the private life of the political celebrity. The magazine profile article, for example, sketches the family life, personal habits, likes and dislikes, and opinions of the politician or his family members. The piece usually includes treatment, however gingerly, of family problems, often with frank discussion with, say, the politician's wife about concerns over the children.

This is but another variation on soap opera politics (see Chapter 2). We refer to that genre of melodrama that focuses on the personal relationships of media characters. From the old radio soaps ("Ma Perkins," "Guiding Light") to pop magazines (*True Romance*) to today's sophisticated TV vehicles ("General Hospital," "All My Children"), Americans are endlessly addicted to the soap opera formula. The soap opera deals with a collection of characters, many of them glamorous and wealthy, who involve themselves in intricate and ever-changing relationships. Interest in such characters and tales stems in part from the same vicarious roots as our interest in real-life celebrities. Both soap characters and political celebrities are involved in a celebrated melodrama of interpersonal relations. In both cases the vicarious fantasy is constructed from our interest in the personal lives of mass-mediated characters who have problems and failings just like you and me. Soap opera politics humanizes politicians and their families. For many of us politics is part of a larger national soap opera. Our rhetorical vision includes generalized fantasies about the private lives of political and nonpolitical celebrities, their families, and their friends. Gossip and tidbits about how the great and mighty live enliven our vision. If politics were merely abstract issues and policies devoid of personality, it would be of less interest. The mediated soap opera of politics provides flesh and blood, what journalists used to call human interest.

There are many media forums for the political dimension of the national soap opera—celebrity columns in newspapers, Sunday supplement profiles, TV gossip reporters, talk and interview shows, magazine profiles. When Barbara Walters or Mike Wallace interviews a political figure on TV, this provides a stage for the validation of political celebrity. Publications such as the *National Enquirer, National Star,* and *People* give play to the private lives of the political great, including innuendoes about swinging lifestyles and tales of family woes. But perhaps one of the most important, but lesser-known media forums for soap opera politics is the women's magazines—*McCalls Magazine, Ladies' Home Journal, Redbook, Harper's Bazaar, Good Housekeeping,* and, in a somewhat different sense, *Ms. Magazine, Cosmopolitan,* and *Playgirl.* A glance at the articles about political celebrities in the mainstream women's magazine reveals a gossip fantasy, the domestication of politics as a family affair. The focus is usually on the wives of political celebrities, which, of course, makes wives political celebrities also. Many such articles are collaborative, written in cooperation with the subject of the article and her public relations staff. (First Ladies, for example, have their own PR staff in the White House.) Even if not collaborative efforts, they are very often sympathetic gossip about the lives of political celebrity women in the corridors of power. They appeal to vicarious desires to participate in the lives of celebrities. The result is a fantastic world in which complex political questions are reduced to the province of husband-wife and other family relations. Like the characters on TV soaps, the political characters of a typical women's magazine article live out a celebrated melodrama of interpersonal relations.

In this rhetorical vision the political wife is the central figure in the American political melodrama. Indeed, she may play a variety of roles, depending on how she is cast in the women's magazine article. She may be cast as a *loyal helpmate*, the woman who stands by her political man, and in whom he finds a constant source of strength and encouragement. Or she may be a *concerned parent*, who worries—as we all do—about our children, the high cost of living, the state of the country and the world, all of which she hopes her husband can do something about. Another role is the *social leader*, which casts her as working at some social problem or cause, such as mental illness or art. She may be a *glamorous lady*, who leads a life of elegance and romance with her politician-husband. She is also possibly a *political advisor* to her husband, a power behind the throne. Finally, she can be cast as a *political victim*, someone whom the pressures of power and fame destroy. In each role she is a political celebrity who lives in a world more glamorous, exciting, and dangerous than our own. Yet, at the same time, her relationship to her husband and family is the crucial aspect of her life, as it is for a good part of the readership of women's magazines. Let us look at selected political wives as cast in women's magazines.

Nancy Reagan

Nancy Reagan is cast largely as a loyal helpmate and glamorous lady. From *People*, we learn "The New First Lady is a Former Debutante, But Watch Out: She's a Fighter." In the 1980 campaign, she was the loyal helpmate: "Her performance in the 1980 campaign was flawless. . . . By supernatural discipline, she seemed never mussed or wrinkled, and even in the last days before the election she listened to her husband's campaign litany as if she were hearing it for the first time." She is, we learn, in love with her husband: "Perhaps the Reagans' greatest gift to the style of official Washington will be their unabashedly public romance—which is more openly affectionate than that of the understated Carters."[9] *People* later tells us that she is glamorous: "Elegant, Opulent, Right-Minded," she and her friends are "world-class partygoers and -givers, and all are movers in California society. . . . We are finally going to see some real style in Washington. . . . It's a kind of style that requires effort and inventiveness—and lots of experience."[10] *Harper's Bazaar* tells us how Nancy stays young and beautiful: "Fastidious in her approach to beauty, meticulous in her way of dressing, she is setting a standard of excellence that women everywhere can identify with."[11] Being cast as loyal helpmate and glamorous lady is not necessarily virtuous. The feminist periodical *Ms. Magazine* tells us that we now have a "Total Woman" in the White House, a "winner of best in her class. Queen Nancy. The Marzipan wife. The rare woman who can perform the miracle of having no interests at all; of transplanting her considerable ego into a male body."[12] Overall, women's magazines generally treat Nancy Reagan quite positively and are largely uncritical of her opulent lifestyle; but, then, they might also have taken the same view of Marie Antoinette.

Rosalynn Carter

Rosalynn Carter was rarely depicted in women's and gossip magazines as highly glamorous, but she was cast as a loyal helpmate and political advisor. *Redbook* told us that she is "described by her husband as his first and last love . . . and no doubt will remain Jimmy's best friend and closest advisor. She is a warm and gracious woman who seems to have expanded her capacities with each new phase of her husband's career."[13] *Ladies' Home Journal* ("Love and Power in the White House") gave us "an intimate look into the lives of Washington's most romantic couple—the President and his First Lady." Rosalynn has "verve, intelligence, curiosity, a calm core and strength . . . firm determination." She "does not seem what she is: the Cinderella small-town beauty parlor attendant who is now one of the most powerful women in the world." We also learned that Jimmy and Rosalynn are a "team," that she helps him make political decisions and negotiate with American government leaders, but she still insists on, and directs, a "close" family life. The portrait concluded that Rosalynn is a "pretty young woman from a tiny town in Georgia who married the man she loved, who helped make him a prince—and shared his power."[14] Although in a somewhat different way from Nancy Reagan, she is, like Nancy, a great help to, and still in love with, her husband.

The core of the First Family fantasy seems to be that it is headed by a happy couple, mutually supportive and loving, who are surrounded by close children and relatives, and in that setting the political wife plays a pivotal role. Such a soap-opera depiction is positive gossip about how happy, busy, and useful the First Lady is, living in an exciting world of handsome princes and exotic lands. The use of the Cinderella motif is not misplaced: the fantasy casts the political heroine in a melodrama in which she really does live in a palace, ride in shining coaches, wear elegant gowns to majestic balls, and live happily ever after with Prince Charming. Perhaps this rhetorical vision of political princesses that traditional women's magazines, in collaboration with the princess herself, is one in which many wish to believe. Romantic melodramas tend toward happy endings.

Of course, the reality of the private lives of political couples is probably as fraught with difficulty as are the private lives of ordinary mortals. We now know, for example, something of the private difficulties of the Nixons and Fords. But difficulties aside, the women's magazines offer a profile of celebrity wives that may well fill a need among middle-class women readers. Positive gossip reassures that family values and happy endings still exist, if not among ourselves, at least in the palace of an American Cinderella and her Prince Charming. The fantasy is important enough that negative gossip, which points to family values denied and unhappy endings, can be politically harmful.

Joan Kennedy

Negative gossip may cast the political wife as a victim. Because the political wife is the heroine of the women's magazine story, this means that the politician-husband may become the villain of the piece. If the rhetorical vision of the women's magazine profile combines love and power in a happy political and familial marriage, then, the failure is not that of the woman who loves her man, but of the man who loves power more than her. The neglected wife is a standard melodramatic theme of romance, and here the political ambitions (and the charisma that causes other women to tempt him) of the husband bring the neglect. Abandoned, the wife becomes the tortured victim of a political world she never made. Prince Charming turns out to be a lout. Such casting can obviously be politically harmful to the politician-husband. One has to be, after all, a good husband to be a good politician.

This was never more clearly illustrated than in the Joan Kennedy fantasy. From *McCalls Magazine* to *Ms. Magazine*, Joan became in the late 1970s the paradigm case of political victim. The pressures of the high-powered Kennedy clan, the lurid episode of Chappaquiddick in 1969, the tabloid gossip about her husband's philandering, and his prolonged absences while campaigning all conspired to victimize her. The feminist magazines cast Joan as a victim of political male chauvinism and exploitation. The more traditional magazines cast her as a victim of husbandly neglect in the spirit of "Can this marriage be saved?"

It is true that the villainous casting of Ted Kennedy was oblique and implied. Indeed, he had often been pictured before as a hero. *McCalls Magazine* of February 1974 spoke of "the burden of Ted Kennedy" as "surrogate father of her [Ethel's] eleven children... that means the nurturing of those traits of physical courage and daring, the ideals of public service, the sense of noblesse oblige that attends the rich and fortunate, the incredible mystique of family solidarity and the seriousness of religious observance."[15] But by November 1975, the "troubled marriage of Joan and Ted" is Ted's fault. Ted may run for president in 1976, we learn, and the "state of his marriage" will be crucial to his chances. Chappaquiddick can be defused as an issue if Ted has a happy marriage. Joan is seen as a "nice girl" who has "public sympathy" because she is "unable to cope with the tough and worldly Kennedys." If she refuses to "play the role of happy wife," public perceptions of a "loveless marriage," tied to Chappaquiddick, will be politically devastating.[16]

Joan, the victim, became increasing press fare as the 1970s proceeded. By 1978 the speculation about Ted running for president began anew. However, speculation in women's magazines about the state of his marriage continued. Whether for planned political reasons or not,

Joan Kennedy recounted "her own story" in the August 1978 issue of *McCalls Magazine*. She revealed that she was an alcoholic, separated from Ted, and trying to rebuild her life. The interviewer noted that as Joan poured out her story, "innocently, almost pleading for understanding," she was "discovering herself as she talked." As the story unfolded, the interviewer's mind

went back to a childhood phrase: 'Once upon a time' was the way the tales began, and this one began so easily: 'Once upon a time, there was a beautiful girl with long blond hair and wide blue eyes who met a handsome and very rich prince. . . .' But then the tale would turn tragic, for the next line would be: 'This prince had two older brothers. . . .' Was it possible that her story will, someday, end as fairy stories are supposed to end? Will people ever say, 'And they lived happily ever after?'

The interviewer concluded with

admiration—for her courage, her understanding and her self-reliance. . . . I no longer had any doubt about how the story would end. They would 'live happily ever after.'[17]

There were reports that when Kennedy saw the article, he was furious because it cast him as the heavy, making people ask, "What kind of man would do that to his wife?"[18]

What kind of man, indeed? The negative gossip generated by women's magazines was to haunt the presidential candidacy of Ted Kennedy in 1980. His candidacy brought Joan back into the gossip limelight. And, indeed, the gossip fantasy did harm Kennedy's primary fight against the family man Carter. His marriage to Joan was refurbished, and she joined the campaign trail. *People* in 1979 announced that she has joined her "husband's daring campaign," says "Yes, I still love him," and makes a "gallant defense" of recurrent tales about his "womanizing." But gallant Joan is still the victim: "Playing enthusiastic candidate's wife, some claim, is Joan's most skillful acting job since she made TV commercials for Coca-Cola and Revlon 20 years ago."[19] She appeared with him in public and said she would live in the White House with him if elected. She told *McCalls Magazine* that "this campaign has been wonderful for me, the best thing in the world, next to getting sober. It's been terrific for my self-esteem."[20] Joan was now not so much a victim as a victorious independent lady. Although Kennedy's campaign failed, we learn from a June 1980 woman's supplement in the *Chicago Tribune*, "The 'Kennedy Victory' may be Joan's."[21] The once frail and pitiful Joan was by now "as tough and brave and independent as any Kennedy. . . . Joan may well deserve the label of 'bravest Kennedy'."[22]

Joan Kennedy, then, was in 1980 the heroine of a mass-mediated soap opera with definite political consequences. The mass expectation that political celebrities be good husbands made Ted a villain. If she was transformed in the rhetorical vision of women's magazines from a victim to a brave and independent new person, he was recast in the minds of many as lacking character. The news theater of women's magazine and newspaper political celebrity profiles that the Kennedys had used so well for so long was now ironically helping to undermine Ted's public image. If his wife was the personal victim, now he became the political victim. The 1975 *McCalls Magazine* article cited above was quite prophetic: the state of his marriage was going to be crucial to his political chances, and Joan's inability to play a Nancy Reagan–like happy wife would be politically damaging. The political princess had been betrayed by Prince Charming, and the romantic melodrama was transformed into pathos. The political part of the play had an unhappy ending.

The political lesson of the Joan Kennedy story is quite clear. We have noted that a political figure can only exert genuine influence on the general public to the extent he becomes a celebrity. But he must maintain his celebrity without notoriety. Cast as a bad husband who disappoints, hurts, and uses his beautiful princess, his ability to influence public opinion positively—in the form of votes—is seriously undermined. The melodrama of the soap opera is still a highly moral one: traditional virtue must triumph in the long run. The domestic melodrama of Joan and Ted Kennedy had no such triumph of them living happily ever after. So, at least in 1980, the political melodrama of the Kennedy family did not have a happy ending either.

In early 1981, long after the campaign and election, Joan and Ted Kennedy quietly announced they were getting a divorce. Joan emerged from this with her image as a new woman. *People* of February 1981 said she lost her marriage, "but gains control of her life."[23] Armed with her new "self-esteem," she became the "winner" of the 1980 election. But women's magazines and other media that cater to female and family audiences may have contributed to her husband's defeat through the melodramatic depiction of Joan Kennedy. Yet, the saga is not over for either Joan or Ted. She remains steady fare for gossip columns ("Joan to Wed . . .") and women's magazines. Ted is too, with speculation that he will remarry before the 1984 election.

THE COSTS OF POLITICAL CELEBRITY

The fantasy figures of women's magazines are not necessarily in everyday life as depicted in popular media. The breakup of Ted and Joan may be as much her fault as his. But the logic of the melodrama calls for only one marital partner to wrong, the other to be wronged. The women's magazine political celebrity melodrama includes moral logic: the story reasserts the moral values of the mass. Becoming a political celebrity means serving as a popular representation of that moral logic. Marital fidelity is central to the domestic melodrama of political celebrity. As a popular representation of moral values, the politician must use mass-mediated forums, such as women's magazines, to play the proper role in the melodrama. To the extent he or she cannot, their political ascent will be adversely affected. The politician may be a prisoner of a confining personal reality—say, staying married to someone with whom he or she does not get along—because a celebrity is a political prisoner of other people's mass-mediated fantasies. Political celebrity has its price.

NOTES

1. John W. Ward, "The Meaning of Lindbergh's Flight," *American Quarterly*, 10 (1958): 3–16.
2. Daniel J. Boorstin, *The Image: A Guide to Pseudo-Events in America* (New York: Atheneum Publishers, 1972), p. 57; see also C. Wright Mills, *The Power Elite* (New York: Oxford University Press, 1956), pp. 71–92; see also book-length discussions, Orrin E. Klapp, *Symbolic Leaders* (Frank & Wagnalls Book Publishing, 1962). (Minerva Press Paperback); James Monaco, ed., *Celebrity* (New York: Dell Publishing Co., 1978). (Delta Books).
3. Richard Schickel, "Fairbanks: His Picture in the Papers," in Monaco, ed., *Celebrity*, op. cit., pp. 121–127.
4. John L. Caughey, "Artificial Social Relations in Modern America," *American Quarterly*, 30 (1978): 73.
5. See also Caughey's article, "Media Mentors," *Psychology Today*, 12 (September 1978): 44–45; and Donald Horton and R. Richard Wohl, "Mass Communication and Para-social Interaction: Observations on Intimacy at a Distance," *Psychiatry*, 19 (June 1956): 215–229.
6. Robert Brustein, "New Theater," *New York Times Magazine*, June 16, 1974, pp. 66–67, 74–75.
7. Cf. Klapp, *Symbolic Leaders*, op. cit., passim.
8. Bruce A. Rosenberg, "Kennedy in Camelot: The Arthurian Legend in America," *Western Folklore*, 35 (January 1976): 52–59.
9. *People* (November 17, 1980): 44–47.
10. Kathy Mackay, "Elegant, Opulent, Right-minded: The Friends of Nancy Reagan March on Social Washington," *People* (January 19, 1981): 38.
11. Andrew Kay, "Nancy Reagan—Keeping Young and Beautiful," *Harper's Bazaar* (February 1981): 146–147.
12. Gloria Steinem, "Finally a 'Total Woman' in the White House," *Ms. Magazine*, 9 (March 1981): 13.
13. Doris Kearns Goodwin, "Ford & Carter: The Character of the Candidates," *Redbook*, 148 (November 1976): c–7.
14. Ralph G. Martin, "Love and Power in the White House," *Ladies' Home Journal* (March 1979): 99–101, 168–174.
15. Vivian Cadden, "The Burden of Ted Kennedy," *McCalls Magazine* (February 1974): 48.

16. Penelope McMillan, "The Troubled Marriage of Joan and Ted Kennedy," *McCalls Magazine* (November 1975): 46.

17. Joan Braden, "Joan Kennedy Tells Her Own Story," *McCalls Magazine* (August 1978): 121, 190–193.

18. Eleanor Randolph, "The Kennedys," *Chicago Tribune*, September 10, 1978, sec. 5, p. 1.

19. "Joan Kennedy," *People* (December 24, 1979): 51.

20. *McCalls Magazine* (June 1980): 48.

21. Ann Blackman, *Chicago Tribune*, June 8, 1980 sec. 12, p. 5.

22. Stephen Birmingham, "The Kennedy Women: America's Seven Wonders," *Harper's Bazaar* (October 1980): 29.

23. Gail Jennes, "Joan Kennedy Loses Her Marriage, But Gains Control of Her Life," *People* (February 9, 1981): 37.

5

The View from Sunset Boulevard
The Political Fantasies of Hollywood

A legendary movie mogul was supposed to have remarked, "I never make 'message' films. Leave the messages to Western Union." He meant that Hollywood, in the days of tight studio control over the making of movie fare, made only certain *kinds* of message films. American movies are, and always have been, made by people who are part of their culture and the time they live in. They cannot escape telling stories that say something about America. Too, they make movies to attract mass audiences. Therefore, they must tell stories that are familiar in some sense to that audience. For that reason the cultural messages imbedded in those movies also tell us something about America because they flesh out what's in, and on, the minds of the American mass public. If people go to movies and respond to them, it is because they are familiar with the cultural stories presented.

With movies we have a complex fantasy process at work. In the context of culture and time, movie creators fantasize a story they believe both will be interesting to and will sell tickets to mass audiences. The fantasy takes shape as a dramatic popular story made into a movie and distributed to theaters. If the fantasy is shared by the moviegoing mass, it can become a hit. The success of any artistic creation depends in part on its resonance with a popular audience. The success of a movie depends on the meshing of the fantasy of a small group of people (the moviemakers) with the fantasies of sometimes hundreds of thousands of people (the audience). In that sense the movies really are a democratic art, dependent on acceptance by mass audiences. Those movies that sell and those few that endure do so because they have treated selected cultural themes that were on the minds, or in the back of the minds, of large numbers of people.

We thus regard a movie as a cultural artifact, a piece of popular art that offers us insight into the immediate fantasies and enduring myths of the American people. Like the anthropologist who studies the artistic creations of primitive tribes, we may "read" movies for the same cultural insights. The movie industry, it has long been said, is a dream factory that offers dreams for sale. But those cultural dreams are a mediated reality that has helped to shape and to reflect (however ambiguously) the American consciousness of itself. The movies, some observers argue, helped to create national values and the evolution of America from a Victorian to a modern society. Certainly the movies were crucial in the creation of perhaps our central heroic myth, the myth of the West. The dream factory gave life to our dreams, affecting our images of ourselves and the world. Hollywood filmmakers may claim to avoid messages, but we would not be who we are as a people without the collective representations of the movie industry.[1]

Hollywood makes movies for profit by telling stories. These stories are fantasies about the American Dream. By the American Dream we mean the persistent cultural myth, ever retold in new form, about America's search for, and presumed destiny to realize material and moral prosperity and to achieve individual and collective happiness.[2] The American Dream is given fantastic form in each new age because new problems present new obstacles to the realization of the Dream. Popular art forms like the movies dramatize our anxieties about the present, linking it in fantastic melodramas to the enduring myth of the American Dream. In that sense the movies represent the Dream, and resolve the new problems created by the present. They may, of course, represent and resolve them in either positive or negative ways. The movies have presented stories that encourage either belief or doubt about the realization of the Dream. Images of optimistic order or pessimistic disorder dramatize our fantasies about American society.

The popular tales that Hollywood has produced over the decades of this century do not, however, tell the same cultural story. The many genres (horror, mystery, epic, comedy, gangster, Western, etc.), viewpoints (stemming from the director or studio), or interpretations (by critics or audiences) that Hollywood has generated means that from films we learn and use a variety of social and political messages. Indeed, people sort themselves on the basis of the cultural fantasies that appeal to them. Movie audiences obviously flock to movies that tell tales they want to believe. The most flexible moviegoers select and enjoy plural fantasies. Those who want confirmation of a singular fantasy—that, for instance, heroism is unsullied, as in the classic Western—avoid unheroic or antiheroic tales. The American film audience is like art gallery patrons viewing pictures at an exhibition. They glance over them all, avoid and dislike some, like and linger over others. In any case the paintings and patrons' responses to them define the cultural stories that shape people's images of themselves and their world. Movies are cultural pictures on exhibit for mass audiences; they inform the observer of the twists and turns of the evolving American Dream, how the Dream is depicted in a popular art form.

MOVIES AS MEDIATED POLITICAL MELODRAMAS

The dramatic logic of the movies is patently melodramatic, appealing to popular audiences with the same theatrical devices that always characterize melodrama. True, the stilted plots and overwrought acting of the early silent movies are laughed at today, but although more sophisticated and varied, contemporary films are still well within the bounds of melodramatic fare. Hollywood movies still largely revolve around the theme of moral justice as it affects identifiable, and usually one-dimensional, characters. That movies do not necessarily come to a "just" conclusion or happy ending anymore is an indication both of their sophistication and the fact that mass audiences probably do not agree on what a "just" conclusion might be. Hollywood has developed the canons of melodrama into a popular art form of great power and flexibility, one rich in social and political meaning.

The political messages of Hollywood movies range from overt to covert, the consciously executed to the unconsciously included. Whatever the case, the political theme surfaces in melodramatic story lines and usually dramatizes the American Dream. Although relatively few Hollywood movies treat political subjects directly, they offer a rough calculus of the political fantasies of people at a particular time period. If political events in an era confirm or deny the moral or material promise of the Dream, representative popular movies from that period depict the mass consciousness of that political age.

Consider an example. In the 1950s Hollywood produced a seemingly unending supply of science-fiction movies. Some (e.g., *The Thing from Another World, The Day the Earth Stood Still, Forbidden Planet*) were high quality, but many more were B-movies for drive-in theaters springing up in suburban America during that time. These movies had a recurrent theme: an alien force from outer space invades Earth— almost invariably the United States—and attempts to take over the world either by dehumanizing people or by physically annihilating those who resist.[3] The plot line was always predictable: the aliens possess superior power—usually technological; for one reason or another they are foiled; yet, the threat of another invasion is hinted at the film's end. There were of course other themes in sci-fi flicks of the 1950s (such as what a postatomic-war world would be like), but the invasion-from-outer-space theme dominated.

What was it about the 1950s that made such a plot so popular? This was the period of the Cold War. The United States dwelled in a state of anxious hostility in a world of alleged hostile powers, the Communist nations of the Soviet Union and China. Further, Americans believed that communism was an aggressive menace worldwide that was attempting to subvert friendly governments. Indeed, many people came to feel that communism was a subversive force at home and that efforts should be made to root out domestic communism before it destroyed the American Way. This atmosphere lent itself to political fantasies about subversion, led by such politicians as Richard Nixon, J. Edgar Hoover, and Senator Joe McCarthy. Spectacular trials of alleged spies—Alger Hiss, the Rosenbergs, the Hollywood Ten, and the Army-McCarthy hearings—gave credence to fantasies about the insidious power of domestic communism. The Russians seemed ten feet tall; their clever agents were everywhere and knew everything. The central political fantasy of the Cold War was one of communism as a tide, a tide that was an immediate and present danger that could overwhelm America if the country were complacent. The corollary to that fantasy was the possibility that Americans would destroy themselves through paranoia, self-doubt, and mutual suspicion; the internal corruption caused by the external threat would diminish the ability to resist.

The politics of the Cold War entered some portions of popular culture overtly. Mickey Spillane's fictional two-fisted private detective, Mike Hammer, struggled against "the Commies." Television syndicated shows such as "I Led Three Lives," a weekly dramatization of FBI undercover agent Herbert Philbrick who was a "high level member of the Communist Party," portrayed the foiling of subversive schemes. Television divines, such as Bishop Fulton J. Sheen and Billy Graham, warned of the dangers of godless communism. The movies turned to plots in which heroes played by Ronald Reagan or John Wayne fought a new kind of villain, the Communist agent.[4]

Most of the time, however, popular audiences were not treated to an overt tale of the good guys versus the Reds. Indeed, the more subtle fears raised by the Cold War were only implied in filmed melodramas. The larger fantasies raised by the fear of communism were too mammoth to include in the agent-in-the-back-alleys-of-the-world stories. The larger-than-life but ever-threatening fantasies were more conveniently chained out in stories and settings with which audiences could deal, by which they could be scared, but which they would not take too seriously.[5] We call this *fantastic displacement*, the process of placing fantasies of an age in a melodramatic setting and story that covertly mediates the political fantasy for a mass audience to make their fantasies palatable and entertaining.

In this respect the political root of the sci-fi theme so common to the 1950s was a fear of invasion, dehumanization, and annihilation at the hands of aliens. In actuality, the political fantasy was of faceless inhuman Communist aliens—Russians and Chinese—either directly invading and overwhelming America or taking control by brainwashing, infiltration, and other sinister subversive means. Americans could envision the nation turned into a huge concentration camp with mindless automatons regimented in a totally unfree society that was run by Communist occupiers and enslavers. The enemy was ruthless, technologically advanced, and committed to the enslavement of Americans. The various alien forces that tried to invade and take over the United Sates in the endless sci-fi films of the period reflected the Communist threat displaced into outer space, not coming from Russia or China. But, like our earthly adversaries, the enemies were ruthless, giant sized, and technologically superior; it seemed fruitless to resist. Those who came under the alien spell became slaves, unfeeling robots who would do the enemy's bidding, including killing and regimenting. Those not so dehumanized were annihilated.

This, then, is one process of mediating political realities in popular films. By fantastic displacement the political concerns of a particular era become entertaining film fare. It is unlikely that many moviegoers are aware of the political moral of such tales. But they are aware of the salience of such tales and dimly conscious of something relevant and recognizable about a story involving alien invasion, dehumanization, and annihilation. The melodrama of a science-fiction nightmare was a popular genre through which people could participate, albeit without knowing it, in the political fantasy of an age.

A good deal can be learned about the political fantasies of any age by examining and interpreting the popular movies of the time. The status of the American Dream can be seen implicitly in the movie melodramas of each age. The pictures exhibited in the movie theaters during each era are key cultural artifacts that permit us to interpret the political ethos of the time. To expand this analysis we examine movies from recent decades; in each case the films demonstrate how movies act as popular representations of political fantasies in different epochs.

The Depression Fantasy in the Films of the 1930s

The 1930s is a convenient time to begin our inquiry. It was a highly politicized decade and the first one in which the movie industry grew acutely aware of its own power for social and political commentary. The 1930s were the years of the Great Depression; in one way or another what the movies of that period say relate to that overriding economic fact. The Depression was remarkable in that it produced both great social upheaval, yet social solidarity as well.[6] People yearned for social change engineered by a benevolent government to end the economic crisis, but they also yearned for the reaffirmation of traditional American values and institutions. The 1930s were both liberal and conservative, reflecting both a desire for a political new deal to reform capitalism and a social old deal to preserve what had made America great.

For the movies, the political atmosphere suggested that specific types of fantastic displacement would be accceptable to mass audiences, and through the usual trial-and-error process of movie marketing, film producers discovered the appealing rhetorical visions. The movie formulas we associate with the 1930s—the gangster movie, the screwball comedy, the social-conscience film, and so on—all developed as stories that permitted audiences to displace their anxieties about the present into screenplays. The material prosperity promised by the American Dream was never in greater doubt. Nor was there more acute need for people to be reassured of the moral component of the American Dream. The various movie genres of the 1930s depicted the middle-class poverty of the Depression and the ways people could cope with it as well as the moral strength that permitted them to cope. The American Dream was alive and well in the films of that decade; ordinary Americans still possessed the moral power to overcome a temporary material setback. Andrew Bergman sums up nicely what the movies did:

What happens in depression movies is that traditional beliefs in the possibilities of individual success are kept alive in the early thirties under various guises, that scapegoats for social dislocation are found and that federal benevolence becomes an implicit and ultimately dead-ended premise by the end of the decade. Hollywood would help the nation's fundamental institutions escape unscathed by attempting to keep alive the myth and wonderful fantasy of a mobile and classless society, by focussing on the endless possibilities for individual success, by turning social evil into personal evil and making the New Deal into a veritable leading man.[7]

Hollywood accomplished this through ingenious film formulas, not the least of which was the gangster genre. The gangster melodrama was a fantastic displacement about what had happened to ambition and the achievement ethic. The gangster film was both a positive and negative commentary on what was supposed to be the central motivating force of capitalism. Audiences could witness in films, such as *Little Caesar*, *The Public Enemy*, or *Scarface*, how a poor boy could rise to the top in the best Horatio Alger fashion, but now he had to become a criminal to acquire wealth and power. The irony attached to success provides a clue to the political ethos of the early 1930s: films reflected both mass desire for, and suspicions about, material prosperity. The price paid for wealth was great, but it beat being poor. In the gangster film, crime both did and did not pay. Were the gangsters who succeeded and then failed any different than the captains of industry who were responsible for both the 1920s' prosperity and the "Hoover depression"? That ambivalence repeats itself in 1930s' movies.

The reaffirmations made in Hollywood movies included no tinge of political radicalism, but rather a brand of political populism that exhalted the wisdom and endurance of the common people. The gangster was no common man; and it was his rejection of traditional values that made him, like the industrial magnate, uncommon and tragic. The wealthy families depicted in screwball comedies, such as *My Man Godfrey* and *It Happened One Night*, are idle, useless, and corrupt, whereas ordinary people—servants for example—are wise and functional. The implicit political fantasy is that the people who got us into this economic mess—the plutocrats—are not sinister, but silly; and common folk will get us out of it by common sense. The message of the screwball comedy is certainly not a Marxist criticism of the class structure, but rather a reaffirmation of democratic man. The populace may not have the money, but they are superior in wit and wisdom.

This Depression movie fantasy reached its artistic epitome in films directed by Frank Capra in the late 1930s—*Mr. Deeds Goes to Town*, and *Mr. Smith Goes to Washington*. These films involve the story of an ordinary individual, born and reared in the great American heartland, who comes to the "big city" armed only with that hard core of traditional, popular, individual values and grit. The "big city" is peopled by evil plutocrats, shysters, hardbitten newspaper reporters, cynical women, all of whom sneer at and try to use the rube. But in the end the common sense and idealism of the rube overcomes. This is most directly political in *Mr. Smith Goes to Washington*, which depicts a naive but idealistic Jefferson Smith (Jimmy Stewart) who is appointed to the U.S. Senate by a political machine in a Western state. The state boss, in league with the senior senator from the state, appoints Smith for political reasons, believing him a popular choice for the interim seat and easily manipulable. When Smith uncovers a scandal involving the machine, the politicians attempt to destroy him. He counters with a one-man filibuster on the Senate floor. As he espouses the timeless truth of democratic and Christian values on the floor, his cynical office aide (Jean Arthur), the reporters in the gallery, and some of the senators (and the presiding vice president) begin to root for him. In the end, he collapses, thinking that he has failed, but the guilt-ridden senior senator repents, and at the last moment Smith is vindicated—and by extension so are democratic ideals.

Capra movies from the 1930s evoke much of that era. *Mr. Smith Goes to Washington* in particular spoke to the desire for social solidarity and belief in traditional values and solutions that characterized the decade. The senators, reporters, and other denizens of the "big city" are remote from the true heartbeat and lifeblood of the republic—kids, mothers, and ordinary folk in the American heartland. The message? The fantasy? Simply put, when the sophisticates of the Capital remember their roots and abandon their cynicism for restored belief, the true promise of America can be realized. *Mr. Smith Goes to Washington* says naught about the problems and solutions that spawned the New Deal; but it says much about the old deal, that the political salvation of the country is, in a sense, nonpolitical, rooted in national character and not in a political program. It is the same fantasy that made Will Rogers popular, and for that matter Jimmy Stewart, too. Stewart brought to the Smith role the kind of Lincolnesque down-home "aw shucks" manner that evoked in his persona those enduring values moviegoers of the 1930s sought. It was the same style adopted by 1930s' actor Ronald Reagan, a style he was much later to adopt nicely to politics when he became a citizen-politician who would bring belief and change first to Sacramento and then to Washington. (The story goes that when a senile Jack Warner was told that Reagan was running for governor in 1966, he responded, "No, you've got it wrong: Jimmy Stewart for governor, Ronald Reagan for best friend.") In any case the Depression fantasy included both pessimism about institutions (in *Mr. Smith Goes to Washington*, the Senate and political machines) and optimism about the values and abilities of ordinary folk. The American Dream was alive, but it was alive in the hearts and minds of the democratic mass who kept the faith—and went to the movies.

Hollywood Goes to War in the 1940s: The Commitment Fantasy

The political ethos of the 1940s was dominated by World War II. The melodramas of the 1930s had offered a domestic fantasy that everything would work out all right here at home. The melodramas of the 1940s' films reassured Americans that the war was worth fighting, that U.S. allies were gallant and U.S. enemies evil, that America was in the right, and that after the war there would be a better world. The recurrent fantasy was that everything would work out abroad (the United States would win the war) and that the resulting peace would ensure the final realization of the American Dream. Indeed, there were many cinematic suggestions that we would not only win the war and ensure the peace but also spread the American Dream abroad. When other peoples learned the promise and truth of the Dream and adopted it, the peace and prosperity it offered would be theirs as well. Jefferson Smith had to sell the Dream anew to the "big city." Now U.S. heroes would sell the American Dream to the world. Americans did not go into, or out of, World War II cynically; there were ideals for which to fight and, if necessary, for which to die with courage and vision.

It is no surprise to us, then, that many Hollywood movies of the war years were fantasies of commitment. Anxieties and doubts about the war were displaced into melodramatic settings that helped convince the weak of heart of the wisdom and necessity for the war. As Hollywood depicted it, nothing less than the survival of the American Dream was at stake. This was most obvious in the frankly propagandistic war movies of the period, such as *Wake Island, Thirty Seconds over Tokyo*, and *Operation Burma*, all of which portrayed the culpability of the Japanese. The heroism of U.S. allies was dramatized in *Mrs. Miniver, Paris Calling*, and *The Commandos Strike at Dawn*. Indeed, in a movie that became an embarrassment after the war, *Mission to Moscow*, the Russians were not only depicted as heroic but also Stalin was portrayed as kindly, thoughtful, and democratic at heart. Conversely, Hollywood fantasized the Nazis as urbane and ruthless villains, much more malevolently sinister than any social type the Great Depression had conjured up. *Hitler's Children* was a melodramatic account of how the Nazis turned their own people into robots, flogged young girls, and coveted world domination. To the extent that Hollywood film makers of the war years had conscious propaganda motives, they were trying to shame or scare citizens into buying more war bonds, enlisting, conserving scarce materials for the war effort, "backing our boys," and so forth. But in all cases the films depicted commitment: the guys who died at Wake or bombed Tokyo were committed, the allies were committed, and the Nazis and Japs were committed to America's destruction. Even familiar movie stars with whom people identified—Gary Cooper, Errol Flynn, John Wayne, and others—made a symbolic commitment to the war by fictional appearances in Bataan or Burma or Nazi-controlled Europe.

But perhaps the most famous, and certainly most enduring, Hollywood fantasy about commitment is Warner Brothers' *Casablanca*, released in November 1942. *Casablanca* was filmed and released at a time early in the war when Americans were still uncertain about their commitment to fighting Nazi Germany. Indeed, *Casablanca* is set in Vichy France and its territories in Africa—one of the puzzling diplomatic quagmires of those days—with which the United States maintained relations even though it was clearly a puppet of the German Reich. President Roosevelt viewed the movie on December 31, 1942, and soon thereafter severed relations with Vichy. He then traveled to Casablanca in January 1943 to confer with Churchill and the new leader of the Free French, General De Gaulle.[8]

Casablanca is a story about Rick Blaine, a mysterious and cynical

American, who has been disillusioned by both politics and love. He has anti-Fascist credentials from the 1930s, having fought in Spain and run guns to Ethiopia. Blaine is symbolic of many things, not the least of which is the new international status of Americans. The fantasies of the Depression were domestic, concerned with America at home; now suddenly war thrust the United States into an international role. The fantasy of the 1940s envisioned Americans in a variety of exotic climes (and the promise of adventure and romance there) and cast America itself in the role of the Promised Land, the country that was the hope of the world at war. Rick is wary of commitment to the anti-Fascist cause and refuses to aid the leader of the Underground, Victor Laszlo, partly because Laszlo is married to Ilse, the woman Rick loves but who Rick thinks jilted him. Superficially, then, the plot is the melodrama of pure soap opera.

But clearly Rick's agony with the reappearance of Ilse is not simply romantic. After his encounter with her in his Café Americaine (he had not seen her since she mysteriously left him years earlier in Paris), Rick seeks solace in drink. Sitting alone, drinking and feeling sorry for himself, he says, "It's December, 1941, in Casablanca. . . . What time is it in New York? . . . I bet they're asleep in New York—I bet they're asleep all over America. . . ." The fantasy of America being asleep at the fateful time of Pearl Harbor reminds us of international menace, of which Rick is experiencing the European version. Rick cannot decide whether the menace is worth fighting. Laszlo reminds him later of his "responsibility," despite Rick's protestations that "I'm the only cause I'm interested in." Finally, in a closing airport scene, Rick puts Ilse on the plane to Lisbon with her husband. She does not want to go, but Rick says her responsibility is to Victor. Anyway, Rick has "a job to do," their romantic problems "don't amount to a hill of beans in this crazy world." Laszlo welcomes Rick "back to the fight. . . . This time I know our side will win." The Laszlos fly off to Lisbon and America, and Rick walks into the mist, toward, we are told, a Free French garrison in central Africa.

By his act of commitment, "Rick has become a patriot;" he says casually, "It seemed a good time to start." The political message of *Casablanca* is one of a necessity for individual commitment. Everyone must fight, even those who have a lot to lose, such as Rick Blaine. The menace to the American Dream is given sinister reality in the Nazi characters, one of whom speculates about invading New York. The refugees from other places such as Bulgaria universally share the American Dream—their one great hope is to get to America. Rick's commitment symbolizes the need for national commitment to aid those abroad, Americans and otherwise, who believe in the American Dream and are already fighting for it in dangerous places. Rick is a sophisti-

cated blend of American and European, signifying the union of purpose of the two continents. The motley international flavor of the anti-
Fascist cast—Russians, Jews, Czechs, Norwegians, French—suggests
the universality of the Grand Alliance. The character of Laszlo embodies the moral purpose of "the Cause," and his flight to America links
that international cause to the American cause. *Casablanca*, then, is a
rich fantasy of commitment that, in its plot, lets audiences solidify their
own commitment. It evokes both a call for popular concern and individual sacrifice on the part of moviegoers. It remains a timeless romantic film, but the implicit political message it carries cannot be ignored.

The Alien Fantasy in 1950s' Films

The political atmosphere of post-World War II America derived from a
disillusionment with the emerging international order and efforts to
adjust to domestic changes stimulated by the war. The threat of international communism and a failure to secure the peace and prosperity
promised by war propaganda was profoundly disillusioning. The
domestic problems that persisted—unemployment, inflation, scarcity—
gave impetus to a sense of injustice, that somehow the sacrifices of
the war had been betrayed and that the American Dream was still un-
fulfilled. Movies began to display themes indicative of the mood. The
"dark" movies (film noir) depicted a bleak world of evil filled with disillusioned, burnt-out heroes trying to cope in an unregenerate society.
In response, family movies attempted to reinforce the familial core of
the American Dream. The most remarkable of these was probably *The
Next Voice You Hear*, in which God speaks on the radio to reassure middle-class Americans of the truth of the American Dream.[9] And, of
course, many adventure films picked up directly on the anti-
Communist theme, such as *I Was a Communist for the FBI*, in which
domestic Communists attempt to infiltrate American steel unions.

But perhaps the central theme of the politics of that era relates to
what we discussed earlier in this chapter, the extent to which people
thought that the American Dream might be undermined, either by subversion from without or paranoia from within. The issue of communism
was much on the minds of Americans, and both liberal and conservative political agendas were oriented to the proper response to the Communist threat. The political careers of Richard Nixon, Joseph McCarthy, and Ronald Reagan date back to this era, and the witch hunts (investigations of alleged Communist infiltration) gave focus to the issue.
The movies, in one way or another, treated these themes, a point
noted in our discussion of the political fantasies implicit in 1950s' sci-fi
flicks.

The most notable, and perhaps the best, of the sci-fi movies is *Inva-*

sion of the Body Snatchers, which was released in 1956. It is possible to give this film both a liberal and a conservative interpretation, but in any case it speaks in allegorical form to the fears and doubts about the American Dream that people in the 1950s entertained. The story is set in an idyllic, typical American town in which a local doctor, Miles Bennell, finds that people suddenly think other people they know have changed. Are they paranoid, hysterical, or correct? Bennell eventually finds that people are being taken over by duplicate bodies of an alien origin. The aliens have no emotions—"no more love, no more beauty, no more pain," one alien explains. They are obedient and ruthless robots whose purpose is to convert and regiment the rest of the country. Their possession robs them of their humanity, and they claim to be superior to the merely human. The doctor's friends and allies eventually succumb. Finally, he is alone in his humanity, pursued by former humans now only vegetable-pod beings. Bennell barely escapes, sees that the alien pods are being shipped to other cities, and warns motorists: "They're here. . . . You're next."

The political fantasy of the *Invasion of the Body Snatchers* is complex and has been variously interpreted.[10] It can be viewed as a parable on the Communist menace. The inhuman and technologically superior aliens have invaded the peaceful American community of Santa Mira and desire to control it (and by extension America as well) through dehumanization and even annihilation. The film can also be read as a statement about the dangers of domestic paranoia in which we deteriorate into madness by believing that familiar people are in league with some subversive alien force. (The movie begins and ends with the doctor being held in a hospital insanity ward with the psychiatrists incredulous about his story; it is thus plausible to think the whole story a fantasy of a paranoiac.) And certainly the movie is amenable to another politically relevant interpretation—the larger theme of the conformity and alienation emergent in the America of the 1950s, attitudes that dehumanized by annihilating individuality. In that sense the external Communist menace is simply a political projection of what was happening domestically, the destruction of individuality and diversity by the demand for group conformity. Santa Mira is simply a cinematic example of the basic social trend of the time, the creation of a uniform and mindless mass society that includes powerful pressures for everyone to be the same and to be intolerant of those who are different. This was backed up by a political milieu that enjoined banality and conformity as well. Jefferson Smith and Rick Blaine would not have been welcome in such a social and political cosmos.

The 1950s' movies reflected the insidious trouble in paradise that lay beneath the affluent and peaceful surface. Films such as *Invasion of the Body Snatchers* developed plots that displaced fantasies about the status of the American Dream. The threat to the Dream during the Depression was a domestic loss of faith that an indigenous hero from the frontier, like Jefferson Smith, could combat. During World War II the threat to the Dream was an identifiable alien force that could be defeated by the commitment of Americans both at home and abroad. But the threat to the Dream of the 1950s—as dramatized by the *Invasion of the Body Snatchers*—was more puzzling, insidious, and ambiguous. Both the failure of the postwar peace and the nagging sense of unfulfillment in the presence of postwar affluence contributed to the political unease. The moral ideals that motivated Jefferson Smith and even Rick Blaine seem notably absent in the doctor of the *Invasion of the Body Snatchers*: he is simply afraid of being dehumanized and flees the community. The fantasy was a powerful one for 1950s' audiences because, for most of them, there was no place to flee. And the body-snatcher fantasy surely raises the question that nagged at the consciousness of the time: Who is the enemy? Is it them, as the orthodox political interpretation went, or is it, as Pogo Possum thought, us?

Violence and Transcendent Hope in the 1960s

Like other eras, it is difficult to pin down exactly when the fantasy of the 1960s begins and ends. We may take an arbitrary political definition: the 1960s begins with the assassination of President John Kennedy in 1963 and ends with the defeat of George McGovern in 1972. Before Kennedy's death, what the era was becoming socially and politically was still anchored in the 1950s (as nostalgically depicted in the movie *American Graffiti*). The trauma of the assassination was the first blow to an era that vacillated between cosmic hopes and claustrophobic despair; that witnessed the vision of a Great Society, but the turmoil of urban riots; and that saw the moon landing and Vietnam, the student movement and the Wallace movement, and the rise of the counterculture and the silent majority. It was a breathless, turbulent era, somewhat awesome in retrospect. As one writer about the 1960s has remarked, "Did all that really happen?"[11]

The 1960s involved extreme reaffirmations and doubts about the American Dream. The civil rights movement and the Great Society posited the expansion of the Dream to those who did not share it. The politicians who emerged in reaction to that enlarged rhetorical vision— Nixon, Agnew, Wallace, and Reagan—thought the American Dream was being undermined by those who opposed the Vietnam War or who sought a redistribution of wealth. Such politicians mobilized support among those who disliked the critics of their all-too-narrow Dream. The supporters of the war (as exemplified in John Wayne's movie *The Green Berets*) thought U.S. motives in Vietnam benevolent, an extension of the anti-Communist good works performed earlier in China, Japan, and Korea. The opponents of the civil rights, student, feminist, and other movements regarded proponents of change as perverters of the Dream. They condemned the Great Society giveaway as catering to the wrong people and ideologies. The generation gap and other divisions and conflicts in society burst forth in the 1960s. It was as if all the suppressed forces of the silent generation of the 1950s were compensated by the outburst of energy, political and social, that characterized the decade.

The movies depicted these social and political themes, which flowed like a current throughout the period. The most obvious politically charged theme that recurred in the films was violence. The decade itself included assassinations urban riots, fights between students and police or hardhats, the Kent State shootings, and most of all, Vietnam. These events appeared seemingly every night on TV in vivid color. Violence and the questions it evoked haunted the decade: Was the violence of Vietnam justified? Were violent uprisings and even revolution justified? Was violent suppression of violence by society justified? Violence, said a black radical of the period, is as American as cherry pie. The omnipresence of violence seemed a threat to the American Dream to some, a necessary way to defend the Dream to others.

The theme of violence made its way into the popular movie fare of the time. The Western, for example, had always included violence, but now the violence seemed gratuitous, done for its own sake without some redeeming purpose. In the man-with-no-name movies, Clint Eastwood was a softspoken murderer who killed for revenge or money, but also at times for the slightest of provocations. In Sam Peckinpah's Western, *The Wild Bunch*, violence takes on a kind of beauty, with long, slow-motion shots of killing and dying and a final orgiastic shootout of overwhelming proportions. In *Straw Dogs* the hero must turn to violence for survival and retribution but discovers he likes it. It was hard to escape the conclusion from such films that violence was anything more than nihilistic, appealing to the fantasy that the world was one of meaningless violence.

Indeed, violence in 1960s' movies could even be funny, something done as play. In the controversial *Bonnie and Clyde*, the two young bank robbers become criminals—and killers—just to have some fun. Their killing is nihilistic, to be sure, but antisocial play was a stance taken in the 1960s from the Green Berets in Vietnam to the antiwar activities at Columbia University. Trashed were the Vietcong and trashed were the police pigs, simply as objects of antisocial play. Bonnie and Clyde are young and disenchanted with normal bourgeois life and ready to flirt with death to have some fun. Like the youthful rock singers of the time—Janis Joplin, Jimi Hendrix, and Jim Morrison—

they live hard and die young. Because social values had no meaning anymore, their only use was to justify fun at society's expense—including killing.[12]

The negative theme of violence was clearly a disturbing aspect of the American Dream for the 1960s because the atmosphere of violence was much on the minds of people. For that reason, it should not surprise us that another powerful theme emerged in the consciousness of the 1960s: transcendent hope. The omnipresence of death and conflict brought by violence was counterposed by the emergence of new hope. This was clearly the case in the nascent youth culture of the time, those who yearned for, and even believed in, "a new world in the morning." While middle America clung desperately to the materialistic and traditional moralist version of the Dream, many of the 1960s' youth rejected materialism (in an era of unparalleled prosperity and opportunity that permitted them that luxury) and sought a new morality. The 1960s produced idealism and a search for new forms of living—various movements, the sexual revolution, the emergence of counterculture hippies and flower children, the popularity of idealistic gurus and writers.

Transcendent hope was given impetus in a variety of ways. The hope for racial equality, peace, and a solution to social problems helped define the political perspective of 1960s' activists. The desire to reform the present made people hope for a better future. But there were more cosmic symbols of transcendent hope. The space program, culminating in the moon shots, made people aware of the cosmic place of the Earth. Consciousness-expanding drugs allegedly held out the promise of a consciousness beyond rationality. Mysticism flourished, with renewed interest in exotic religions, pagan gods, and the occult. Man had too long confined his perspective to this Earth; now he needed to think in more cosmic and transcendent terms. "Why can't politicians take the larger view of things?" was a common lament. Themes of peace, universal brotherhood, ecological balance, and cosmic piety emerged from man's hopefulness.

Popular culture included many artifacts of 1960s' transcendent hopefulness, but the most remarkable is probably the movie *2001: A Space Odyssey*. Stanley Kubrick's 1968 movie in many respects came to symbolize the mood of transcendent hope of the era more than any other film. *2001* offered a fantasy of contradictions and possibilities that typified the decade. *2001* is a tale about technology—how protomen discover how to use a bone as a weapon (the violence theme) and how that leads, eventually, to space stations and flight (transcendence). Yet for all the high-tech existence, men are very much as they are in the 1960s: rational technocrats who manipulate machinery. The two astronauts aboard the flight to Jupiter space are as emotionless and inhuman as the pod people of *Invasion of the Body Snatchers*. They are the ultimate technological men, devoid of poetry, feeling, and self-doubt. Yet the technology they master is leading them to an ultimate destiny, indeed, man's destiny—the discovery of superintelligent, godlike life from another world. For the black monolith which had given the proto-men the spark of intelligence to begin with had buried a slab on the moon that would signal the protomen when man had advanced to the point of discovering that slab. The movie hints that man will triumph in spite of himself, through the technology that he creates. Thus, man does not have to use technology for death, as in Vietnam; rather, he can use it for exploration, and exploration leads to trans-cendence. In the climax of *2001*, the surviving astronaut is "reborn" into a "star-child" who will begin man's quest anew. *2001* is the ulti-mate 1960s' statement about man's possibilities, and how, if he adopts the cosmic view of things, man can transcend the evils of the present for a consciousness-expanded and mystical future. The political odyssey need not be one of conflict and violence; technology can be benevolent, and man can transcend himself through it. This was a fantasy that the strife-torn 1960s desperately wanted to believe, that is, that the Amer-ican Dream would not be perverted but rather saved by technology. It was a shred of hope in a decade when everything seemed to be coming apart.[13]

The Abandonment of Hope in the 1970s

The 1970s was a decade of the decay of hope. Whatever political opti-mism the previous decade might have entertained dissipated in the gloom of the 1970s. The cosmic hopes of the 1960s disappeared as peo-ple retreated into self. Observers began to speak of America as a cul-ture of narcissism; the decade was dubbed the "me decade." Books ex-tolled again the materialistic aspect of the American Dream. The moral and reformist fervor of the 1960s disappeared. The political drift of the decade was into either a renascent individualistic conservatism or, more commonly, into cynicism and apathy. The political scandal of Watergate, the flounderings of Presidents Ford and Carter, the rise of OPEC—all added to the sense of corruption and decay in the political and social order. Both the moral and material dimensions of the Amer-ican Dream seemed failures as the sense of community purpose that had given the Dream its moral thrust and the widespread prosperity and abundance that had given the Dream its material thrust con-tracted. It was a claustrophobic age with fantasies about saving oneself (through religion or some human-potential method), about death (as in the popularity of books on death and movies, such as *All That Jazz*), or in establishing stable relations with others (satirized in the Woody Allen movies and in the many family films). The 1970s did not put much hope in politics; if the American Dream was to be realized, it would have to be achieved by the individual.

The popular fantasies of the 1970s found their way into movie melodramas with implicit political themes. Watergate and its attendant mysteries helped to define the themes in movies of the time. *The Godfather* movies dealt with illegitimate power, which many people in the 1970s had come to think of as all power. (Conversely, at least the Corleone godfathers were efficient, which was more than could be said for a lot of politicians.) *Chinatown* dealt with themes of lying, immoral purpose, hidden scandal, and the fact that "nobody knows what's going on." *The Conversation* depicted the world of electronic surveillance and the paranoia it engenders. Most directly, of course, *All the President's Men* depicted a Washington that was dark and somber with hidden secrets discovered in whispered conversations in underground parking lots.

Perhaps the 1970s' fantasy of decay and hopelessness was best exemplified in the movie *Taxi Driver*.[14] (This particular film has now become infamous because the man who attempted to assassinate President Reagan appeared to be acting out some sort of bizarre mimicry of Robert de Niro's role in the movie.) *Taxi Driver* tells the tale of a Vietnam veteran who drives a cab in New York City. As the movie progresses, we are aware that the taxi driver inhabits a corrupt, insane world, and that he is going mad. The taxi driver is driven by devils, even moral purpose, but he is about as far removed from the American Dream as one can be. With the acquisition of guns, he becomes a potential assassin, first stalking a politician, but actually killing Jodie Foster's pimp. Ironically, he becomes a hero because of this. But the lingering fantasy conjured up by *Taxi Driver* is the unredeemable corruption of the city, a symbol of American civilization gone wrong. The taxi driver is driven back into a claustrophobic reliance on self because there is no moral or material community to which it is worth belonging. His individualism is the result of total alienation. Yet, he is at one with his environment: in a world gone mad, so has he. If there is an implicit political fantasy at work in *Taxi Driver*, it is that the American Dream has failed because society has failed the individual. Politics has become a remote sham, something to be killed; government is irrelevant to the urban underworld the taxi driver inhabits. If the 1970s was a decade of the decay of political and social hopes, then it was disturbingly reflected in the nightmarish world of *Taxi Driver*.

THE 1980s: REBIRTH OR RETRENCHMENT?

At this writing the 1980s are too unformed for us to select films that reflect the political fantasies of the decade. But we may speculate. The popularity of movies such as *Raiders of the Lost Ark* may augur a new desire to believe in heroism, including political heroism. Perhaps the 1980s will include political fantasies of rebirth, revitalization, and renewal. President Reagan called for a "New Beginning" as his administration began in 1981, and the release of the hostages in Iran brought a patriotic outburst. The American Dream requires belief, and people want to believe in it. Thus, it may be that movies will reflect a new heroic fantasy of restored institutions, adventures in which the good guys clearly win, and focus on upbeat plots and happy endings. But this will only happen if political, economic, and social conditions cooperate. If we have another economic depression, the mediated political realities of Hollywood may not give us another Jefferson Smith. If we have World War III, we may not have another Rick Blaine (we may not even have time to make movies in a nuclear war!). If we have renewed searches for scapegoats, the depiction of it may not resemble the 1950s. And so on. The mediated political realities of Hollywood are specific to an age, and just as history does not repeat itself, neither does Hollywood. So we shall have to interpret both the politics and the movies of the 1980s after the fact, but that interpretation will be no less illuminating than that of previous decades. As the drama of politics is acted out in this and future decades, it will appear, in subtle and covert forms, in the flickering images we shall watch in the dark at the movies.

NOTES

1. The literature on the movies is now vast. See, variously, Charles Eidsvik, *Cineliteracy* (New York: Random House, 1978); George Wead and George Lellie, *Film: Form and Function* (Boston: Houghton Mifflin Co., 1981); Lary May, *Screening Out the Past* (New York: Oxford University Press, 1980); Jack C. Ellis, *A History of Film* (Englewood Cliffs, N.J.: Prentice-Hall, 1979); Phillip French, *The Movie Moguls* (Chicago: Henry Regenry Co., 1969); Hugo Munsterberg, *The Film: A Psychological Study* (New York: Dover Publications, 1969); Garth Jowett, *Film: The Democratic Art* (Boston: Little, Brown & Co., 1976); Marjorie Rosen, *Popcorn Venus: Women, Movies, and the American Dream* (New York: Avon Books, 1973); Robert Sklar, *Movie-Made America: A Social History of the American Movies* (New York: Random House, 1975); I. C. Jarvie, *Movies and Society* (New York: Basic Books, 1970); Hortense Powdermaker, *Hollywood: The Dream Factory* (Boston: Little, Brown & Co., 1950); Martha Wolfenstein and Nathan Leites, *Movies: A Psychological Study* (New York: Atheneum Publishers, 1970); Michael Wood, *America in the Movies* (New York: Basic Books, 1975).
2. See Walter R. Fisher, "Reaffirmation and Subversion of the American Dream," *Quarterly Journal of Speech*, 59 (April 1973): 160–167.
3. Susan Sontag, "The Imagination of Disaster," in Fredric Rissover and David C. Birch, eds., *Mass Media and the Popular Arts* (New York: McGraw-Hill, 1977), pp. 370–381.
4. See J. Fred McDonald, "The Cold War as Entertainment in 'Fifties Television," *Journal of Popular Film and Television*, 7 (1978): 3–31.

5. William Blake Tyrell, "Star Trek as Myth and Television as Myth-maker," *Journal of Popular Culture*, 10 (1977): 711–719.

6. See Andrew Bergman, *We're in the Money: Depression America and Its Films* (New York: Harper & Row, 1971). (Colophon Books)

7. Ibid., p. xvi.

8. See Umberto Eco, "*Casablanca*: The Archetypes Hold a Reunion," *Decade* (1978): 19–21 (premier issue); Harvey R. Greenberg, *The Movies on Your Mind* (New York: E. P. Dutton & Co., 1975), pp. 79–105.

9. Frederick Elkin, "God, Radio, and the Movies," in Bernard Rosenberg and David Manning White, eds., *Mass Culture* (Glencoe, Ill.: Free Press, 1957), pp. 308–314.

10. Stuart Samuels, "The Age of Conspiracy and Conformity: *Invasion of the Body Snatchers*, 1956," in John E. O'Connor and Martin A. Jackson, eds., *American History/American Film: Interpreting the Hollywood Image* (New York: Fredrick Ungar Publishing Co., 1979), pp. 203–218.

11. Morris Dickstein, *Gates of Eden: American Culture in the Sixties* (Basic Books, 1977), p. ix.

12. Lawrence L. Murray, "Hollywood, Nihilism, and the Youth Culture of the Sixties: *Bonnie and Clyde*, 1967," in O'Connor and Jackson, *American History*, op. cit., pp. 237–256.

13. Jerome Agel, ed., *The Making of Kubrick's 2001* (New York: American Library, 1970). (Signet)

14. Colin L. Westerbeck, Jr., "Beauties and the Beast: 'Seven Beauties' and 'Taxi Driver'," *Sight and Sound*, 45 (Summer 1976): 134–139.

6

Fantasies of the Arena

Popular Sports and Politics

By the rude bridge that arched the flood,
Their flag to April's breeze unfurled,
Here once the embattled farmers stood,
And fired the shot heard round the world.

To generations of American schoolchildren required to memorize Ralph Waldo Emerson's *Concord Hymn*, the "shot heard round the world" opened the war for America's independence. Since 1951, however, another "shot heard round the world" has become almost as equally famous. It goes like this:

Bobby Thomson up there swinging. He has two out of three, a single and a double and Billy Cox is playing him right on the third base line. One out, last of the ninth. Branca pitches; Thomson takes a strike called on the inside corner. Bobby hitting at .292. He's had a single and a double and he drove in the Giants' first run with a long fly to center. Brooklyn leads it 4 to 2. Hartung down the line at third not taking any chances; Lockman not too big of a lead at second but he'll be running like the wind if Thomson hits one. Branca throws. There's a long fly that's going to be it, I believe. THE GIANTS WIN THE PEN-NANT. THE GIANTS WIN THE PENNANT. THE GIANTS WIN THE PEN-NANT. THE GIANTS WIN THE PENNANT. Bobby Thomson hits one into the lower deck of the left field stands. The Giants win the pennant and they're going crazy, they're going crazy. Aahh Oohh. I don't believe it, I don't believe it, I do not believe it. Bobby Thomson hit a line drive into the lower deck of the left field stands and the whole place is going crazy. . . . The Giants win it by a score of 5 to 4.

It may seem a long way from Russ Hodges's radio account of Bob-by Thomson's "shot heard round the world," which won the 1951

National League baseball championship for the New York Giants over the Brooklyn Dodgers, to the realm of politics. Certainly the relationship is more tenuous than the tie between politics and Emerson's first "shot heard round the world." Or is it? Noted historian and critic Jacques Barzun did not think so. In an oft-quoted line he wrote, "Whoever wants to know the heart and mind of America had better learn baseball, the rules and realities of the game." He compared the game to high drama, even melodrama. "The wonderful purging of the passions that we all experienced in the fall of '51, the despair groaned out over the fate of the Dodgers, from whom the league pennant was snatched at the last minute, give us some idea of what Greek tragedy was like. Baseball *is* Greek in being national, heroic, and broken up in the rivalries of city-states."[1] Barzun did not stop there. He went on to imply that baseball with its imaginative rules is much like the U.S. Constitution, a creation that fits the richness of change in American life, just as cricket with its less formalized rules parallels the unwritten British Constitution that matches the customs and conventions of societal tradition.

We, too, believe there is much to learn about politics in America from examining the national pastime, baseball. But much can also be learned about politics by going beyond baseball to a variety of popular sports. Historically Americans took to sports with the same gusto they did to business and politics. It is no secret that we are still a sports-happy nation. We created indigenous games—baseball, football, and basketball—and follow professional leagues of highly paid athletes with avid interest. The popularity of sports makes the subject a natural for the mass media; newspapers, radio, and television devote considerable attention to sports reports and programming. American interest in sports appears inexhaustible; now there are even all-sports cable TV channels broadcasting nothing but sports news. There are specialized magazines that deal with what is happening in each of a variety of sports—tennis, boxing, wrestling, golf, and so on. The drama of sports, both as acted out by spectators and players, is integral to our lives.

People who study sports have long pointed out that sports are an important indicator of how we live and what we believe.[2] Sports reflect the values and institutions of a society in many ways, and it is fair to paraphrase Barzun: if one is to understand a country, such as the United States, one must study its sports-mediated reality, given dramatic construction by its mediators. The fantasies that sports conjure are socially significant for the mass public that accepts them. Further, the student of sports must be aware that both the sport itself and its mediation include implicit political content. Even though sports may seem at first glance remote from the corridors of political power, we believe that there are connections that make the fantasies of the playing field relevant to politics.

SPORTS AS MELODRAMA

Americans' fascination with sports derives from a variety of sources, not the least of which is the fact that sports contests are exciting popular fare. Moreover, for the same reason that movies and other forms of entertainment appeal to mass audiences, sports quickly became an integral part of American popular culture and a subject of mass mediation. Sports contests, after all, are great melodramas and thereby appeal to the popular mind. The appeal is not simply for the game-in-itself but to what uses people make of sports and the gratifications that fans gain from sports. A sport such as baseball very quickly acquired all the characteristics of melodrama—the contest between the virtuous and villainous, the suspense of the contest, the triumph of justice or the intervention of fortune, anxiety as the game proceeds, heroic deeds and untimely errors, dramatic climaxes, and the euphoria of the victors along with the gloom of the vanquished. To these attributes the mass media in the process of reconstructing the realities of a sport like baseball has added soap opera elements—the rivalries of players, petty quarrels, salary disputes and team jumping, fights and fines, romances and deaths. Through mass mediation, people could delight in not only the play of Ty Cobb, Babe Ruth, Lou Gehrig, and Christy Mathewson but also in their personalities, exploits off the field, high salaries, and personal tragedies. The "boys of summer" were heroes, villains, and fools, yes, but also very human types with all the failings and foibles of ordinary people.

Sports, then, bend to the melodramatic imperative as much as other areas of popular culture. Sports contain elements of epic, romance, tragedy, comedy, and farce. Basically people enjoy sports and the mass media report sports because, in part, of the melodramatic structure of the contests. But what makes sports politically relevant melodrama? Basically, the fantasies people draw from sports as interpreted by the mass media. Let us point to some of these fantasies.

SPORTS AND HEROIC FANTASIES

Popular sports are universally one of the great bastions of cultural heroism. The melodrama of American sports includes identifiable and personable heroes. By this we mean that they can be identified as "one of us," clearly a part of American culture; yet, they are personable in the sense of being larger than life. In short, a sports figure is a democratic persona. American heroes—in sports and elsewhere—conform to the cultural demand for both equality and achievement; that is, they have both the common touch and uncommon ability. In any case American sports heroes are objects of popular veneration, fascination, desire, awe, and hatred. As a nation, Americans entertain a variety of fantasies about the men and women on the playing field.

It may well be the case that the primal psychological root of sports heroism derives from a person's early experience in life with sports. As children, people acquire, through peers, an interest in sports and, by playing kids' games, a notion of what sports means. Americans often admire those accomplished at sports; schools reinforce the admiration because agility at sports and games is rewarded. People even learn that the role of player implies a heroic ideal: the player strives for excellence, records, winning. The heroic fantasy includes a role model of what athletic achievement entails. Because most Americans are not great athletes—and certainly not among the select few who achieve fame in the higher reaches of collegiate or professional sports—the heroic fantasy is largely vicarious. Average people fantasize about performing great deeds and winning admiration and thereby enjoy the mass-mediated fantasy of sports heroism presented to them.

If the roots of sports heroism is in childhood fantasies, the social and political uses of heroism find expression in institutional forms. It has not been lost on institutions that sports can teach us many things useful for a society and that the heroic ideal is something to strive for because of that. The heroic role model includes many nonathletic aspects—leadership, clean living, moral purity, hard work, religious piety, suffering, and so on. The classical American sports hero was a "natural aristocrat," for example, as portrayed in Ivy League sports stories at the turn of this century. Later on, he (and eventually she) became a moral aristocrat by the grit to overcome poverty and through athletic prowess. (Lou Gehrig of the New York Yankees exemplified heroes of such Protestant ethic fables.) The sports literature that developed concurrently with popular interest in collegiate and professional sports did much to codify the melodramatic formulas that later catered to, and helped to shape, the mass fantasy about sports heroes. Frank Merriwell's heroics were only the most unbelievable of a range of sports stories that continue, in a variety of media, to the present.[3] Now there is also an antiheroic literature, which details the idiocies and failings of sports heroes. But the heroic ideal remains a cultural norm that is deeply embedded in the popular consciousness. That adults still organize, and kids still play in, baseball Little Leagues and football Pop Warner Leagues testifies to the survival of the norm.

The fantasy of sports heroism is most evident in the mass media— newspaper sports pages, sports magazines, radio and video sports broadcasts. Sportswriters and broadcasters chain out mass fantasies about heroism and, in most cases, believe in sports heroics themselves. Whatever their private beliefs, their public rhetoric—in the paper or on the air—is largely supportive of the heroic fantasy if for no other reason than that they sense that their audience expects it. Too, sports heroism has the sanction of institutional approval. There are powerful pressures for sports-media people to boost and not debunk. Howard Cosell's "telling it like it is" involves much more heroic affirmation than cynical doubt.

A recent analysis of the rhetorical visions implicit in the popular ABC-TV series "Monday Night Football," exemplifies the penchant for melodramatic and heroic presentations by sportscasters.[4] The researchers, Jack E. and Jacqui S. Wallace, argue that the actual National Football League game carried by the network on the telecast is but a pretext for the TV show, a show that emphasizes only marginally the contest on the field. Instead, what the telecast stresses is a three-part melodrama—a moral, epic, and comic tale. Each melodramatic emphasis derives from the performance of one of the show's three principal announcers. Frank Gifford, although seeming only to offer a running account of the context, extols the virtues of the National Football League (NFL). He reflects the fantasy that athletics is both cause and consequence of moral virtue. Hence, Gifford says little of a star player's vast salary but speaks instead of the "pressures upon this deeply religious man." Gifford is the moral voice. Howard Cosell interprets the game in epic proportions. No contest is but a mere game. It is, instead, a critical contest wherein Cosell chastises a team whose offense is "timid," praises players' "courage," and talks of "tragic errors," "startling upsets," and "humiliating defeats." It is for Don Meredith to provide comic relief. If the hero is a democratic persona, then Gifford offers the moral side of democratic character, Cosell makes him bigger than life, and Meredith renders him the populist democrat, one of us. And, in comic character, it is for Meredith to sound the denouement of each Monday's contest with his rendition of "Turn out the lights, the party's over."

The widespread advocacy of sports heroism as a norm and ideal suggests a semiofficial fantasy with political implications. Heroes are, after all, models of excellence that an achievement-oriented society should emulate. The prototypical sports hero is a good citizen and no amount of debunking apparently can totally undermine the role model. People still believe that sports build character.[5] This implies a fantasy with an important political connection: a nation that is "soft" cannot compete in international political struggle; thus, physical fitness, competetive achievement, and the tough character building that sports allegedly offer is valuable for political purposes. President John Kennedy created the President's Council on Youth Fitness to organize sports programs (often compulsory) in schools to reverse the feared decline of fitness, strength, and, by extension, character in American youth. "Our growing softness, our increasing lack of physical fitness, is a menace to our security," he said.[6] The equation between heroism on the playing field and the battlefield is ancient, and the fantasy that the absence of sports heroism will affect national security has enduring appeal.

There is a more direct connection of sports heroism to the political fantasies of Americans: political recruitment. Sports heroes have long been exploited by politicians who desire to associate with such admired celebrities. Presidential candidates seek the endorsement of athletes—as if sports heroism qualified athletes to make political judgments with more assurance than the rest of us. Both Herbert Hoover and Al Smith sought the endorsement of Babe Ruth in 1928, hoping to mobilize Ruth's popular magic in their campaign. In 1976 Gerald Ford ran a radio spot that featured Joe Garagiola, TV sportscaster and former major league baseball catcher, reading an endless list of "athletes for Ford," connecting Ford's own sports heroics with sports heroes who supported him. (Both Al Smith, whom Babe Ruth backed, and Gerald Ford lost.)

But fantasies of heroic association are not as powerful as fantasies of heroic background. A record of sports achievement in one's background is valuable. A political aspirant who has been a sports hero takes an added luster. Two recent sports heroes-politicians have traded directly on their sports background. Senator Bill Bradley of New Jersey played a decade with the New York Knicks of the National Basketball Association. In his campaign for the Senate, he stressed that his sports role taught him competitiveness, being part of a team that works, exposed him to "many layers of national life," and gave him "a unique perspective of our problems, particularly since I was a white man in a predominantly black world." Even though he tried (often to no avail) to stress other qualifications, he did not ignore his sports background. He even ran a TV spot in which he crumpled up a piece of paper and hit the wastebasket from ten feet.[7] Representative Jacks Kemp of New York is a second example. He campaigned in the House district where he once played professional football (Buffalo). He stressed that having been a quarterback trained him for "leadership." As a conservative, he compared the virtues of a "competitive economy" with athletic competition and defended his support of low-paid apprenticeship jobs for the unemployed by comparing it with his own apprenticeship as quarterback in pro football.[8] The analogy is fantastic, not only because sports careers are rare experiences but also because lessons learned from a game may not apply to economic and political realities. But, in any event, these two successful politicians indicate that the fantasy of sports heroism can promote political victory.

SPORTS AND POLITICAL VALUES

Sports heroism is the personification of the value fantasy derived from sports, a fantasy with rhetorical and ideological uses in a variety of contexts. By value fantasy we mean a melodramatic account that provides people "proof" that culturally prescribed values work. The sporting life frequently promotes value fantasies that, employed as analogies, inform people of the values that work in politics. Values tested in the melodramatic structure of a sport, through various mediated interpretations, offer analogies to the "real world" of politics. Fantasies evident in the sports banquet speech, sports page editorial, or politician's oratory using sports as a political metaphor all contribute to the analogy. In this respect the value fantasy involving sports is didactic: it teaches political lessons.

Sports, of course, means different things to different people, depending on the fanciful interpretation they give to sports events, figures, and accounts. Given the variety of sports and the people who comprise their various followings, it is obvious that numerous value fantasies can generate from the sports world. From all of those possibilities we shall address four major and recurrent value fantasies: sports as patriotic inspiration, sports as a lesson in democratic sportsmanship, sports as a teacher of winning and achievement, and sports as an exemplar of political evils.

In its broadest aspect, the politically charged value fantasy derived from sports is that athletics embodies the American way of life. Sports thereby yield patriotic inspiration. In particular, our major indigenous sports dramatically portray the American way. Polls consistently show that people believe sports have positive consequences for American society, indeed, that "sports are valuable because they help youngsters to become good citizens."[9] Many people in sports—coaches, owners, players, sportswriters, and so on—share that popular belief, as do military generals and civilian politicians. In theory, the young learn from this inspirational analogy, thus enhancing love of country and appreciation of American values. It is no accident that patriotic and religious ritual—the Pledge of Allegiance, the national anthem, prayerful invocations—are included in game ceremonies. But inspirational learning extends beyond ritual to the sports experience itself. American values, such as competitiveness, desire to succeed, belief in progress, the necessity of hard work, and pragmatic efficiency, are instilled through playing the game, which can by extension apply to the game of life. Skeptics doubt that such lessons are in fact learned or point out that what is learned may be contradictory (e.g., individual achievement versus teamwork). But no one can deny that the value fantasy of sports has a powerful grip on the American consciousness.

Sports fantasies also teach us the political value of democratic sportsmanship. The heroic model of the sportsman is of an aristocratic cultural figure dramatized through sports fair play. The sportsman plays fair, fights hard, treats opponents with respect, enjoys the contest, and accepts victory with magnanimity, defeat with grace. Being a good sport even now is a trait admired in everyday life. At one time many high schools in America issued report cards with students' grades bearing the rhyming aphorism:" For when the great scorer comes to write against your name, he'll write not that you won or lost but how you played the game."

A sportsman is a gentleman committed to excellence within ethical bounds that prevent unethical means or cheap tactics to win. A classic book on the democratic way of life describes the value fantasy of "democracy as sportsmanship." The sportsman, on the playing field or in politics, likes the game for its own sake, tolerates and honors the opposition, plays by the rules, and strives for victory but accepts defeat with dignity. The true democratic man is a good loser and winner. He or she learns from sports valuable lessons about the game of politics.[10] A comprehensive analysis of the role of collegiate sports in American life suggests how forms of winning and losing are analogous to politics. In *The Big Game* Edwin H. Cady talks of the esthetics of winning and losing. There are, he writes, four kinds of winners/losers: "*Winner-winners* triumph with decorum, with class. *Winner-losers* top the score but act bush. *Loser-winners* lose the game, but they win the experience, lose while gaining the rewards of the tragic sense of life, with class. At poor last come the *Loser-losers*: they lose and act bush to boot."[11] Consider by extension the application of this sports metaphor to the outcomes of recent American presidential elections. It should not be difficult to think of candidates for each category.

But the sportsmanlike code of conduct for players in political games runs counter to another value fantasy: the necessity to emphasize *winning* at all costs and, thus, being tough, mean, and willing to break the rules. "Winning isn't everything," goes Lombardi's Law (after Hall of Fame NFL coach Vince Lombardi), "it's the only thing." "Nice guys finish last," goes Leo Durocher's dictum. Sports prove that winning is what life is all about and, thus, that winning in politics is the bottom line: all other moral or social considerations bend to that harsh fact. Winning is the goal of those who wish to achieve, and one cannot be too fastidious about the means. The metaphor has been applied to business, war, and politics. As in sports, the successful businessperson achieves wealth at the expense of others. In war it is kill or be killed. In politics one becomes "King of the Hill" only by being meaner and more cunning than everyone else. A sport such as football is competitive, aggressive, and violent. The success of a player or team that has a reputation for mean tactics provides dramatic evidence of the necessity of nastiness. Sports melodramas where unsportsmanlike conduct triumphs validate the fantasy.

Such a value fantasy is obviously outside the moral code of American society, at least in an "official" sense. Therefore, it cannot be overtly stated by, say, TV sportscasters, but only subtly suggested as integral to success. The sportscaster reporting an NFL game is supportive of playing by the rules but also may obliquely suggest that "cheating," rough and cruel play, and endless struggle are necessary for victory. The mass-mediated fantasy, thus includes an undercurrent of immoral or amoral lessons. These conflicting value fantasies drawn from sports and applied to such areas of activity as politics are an example of *popular Machiavellianism*, the eternal moral ambivalence in the popular mind about what strategies get you what you want in sports or politics. The nasty interpretation of sports appeared in the Watergate mentality of the Nixon administration, whose members used sports metaphors to dramatize to each other and the world the necessity for bending the rules. The political world to the Nixon White House, like sports, seemed a zero-sum game of winners and losers locked in relentless strife (be the opponents Soviet Communists or American Democrats). Because the "other side" are rogues who do anything to win, "we" are justified in being just as mean and cunning. The infamous plumbers office in the basement of the Nixon White House had a sign that paraphrased Lombardi: "Winning in politics isn't everything, it's the only thing." But the blatant appeal to political necessities upset people— both in politics and in sports—who held to the more overt value fantasy of sportsmanship and moral and political rules. The fact that both the nice-sportsman and the nasty-winner fantasies exist indicates a tension in the popular mind about appropriate political conduct, a conflict dramatized in sports.

This conflict is probably highlighted more now because of changes that have occurred in sports over recent decades. The intensity and scope of trends in sports make the contradictions in value fantasies all the more confusing. There is fragmentary evidence that intense sports fans are more authoritarian, nationalistic, and conservative in their political orientation than the rest of the population.[12] There are certainly large numbers of people—fans or not—who draw a negative value fantasy from sports. These critics argue that popular sports symbolizes the negative qualities of American society and politics. They share with the sports booster the fantasy that sports reflects society and teaches values, but unlike the booster they think sports a mirror and teacher of evil: mass-mediated sports melodramas demonstrate the American way of violence, social injustice, and political failing.

If, for the sports booster, the competitiveness and emphasis on winning in sports is a positive analogy for what politics and economics are like, for sports skeptics the analogy has negative implications. Their sports fantasy demonstrates that America is obsessed with power and money, with getting ahead at all costs and exploiting other people in the process. Capitalist competition and political competition alike are destructive; this destructiveness is ludicrously illustrated by athletes getting obscenely high salaries and by the intrigues and petty quarrels of sports franchises and owners. Sports is not pure or innocent, and healthy, playful fun is corrupted by an emphasis on power and greed. In this fantasy, sports teaches imperialism by emphasizing winning and domination; it teaches greed by emphasizing acquisition. Even the Little League, these people point out, is ruined by parents and coaches pushing the kids to win, a corruption confirmed by repeated news accounts of little leaguers sobbing over critical losses.

For others, the negative analogy of sports to life focuses on the violence fantasy. Because sports such as football emphasize winning through aggressive violence, this but underwrites the tendency of American society toward violence and war. Sports, ranging from the computer war games of shopping center arcades to the National Football League, teach that aggressive violence is how you get what you want. This fantasy implicates militarists as advocates of violent sports that prepare people for aggressive military actions. Professional football in particular demonstrates the organized aggression of a specialized team—much like an army—that attempts to conquer turf and defeat the enemy with violent play. A team such as the Dallas Cowboys dramatizes the inhuman, machine-like efficiency associated with the military. Too, the violence fantasy includes the notion that the melodrama of sports supports the unorganized violence of individuals in society. When NFL defensive back Jack Tatum seriously injured an opposing player and then wrote a book (*They Call Me Assassin*) defending such calculated violence, the episode was melodramatic credence for the violence fantasy.[13]

Neither broadcasts of sporting events nor postgame accounts glorify such violence for violence's sake. But critics of big-time sports do not thereby absolve the sports media for contributing to a widespread political attitude. Sports coverage by the media, skeptics argue, does not promote political violence but rather political passivity. The sports fan, so the critic argues, sits before TV, radio, newspaper, or sports magazine; the sports entertainment such media provide lulls the fan into a passive acceptance that violence is normal, there is nothing to be

done about it, therefore, life as a spectator is superior to that of the glad-
iator. But a nation of spectators, say sports critics, is not a nation of
responsible citizens. Thus, popular sports, rather than being the bul-
wark of democracy that sports enthusiasts extol, is a threat to democratic values.[14]

Finally, critics affiliated with a particular political ideology or interest often hold a view of sports that conforms to their own particular
concern. The mediated melodrama of sports as they see it is one that
dramatizes the failings of American society—or conversely, that
dramatizes the struggle of the group with which they identify—to
overcome sports obstacles and, by extension, political obstacles. This
kind of rhetorical vision of sports is perhaps most evident among those
associated with a racial, ethnic, or sexual group. A feminist may see
sports as a bastion of male chauvinism and sexual exploitation; episodes of such conflicts, then, are taken to reflect the pervasiveness of
such attitudes and practices in the larger society. On the other hand,
a successful woman athlete can become a heroine by overcoming bar-
riers in sports. A figure such as Janet Guthrie, who broke the sexual
barrier in race car driving, becomes a heroic pioneer. But the NFL's use
of cheerleader groups in scanty costumes with erotic routines for the
benefit of largely male audiences (and with names like the Rams's
Embraceable Ewes) is proof positive of the chauvinism and hypocrisy
of a male establishment.

The fantasies discussed here involve diverse political values. The
rhetorical visions connected with sports come and go, shift and focus,
as part of the "waves of linguistic behavior" described in this volume's
introduction. The analogies of sports alter with changes in public opinion and politics. However subtle the relationship may be, and however
difficult to pin down, nevertheless popular sports are popular melodramas in mass-mediated form that help shape political consciousness
through value fantasies.

SPORTS AS A DRAMATIC MICROCOSM OF POLITICS

In even a more overt and direct way sports offer politically charged
melodramatic fantasies. This is through the settings of sports events—
either for the actual game or for activities involving the game—used for
political purposes. The mass-mediated fantasy is directly political, a
dramatic microcosm of politics. There are two important politico-sports
melodramas in this respect: the game ritual and the game itself.

Political dimensions of sports appear in formal rituals performed
for the pleasure of mass audiences. These rituals are patriotic melodramas that celebrate both national and ideological identities and regional

and institutional loyalties. The dramaturgy of the pregame patriotic ritual (flag raising, reading the Pledge of Allegiance, playing the national anthem, and so on) invokes a sense of communal unity and deference to the political values symbolized by the game. The drama involves the stadium and TV viewer in a politically charged ritual. Even more directly, many half-time shows at college football games have patriotic aspects. During the height of the Vietnam War, with mounting opposition and confusion over the rationale for the war, many half-time shows were intensely patriotic. In 1970 ABC refused to televise an antiwar half-time show which the University of Buffalo band planned to perform, on grounds that it was a political demonstration, but later that year ABC did broadcast a half-time show at the Army-Navy game that featured, first, the Green Berets who had staged an unsuccessful raid on prisoner of war camps in North Vietnam and, second, a speech by a general condemning antiwar activity at home. The Army-Navy half-time was obviously a political demonstration, thus suggesting the network was selective in the political melodrama it chose to broadcast. The close relationship of sports and nationalism impels the exclusion of ritual fantasies that question patriotic motives. Indeed, mass-mediated melodramas critical of U.S. policies are condemned. When black athletes raised clinched, black-gloved fists and bowed their heads during televised ceremonies at the 1968 Olympics, they were stripped of their medals and banned from further Olympic competition even though the Olympics are nonpolitical. Such a gesture intrudes on the ritual fantasy of national sports affirmation, robbing it of its intended melodramatic power by making it into a negatively charged spectacle.[15] Ritual affirmation can reach awesome proportions as in the love feast for the released American hostages at the 1981 Super Bowl, complete with yellow ribbons everywhere, on everyone, and including a huge yellow ribbon on the New Orleans Superdome itself!

Sports events become political melodrama when the *game itself* has political overtones. The sports event becomes a dramatic microcosm with political conflict inherent in the game. This frequently occurs in Olympic contests. Nations bring political differences into the games and make them tests of national and political superiority. The Hungarian and Soviet water polo teams played a memorable—and bloody— match at the 1956 Olympics held shortly after the Soviet suppression of the Hungarian revolution. Indeed, that two national teams play each other at all can often convey a dramatic political message. An American table tennis team touring the Far East in 1971 was unexpectedly invited by the People's Republic of China to play in Peking. This "ping pong diplomacy" was a signal that China was prepared to end its isolation from the United States and resulted in President Nixon's celebrated trip to China in 1972. The match was thus not just an impromptu sporting event but part of a political melodrama of international significance.

Perhaps the most spectacular sporting event with political significance for Americans was the success of the Olympic hockey team of 1980. What happened at Lake Placid in February was merely the last act of a politically emotional melodrama involving a president seeking reelection, Soviet foreign policy, and a public yearning for reassurance and retribution. Iran and Afghanistan may seem far removed from either amateur hockey or the upstate New York event that tied them together. The seizure of hostages at the American embassy in Teheran and the Soviet invasion of Afghanistan in late 1979 were profoundly upsetting political events to Americans. Both events moved the world into a period of international tension and intensified a chauvinistic and retributive mood in America. President Jimmy Carter, campaigning for reelection, attempted to mobilize the public mood. He dispatched the naval fleet to the Persian Gulf, attempted to negotiate the release of the hostages, agitated for resistance among Persian Gulf states to Soviet expansion, and embargoed the shipment of grain to the Soviet Union.

Carter probably may have understood that the political melodrama he was enacting would not alter Soviet behavior. But dramatic logic demanded the Soviets be punished in the eyes of the American public. Because Carter could not boldly intervene in the Afghan conflict, he sought ways to punish the Russians through propaganda. He called for an American and international boycott of the summer Olympic games, which were scheduled to be held in Moscow in 1980. He pressured European countries not to send teams. He sent boxer Muhammad Ali to Africa to promote the boycott among African states. He advocated and arranged for "alternative" games to be held somewhere other than Russia. He successfully pressured NBC to drop plans to televise the games. He stopped American companies from sending Olympic-related materials to the Russians. He sought the support of American athletes and of the international sports community. All of this dramatized Carter as the hero standing tough and firm against the villainous Soviets—saying that if they were going to act that way, we were not going to play. The fantasy took the form of a political morality play casting the president as the moral agent of the drama whose motive was to express America's collective moral outrage for such villainy. If Carter realized that the Soviets were not about to end their Afghan invasion for the sake of the Olympics (however much they wanted the games to be a propaganda showcase for Soviet achievements), then the melodrama was for largely domestic political consumption.

In the wake of political tension, the winter Olympic games took place in February 1980. To the surprise of everyone (including the team itself), the American hockey team won the gold medal. The sporting saga constructed by ABC–TV, which was telecasting the games, chained out to other media: a Cinderella team thrown together and trained overcame the hockey giants of the world—Sweden, Norway, Finland—in the finals, but, most important, it overcame the Soviet Union in the next-to-last game. The team appealed to Americans as a Horatio Alger phenomenon—the unknown and unheralded who through hard work, grit, and luck triumph over adversity and win game and fortune. Dramatic timing and the outcome of the play in the match with the USSR could not have been more appropriate: defeat of the vaunted Soviet team (which had won four straight gold medals in previous Olympics and regularly defeated National Hockey League teams) was the fantasy that the good guys win. The game had all the elements of melodrama—clearly drawn heroes and villains, intensified peril and anxiety, the pluck and tenacity of the victors, a moral to the story, and a happy ending.

The U.S. victory was an occasion for national celebration, one giant party involving not only hockey fans but also people who cared nothing about hockey and had never seen a hockey game. The sports victory served as the melodramatic substitute for political victory over Soviet aggression. As the news flashed across the country in the minutes after the 4 to 3 triumph, there was spontaneous joy—people honking their car horns, cheering in bars, even ringing church bells. On airplanes in flight, when pilots announced the score, the aisles filled with rejoicing passengers. Exactly how many people did respond to the event is unclear: the extent of such celebration, as reported by the media, was probably a smaller portion of the American population statistically than the news suggested. In any case the sports victory was politically significant, a dramatic microcosm of international tensions with a desirable climax for the mass audience.

The defeat of the Soviet team, however, was not the end of the fantastic drama. The euphoria created by that win was tempered by the fact that to win the gold medal, the American team still had to defeat the formidable Finns in the Olympic final. Dramatic logic called for the U.S. to win because the team was now the focus of national attention and adoration. And it did, coming from behind in the last quarter. The patriotic fantasy stirred and represented by the team was evident in the Olympic fieldhouse and throughout the country. Each time the U.S. team scored, hundreds of American flags waved in the arena as the fans chanted "USA ... USA ... USA ...." Crude signs flourished that said simply "Gold." When it was clear that the U.S. was going to win, the crowd chanted "We're number one ... We're number one ...." The chants of the crowd probably referred not only to the hockey team but also to the country: it was not just a sports victory but a national victory as well. At the end impromptu choruses of "God Bless America" began, and the crowd remained in the fieldhouse, refusing to leave and continuing to celebrate. The hockey team had become America's heroes.[16]

The political significance of the Olympic victory was not lost on the mass media nor on the president. President Carter brought all the U.S. Winter Olympic participants to the White House, but obviously the central characters in the melodrama were the hockey team. In a nationally televised spectacular, the Olympians were cheered by crowds, hailed by the U.S. Marine Band, and praised and greeted by the president. Carter judged they were "wonderful young Americans" who had "thrilled the entire world" (one wonders how thrilled the Russian audience was!) and produced a "wonderful week for our country." Thus, the entire drama culminated in a mass-mediated ceremony of national congratulations. Everybody was happy: Carter was happy because the hockey team had helped him "win" the moral melodrama and enhanced his reelection chances; the team was happy for being victors and celebrities; the media was happy for having a fantastic story; and the nation was happy for having experienced a cathartic victory over the villainous Russians. People projected onto the episode anxieties about Soviet expansion (and also, in the back of their minds, the Iranian hostage crisis); the mass-mediated fantasy relieved fears by a substitute victory, albeit sports and not political. We label this *fantastic substitution*, the process of a mass-mediated nonpolitical fantasy alleviating political anxieties by allowing the projection of unresolved political tensions onto another substitute melodrama. Rather than projecting private anxieties on political objects, people project political anxieties on mass-mediated objects, in this case a sports event that dramatized, and in some sense resolved, the political anxiety. Such displacement and resolution is, however, probably temporary. The Americans won the game and rejoiced briefly in it; but in the cold light of dawn it was clear that the Soviets were still in Afghanistan and the threat of Soviet power was still there. In the wake of political frustration in the future, sports will undoubtedly serve, as the hockey victory did, as a fantastic substitution.[17]

THE ROMANCE OF SPORTS AS THE REALITY OF POLITICS?

The mass-mediated world of popular sports is related, in the ways we have tried to specify, to our political fantasies. Our vision of politics is affected by our consciousness of the lessons of sports. That both sports and politics in a media democracy are melodramas structured for popu-

---

lar audiences is a clue to the affinity. One critic has noted that the "social function" of melodrama "is to engage the communal emotions of an audience through the representation of an ideal world of certainty and justice, which simultaneously offers excitement and spectacle not available in the day-to-day world of that audience." He cites G. B. Shaw's thought that "melodramatic stage illusion is not an illusion of real life, but an illusion of the embodiment of our romantic imaginings."[18] It is not too farfetched to think of both sports and politics that way. The mass-mediated worlds of sports and politics, at least at those moments when things are going the way we want them to go, appeal to our romantic imaginings. We entertain both sports and political fantasies in which the good guys win, poetic justice triumphs, our moral code is vindicated, and the drama turns out the way we want. In the case of the American hockey team, the two fantasies blended together and became an example of what we call fantastic substitution. Thus, our romantic imaginings about politics can be satisfied by sports, given the right melodramatic circumstances. Sports is a world of play and does not alter the world of political power. But its participation in our political fantasies does mean that it helps to shape our vision of politics.

NOTES

1. Jacques Barzun, *God's Country and Mine* (Boston: Little, Brown & Co., 1954), pp. 159–160. Emphasis in original.
2. See, for example, Richard Lipsky, *How We Play the Game* (Boston: Beacon Press, 1980).
3. See most of the essays in Eldon E. Snyder (ed.), *Sports: A Social Scoreboard* (Bowling Green, Ohio: The Popular Press, 1975). (Bowling Green University Popular Press)
4. Jack E. Wallace and Jacqui S. Wallace, "Story-telling in Monday Night Football." Paper delivered at the annual meeting of the American Popular Culture Association, Cincinnati, March 1981.
5. See the discussion in various texts, such as Eldon E. Snyder and Elmer Spreitzer, *Social Aspects of Sports* (Englewood Cliffs, N.J.: Prentice-Hall, 1978); Jay J. Coakley, *Sport in Society* (St Louis: C. V. Mosby Co., 1978); and D. Stanley Eitzen and George H. Sage, *Sociology of American Sport* (Dubuque, Iowa: Willian C. Brown Co., 1978).
6. Quoted in Christopher Lasch, *The Culture of Narcissism* (New York: W. W. Norton & Co., 1978), p. 101.
7. John Husar, "Their Goal Is the Same, but Not Their Approach," *Chicago Tribune*, October 27, 1978, "Sportsweek," p. 1.
8. Martin Tolchin, "Jack Kemp's Bootleg Run to the Right," *Esquire* (October 24, 1978): 59–69.
9. Coakley, *Sport in Society*, op. cit., p. 16.
10. T. V. Smith and Edward C. Lindeman, *The Democratic Way of Life* (New York: New American Library, 1963), pp. 81, 83, 88. (Mentor Books)
11. Edwin H. Cady, *The Big Game: College Sports and American Life* (Knoxville: University of Tennessee Press, 1978), p. 107. Emphasis in original.

12. Robert H. Prisuta, "Televised Sports and Political Values," *Journal of Communication*, 29 (Winter 1979): 94–102.

13. Jack Tatum, *They Call Me Assassin* (New York: Avon, 1980).

14. The classic statement of this thesis is Lewis Mumford, "Sports and the 'Bitch-Goddess'," in Marcia Stubbs and Sylvan Barnet, eds., *The Little-Brown Reader* (Boston: Little, Brown & Co., 1977), pp. 238–241.

15. Eitzen and Sage, *Sociology of American Sport*, op. cit., pp. 146–148.

16. Bob Verdi, "A Dream Come True: U.S. Hockey Team Good as Gold," *Chicago Tribune*, February 25, 1980, sec. 5, p. 1.

17. This notion is adopted from Harold Lasswell's theorem: cf. his statement in *Power and Personality* (New York: Viking Press, 1962), p. 38.

18. Earl F. Bargainnier, "Hissing the Villain, Cheering the Hero: The Social Function of Melodrama," *Studies in Popular Culture*, 3 (Spring 1980): 49.

Part II
Group-Mediated Politics

The mediating of political realities through mass communication contains the potential for creating and sharing fantasies throughout entire communities by means of news, entertainment programming, popular films, celebrity magazines, sports, and other media. Precisely what proportion of persons exposed to the fantasy content of mass media respond to it and how they respond, current research does not permit us to say. Yet, the potential is there, in part because people do not have the opportunity to deal directly with the things they view and hear in the entertainment and news media. If they did have that opportunity, say through their personal or group experiences, the results would be worlds of reality not fantasy. Or would they? We address that question in Part II. We look first at how, even among group members dealing directly with tangible problems, there is a strong tendency to construct and share fantastic political worlds. Then, we examine how this process operates in various areas—among public officials, political journalists, selected religious groups, and highly publicized movements on the political right.

As with mass-mediated politics, our discussion depends on both studies of communication within political groups and speculations about the process. Consequently, we offer the same disclaimer—plus an invitation—to readers that is contained in Part I. The following chapters suggest propositions about how group experience mediates political realities and thereby frequently builds fantastic worlds. We urge readers to reflect on these propositions and examine them further, something they can do in their own group life. In that way, they, too, can participate in the research scholar's version of the American Dream, that is, the quest for a tested body of knowledge explaining how and why the members of the human family behave as they do.

7

Elite Political Fantasies
Groupthink, Decisionmakers, Gatekeepers

1984! To George Orwell it was more than a year. It was a world, a world depicted in his classic novel published nearly three and a half decades earlier.[1] It was not a pleasant world; there was no privacy, no individuality, no love. Virtually every movement and every idea of every citizen was closely monitored by the Thought Police using highly sophisticated techniques of electronic surveillance. Personal considerations counted for nothing; loyalty and service to the group were the be-all and end-all of living.

Orwell's *Nineteen Eighty-Four* takes place in the fictional society of Oceania. The political realities of Oceania's citizens are totally mediated from a central governing power known only as Big Brother. The oft-repeated phrase, "Big Brother is watching you," reminds people that they have no lives of their own independent of the totalitarian regime. Big Brother exerts total control in a number of ways. The mass media are one means. There is only one source and, hence, one mediated political reality of political information for Oceanians, that is, the regime's news service. Moreover, recognizing that what things are called determines how people think about them, Big Brother uses an official language devised solely to meet society's needs, *Newspeak*. Newspeak consists of three vocabularies. One is a vocabulary of a very small number of words, rigidly defined, used for the necessities of everyday living—words like dog, tree, house, and so on. A second vocabulary is made up of scientific and technical terms, such as actinium, which is a word we use for a radioactive element in uranium. The third vocabulary is of particular importance. It consists of words deliberately constructed for political purposes. Each word carries not only a political implication but also imposes an attitude on the person using it. Such words are always compound words, that is, a combination of two or more words or portions of words. Hence, *goodthink* is to think in an orthodox manner, *goodsex* is chastity, *sexcrime* is sexual immorality, and so on. *Duckspeak* (to quack like a duck) is the ritualistic rhetoric of politicians praising orthodox regime opinions. Duckspeak is goodspeak worthy of emulation. If, for example, the Oceania *Times* says that an official is a "doubleplusgood duckspeaker," it is a warm compliment indeed. There is one other facet to this vocabulary, namely, all government organizations and institutions have names that are acronyms. *Minipax* is the Ministry of Peace, *Recdep* the Records Department, and so on. Frequently, the titles are euphemisms that serve the regime. A forced-labor camp, for example, is a *joycamp*.

In 1984 Oceania is at war with Eurasia and in alliance with Eastasia; four years earlier the war had been with Eastasia, the alliance with Eurasia. That is about the whole of the world—Oceania, Eurasia, Eastasia. These are the 1980s and no such alignments exist. Obviously Orwell's world of *Nineteen Eighty-Four* was imaginary. What, then, does it have to do with mediated politics in America? Sufficiently more than appears on the surface to merit pause. Commenting on Orwell's novel, philosopher Erich Fromm observed that readers would err in interpreting the work as simply a description of totalitarian barbarism for "it means us too."[2] It means us not in the sense of how the world is divided between power blocs, perhaps, but in the sense in which our political realities are mediated.

Consider Newspeak. The grooved responses of which we spoke in discussing the rhetoric of presidential campaign debates (Chapter 2) is a form of duckspeak. Catch-phrases of TV news involve duckspeaking: "days of captivity," "body counts," "the horror tonight," and so on (Chapter 1). Students of political language, moreover, point to the euphemisms of political discourse—the neutron bomb is a "clean bomb," there is "fighting in the demilitarized zone," nuclear war is an "all-out-strategic-exchange," old people are "the elderly," and so on.[3] And abridged language is a way of political life: *deeohee* is the Department of Energy (DOE), HUD is not the Hollywood movie of that title but the Department of Housing and Urban Development, the Department of Defense is *deeohdee* (DOD), *Capcomm* relays messages to and from spaceships in orbit, and the *Nissims* (National Security Study Memoranda or NSSMs) of the Nixon administration became the *Pissims* (Presidential Study Memoranda or PSMs) of the Carter White House—for but a single day—to be supplanted by PRMs (Presidential Review Memoranda). Acronym overkill provoked one cartoonist to portray two marching demonstrators with a banner for COCOA, the Council to Outlaw Contrived and Outrageous Acronyms.[4]

But all this is a far cry from the totalitarian mediated politics of *Nineteen Eighty-Four*. We may be near Orwell's imagined year, but not his world. Yet there is one respect in which, from time to time, there is a Nineteen Eighty-Fourlike quality to mediated political realities. That lies in what we refer to in this chapter as *groupthink*, a term that would fit comfortably in the political dictionary of Newspeak and that describes a process often at work when political elites try to come to grips with realities. If most of us are victims of *massthink*, that is, depending on the mass media rather than on direct experience to inform us about politics, political activists sometimes fall victim to groupthink.

GROUPTHINK

In Orwell's *Nineteen Eighty-Four* people engage in *doublethink*. A person doublethinks when holding two contradictory beliefs simultaneously, accepting both:

To know and not to know, to be conscious of complete truthfulness while telling carefully constructed lies, to hold simultaneously two opinions which canceled out, knowing them to be contradictory and believing in both of them, to use logic against logic, to repudiate morality while laying claim to it, to believe that democracy was impossible and that the Party was the guardian of democracy, to forget whatever it was necessary to forget, then to draw it back into memory again at the moment when it was needed, and then promptly to forget it again.[5]

Oceania's *Minitrue* (Ministry of Truth) made a public display of doublethink through an endless repetition of three slogans: WAR IS PEACE, FREEDOM IS SLAVERY, IGNORANCE IS STRENGTH. But doublethink is not confined to the fictional land of Oceania. How often does one hear the phrase *free world* used to include the United States, Great Britain, *and* military dictatorships in South America, *and* apartheid South Africa? Do we not prepare for war to assure peace? Do we not assist the poor by cutting the taxes of the rich? Doublethink, in effect, recognizes contradictory realities, then forces the contradictions into a single, unified reality of truth and falsity, good and bad, yes and no, reality and fantasy. One need not, indeed cannot, check the details of such a single reality for authenticity. Both its internal contradictions and any conflicts with the perceived external world are already accounted for in the doublethink process itself.

Political psychologist Irving Janis has identified what is in effect a form of doublethink. He calls it groupthink. "Groupthink," he writes, "refers to a deterioration of mental efficiency, reality testing, and moral judgment that results from in-group pressures."[6] As we shall see, when people get together to do a job, make a decision, or otherwise act in concert, pressures develop to make group members think alike. As this happens, many of the symptoms of doublethink—holding contradictory beliefs, shutting out information that does not conform to group solidarity, selective forgetting and remembering, and so on—emerge. To see why, it is first necessary to consider the nature of group activity.

When people come together a number of things happen. Two are particularly important in understanding the role of groupthink in mediating political realities. First, there is usually some reason why the group forms. In politics groups form to accomplish something. Groups support and oppose political candidates, try to get their demands converted into government policies, strive to advance their special interests, aim to act in the public good, or attempt to deal with a problem. In short, groups have tasks to perform. Regardless of the size of the group, the key decisions tend to be made by a relatively few group members acting collectively in the name of the organization and with the approval in some form of the total group membership. Be the group as large as a major trade union or as small as a U.S. president's inner circle of advisors, key decisions derive from face-to-face exchanges among a few group members. In that sense all groups are small groups.

Interesting things occur in small, face-to-face groups. Group members have a task to perform—to decide to build a new weapons system, recommend tax reductions, ration paperclips among office personnel, or whatever. But to do that there is a prior goal. That is to build a consensus, cohesion, and solidarity among group members that will permit the group to exist and act *as a group*, not merely a collection of individuals. Normally that cohesiveness emerges as an unconscious byproduct as people go about the social amenities of getting acquainted, exchanging pleasantries, asking and receiving advice, becoming colleagues, friends, and so forth. Soon, two overlapping sets of things are happening among group members, that is, they are socializing and promoting group solidarity at the same time they are confronting the task that brought them together.

Sociologist Robert F. Bales experimented with small, face-to-face groups and observed closely how group members acted as they went about their own work.[7] He classified their exchanges into two categories. One consisted of all the things that dealt specifically with the group's task, for example, members asking and giving information, opinions, and suggestions regarding how the group should deal with a problem. The second consisted of the social relationships between group members, for example, being friendly or antagonistic, joking and laughing, or being tense and withdrawn, complimenting or criticizing one another. One thing Bales concluded from his research was that if the group was to remain in being and, thus, perform its task, it must have means of releasing hostilities and disagreements, of continuously reestablishing friendly relations among group members.

But the desire to promote social harmony and keep the group intact may become an end in itself; indeed, camaraderie may replace the performance of the group's task as the rationale for the group's existence. In the name of group solidarity, disagreements, criticism, information that strains social relations, and other matters *vital to the group's task* are swept under the rug in the name of social happiness. "Don't rock the boat" is the motto.

It was this tendency of task groups to develop into social groups that engaged Janis's interest. He observed that subtle pressures arise in cohesive groups to get members to conform to informal standards of friendly social behavior. These pressures may subvert the original purpose for the group's existence. Instead of hardheaded appraisals of the problems, resources, information, and courses of action before the group, the stress is on amiable relations, warm feelings, and a cozy atmosphere. The pressures are for members to think *as a group* and to arrive at decisions regarding the group's task that do not threaten group solidarity. Loyalty to the group becomes the highest form of loyalty; this requires members to resist raising controversial issues, criticizing weak arguments, or challenging faulty information. A member who persists in dissent from such conformity is ignored, even rejected.[8]

Such, then, is one feature of group life that leads to groupthink, namely, pressures to solve problems in conformity to the dictates of group solidarity and loyalty rather than specifics of the group's task. Janis maintains that this produces a series of defects: groups do not survey a full range of options open to them but seek solutions from a limited number of alternatives; group members reach decisions, then fail to reexamine them in the face of drawbacks; once a course of action has been rejected, the group neglects to reconsider it even though it may have advantages over the chosen option; information from nongroup experts that runs counter to the group's thinking is avoided; group members display selective bias in responding to the assessments by nongroup members, quickly assuming an us versus them posture; and, groups ignore the likelihood that it is impossible to carry out the socially satisfying option.

Thus, when people form groups, social considerations may override hardheaded efforts to solve the problems that brought the group together in the first place. This is one source of groupthink that affects group-mediated realities. We noted earlier that there is a second feature of groupthink that affects mediated politics, that is, the fantasy component of groupthink. We touched on it in our Introduction when we discussed Ernest G. Bormann's theory of fantasy chaining. Moreover, Janis's inventory of the defects inherent in groupthink clearly implies that groupthink is a fantasy-chaining rather than reality-testing process. Hence, we need but comment briefly on how groupthink is fantasythink.

In his study of small groups Bales developed an elaborate scheme for coding the task and social acts of group members toward one another. For example, if a group member gave another help, that reflected the social behavior of showing solidarity; if one asked another to repeat what had been said, that coded as asking for orientation, a task behavior. One social act of importance Bales coded as "shows tension release." If a person joked with others, laughed, showed satisfaction, smiled, and so on, that eased the tension in the group and put members at rest. Bales later relabeled "shows tension release" to "dramatizes." Now recall that Bales concluded that group well-being, even survival, depended on releasing tensions. Hence, groups must show tension release or, as in his later analysis, group members give dramatic performances to build group cohesion.

It was precisely this point of Bales's analysis that Ernest G. Bormann relied on in fashioning his fantasy-chaining ideas. Bormann noted that:

Some, but not all, of the communication coded as 'dramatizes' would chain out through the group. When it did that is when group members got excited, interrupted each other, lost their self-consciousness; the meeting would become lively, animated, even boisterous.[9]

People, in short, were taking part in the drama; the group was no longer a collection of individuals but a being with a life of its own. Simultaneously, groupthink and fantasy chaining begin (see this volume's introduction). Dramatic (social) performance supplants task performance as the first priority of the group.

GROUPTHINK FANTASIES

Potentially anyone can be a victim of groupthink, of fantasyland. Consider the student not doing well in a college course, say in biology. Assume the course ends with a standardized exam. Assume, also, that a few of the student's friends discover a way to steal that exam, work out the answers and, thus, assure themselves of high marks on the final exam and in the course. The student may have all kinds of reasons for looking askance at such a scheme—moral convictions, fear of being caught, and so forth. But the call of group loyalty is higher. The student withholds her reservations, conforms to the group's decision, and goes along. Such things do happen. And, as on one occasion, when the pilfered exam turned out not to be the one given on the day of the final, the student recognized her fantasy for what it was, a product of groupthink.

But what of political groupthink? What lessons can be learned about mediated political realities from cases of groupthink and the fantasies conjured by them? In the remainder of this chapter we consider three types of groupthink. First, we shall look at groupthink among public officials charged with making decisions on important matters. Then, we shall look briefly at groupthink among aspirants to elected office, that is, candidates for election. Finally, groupthink can occur among political journalists who come together to discuss and interpret the news for readers/viewers. We look at a case of that, too.

The Bay of Pigs as a Hornet's Nest: Official Fantasizing

On April 17, 1961, a brigade consisting of fourteen hundred Cuban exiles, intent on establishing a bridgehead from which to topple the regime of Fidel Castro, landed at the Bay of Pigs on the Cuban coast. They were aided by the U.S. Navy, Air Force, and Central Intelligence Agency (CIA). Disaster followed. Ammunition and supply ships failed to arrive, either sunk or forced away by Castro's aircraft. Within three days the brigade was surrounded by Castro's army, two hundred men of the assault force were killed, twelve hundred taken prisoner.

It was the Bay of Pigs fiasco that provoked Irving L. Janis to speculate about groupthink. Why, he pondered, had President John Kennedy's closest advisers failed to detect the faulty assumptions of the Cuban invasion plan? Why had they not pressed the CIA and Joint Chiefs of Staff (proponents of the plan) for justification? Why did the few critics on the president's advisory team keep silent rather than voice their doubts? It was not a lack of competence among Kennedy's advisers. They were all highly qualified, experienced men of public affairs. Nor was it simply a matter of political miscalculation, bureaucratic bungling, or insufficient information. No, thought Janis, the Bay of Pigs plan was a product of groupthink, the result of a group's ability to delude itself into believing that what was ultimately a "perfect failure" was a flawless plan.[10]

Janis argues that there were six key symptoms of groupthink among Kennedy and his advisers in planning the Bay of Pigs invasion. Each symptom tells us something about group-mediated politics among governing elites.

First, there was an illusion of invulnerability on the New Frontier, the slogan of the Kennedy administration. Victory in the 1960 presidential election, a favorably publicized transition, young and fresh faces on the White House staff, a vigorous president—these and other factors combined to lend an aura of activity, strength, even machismo. Phrases, such as "nothing can stop us" and "the future unlimited," fell from the lips of Kennedy's aides. Such optimism led to twin groupthink themes when the subject of the Bay of Pigs invasion came up in the advisory group. One was that, to a strong group of invulnerable people with right on their side, victory could not be denied. The other was to regard Castro Cuba as weak, bad, and vulnerable to a quick strike. Hence, even in calculating the risks involved in the invasion, groupthink dismissed them as easily overcome and, if not, "luck is on our side." The resulting group-mediated reality is likely to have the tone of fanciful, wishful thinking.

Second, as with all groupthink, Kennedy's advisers labored under the illusion of unanimity. By this Janis means the tendency of people who respect one another's opinions to arrive at a consensus and, then, assume that, because "we all think so," it must be true. Instead of checking a decision with outsiders to see if there are risks or errors, group members look inward; thus, consensual validation supplants critical thinking. In the case of the Bay of Pigs plan, the CIA proposal for invasion was adopted in an atmosphere free of dispute, one of assumed consensus wherein silence meant consent.

Third, the illusions of invulnerability and unanimity provide an environment wherein people who have doubts fail to express them. An unconscious fear of being thought of as soft or a deviant produces a reluctance to speak up. Such was the case with respect to the Bay of Pigs plan. One Kennedy adviser, Arthur Schlesinger, Jr., who raised strong objections in memoranda would not speak out against the plan at team meetings for fear of becoming known as a nuisance.

Another factor in the suppression of personal doubts contributes a fourth aspect of groupthink, that is, what Janis calls "self-appointed mindguards." A mindguard is a group member who brings pressure on other members to conform to the body's consensus. The mindguard, thus, enforces cohesiveness. One form of such pressure is to urge members who dissent from group policy to remain silent. Janis relates how Schlesinger was mindguarded during the Bay of Pigs deliberations. Robert Kennedy, his brother's Attorney General and close adviser, asked Schlesinger about the latter's opposition to the invasion plan. Schlesinger explained. Kennedy listened and then informed Schlesinger that the president had already made a decision, that was that; opposition should not be pushed for it was now time to rally around the plan. As a bodyguard protects against physical harm, a mindguard protects against thoughts that might harm the confidence of group members in the soundness of their decisions.

Fifth, groupthink can be enhanced by adroit leadership. Members tacitly accept manipulation from a popular leader, especially one highly respected and suave in manner. President Kennedy exercised such leadership in deliberations over the Cuban invasion plan. By controlling the agenda of group discussion, avoiding controversial issues, deciding what—if any—opponents of the proposal were invited to air their views, and requesting public disclosure of each adviser's opinion, Kennedy unconsciously created the conditions for a single, group consensus on reality rather than fostering the possibility of other visions.

Finally, when new members whom other members trust and respect enter a group, a virtual taboo develops against antagonizing them. If such new members propose a plan that coincides with the group's thinking or support a plan already determined, the pressure on opponents of groupthink to conform is even stronger. If anything, the newcomers instead of being regarded as outsiders serve as external validators of the wisdom and morality of group thinking. Such was the case with two representatives of the CIA who attended deliberations on the Bay of Pigs invasion. Although both were holdovers from the Republican administration of Dwight Eisenhower, they received preferential treatment in group discussions. In spite of the fact that they based their views on questionable, even flawed, assumptions, the Kennedy team deferred to their judgment. Thus, groupthink did not question that the Cuban Air Force would be ineffective, that the brigade of Cuban exiles consisted of crack troops, that Castro's army was weak, that an uprising in Cuba in support of the invasion was likely, or that a CIA cover story that would conceal U.S. involvement would be effective. In the end all of these assumptions were wrong.

There have been other instances of group-mediated realities among governing officials, instances of groupthink rather than of a free rein for individual critical analysis. Janis finds evidence that the failure to take seriously the possibility of a Japanese attack on Pearl Harbor in December 1941 (even as late as twelve hours before the bombing began) was an instance of groupthink. So, also, he argues, was the U.S. escalation of the Vietnam War and the U.S. conduct in the Korean War that resulted in intervention by the People's Republic of China. Without the detailed evidence Janis and others marshal,[11] one can only speculate about the pervasiveness of groupthink in government circles at other times. Was, for example, the abortive rescue attempt to free U.S. hostages held in Iran in April 1980 the product of groupthink in the advisory circle around President Jimmy Carter? Or, on matters of a less publicized nature, how often are the political realities that seem to call for budget cuts or increases, tax increases or reductions, the ever-rising price of first-class postage stamps, registration for a military draft, or other policies, the mediated derivatives of groupthink?

The Wishful Thinking of Political Candidates

A leading symptom of groupthink is the tendency for group members to discount or ignore information that contradicts the group consensus while blowing out of proportion facts and data that seem to support it. Many a candidate for public office as well as the candidate's entourage scoff at reputable opinion polls that predict ultimate defeat and point instead to support expressed through billboards, yard signs, and editorial endorsements.

What may well have been a case of groupthink in this respect—if not groupthink, then surely some variety of group-mediated political reality—took place in the presidential election of 1964. From the beginning of the campaign, preelection polls indicated that Democratic incumbent Lyndon Johnson was well ahead of his rival, Republican Senator Barry Goldwater. In the end the polls were correct in predicting a substantial Johnson victory. Throughout the campaign, however, the Goldwater forces discounted the preelection polls, even those conducted under Republican auspices. In part this reflected the underdog's ritual of always dismissing discouraging poll results, proclaiming instead that, "The only poll that counts is the one in the voting booths on Election Day." But in 1964 there may have been something more at work in the Goldwater camp.

There is evidence that Goldwater and his campaign staff were perplexed by poll soundings, not only because the facts were disheartening but also because they did not conform to a consensus in the Goldwater camp on where the electorate stood in 1964. What was the source of that view? One apparently was the tenor of letters written by citizens to public officials and the editors of newspapers and newsmagazines. Such letters originate from a small segment of the public. A 1964 survey indicated that only about 15 percent of the adult population reports ever having written such a politically relevant letter to a public official; of the total number of such letters two-thirds are sent by 3 percent of the population. And only 3 percent write letters to news media; two-thirds of those derive from 0.5 percent of the population. Given such a circumstance, one might question that political letters are representative of the views of voters generally. But according to the study mentioned, this may not have concerned Goldwater's advisers. In large measure they designed a campaign to appeal precisely to the public opinion reflected among letterwriters. That opinion differed considerably from the soundings of opinion polls. Among letterwriters, for instance, Goldwater never trailed Johnson; he led. Among Republicans and Independents, polls showed Goldwater preferred by a small majority; among letterwriters he had an absolute majority among those groups. Moreover, among letterwriters Goldwater's issue positions and ideological stance met a warm response, whereas in polls the response was negative, neutral, or lukewarm.[12]

The world of letter opinion was a Goldwater world. It possessed a reality that matched the reality assumed by Goldwater strategists. Judgments based on that unquestioned reality led to persistent discrediting of preelection polls and overestimation of Goldwater's strength. As it developed, however, Election Day was the Republicans' Bay of Pigs.

"Washington Week in Review" ("WWR"): Fantasies of Inside-Dopesters

Every week at 7:00 P.M., EST on Friday, five journalists sit around a table in a television studio in Washington, D.C. Unlike a presidential advisory team, it is not the task of this group to make far-reaching policy decisions. The task is, instead, to describe, review, and interpret the meaning of the major political news events of the week. Although not a top-rated news program in size of weekly audience, "WWR", a production of the Public Broadcasting Service, is a prestigious half-hour of commentary. *Newsweek* includes it as "mandatory viewing for much of official Washington," noting that an appearance on "WWR" can boost a reporter's reputation substantially: "'For the first few days after your appearance, the waters part,' says *The Boston Globe's* Martin F. Nolan. 'People return your phone calls quicker.'"[13]

In fact, however, relatively few political journalists comprise the "WWR" group. The show's moderator, Paul Duke, is a permanent member. Four reporters are invited panelists each week, but the same faces appear on the TV screen with remarkable regularity. For example, in one fifteen-week period—when sixty different journalists could have appeared—only seventeen reporters were members of the group, eight of those being on the program but once. A small pool of political reporters appear so frequently on "WWR" that they are virtually regular members of the group: Haynes Johnson of the *Washington Post*, Hedrick Smith of the *New York Times*, Charles Corddry of the *Baltimore Sun*, Jack Nelson of the *Los Angeles Times*, and Albert Hunt of the *Wall Street Journal*. In short, the "WWR" group consists of the national correspondents of the nation's elite press.[14]

The discussion between group members on each week's "WWR" thirty-minute program follows a dramatic format, indeed, it has many of the attributes of a ritual drama (see Chapter 2). Duke, the moderator, provides a brief introduction, taking note of the "top news stories" of the week and presenting the panel. He then asks a leading question of one of the group members. This is the cue for that panelist to make a short presentation (with or without prepared notes) regarding the news item in question. Following this, each of the other three panelists engages in a brief question-and-answer (q&a) colloquy with the reporter. Although promotional spots for "WWR" speak of "frank," "candid," and "heated" exchanges, the questions raised by panelists are rarely critical or argumentative. Instead, they clearly assist the reporter to present a consensus view regarding the topic in the news. After the q&a colloquy has been completed for one panelist, Duke then moves to a second panelist. The ritual repeats itself until all panelists have spoken on a particular news story and responded to inquiries. From time to time the moderator exercises a suave leadership, reinforcing the group consensus and moving the discussion along. Throughout the ritual drama social bonding receives as much, if not more, emphasis as news interpretation and far more emphasis than controversy.

So, although the stakes are not as high as planning an invasion of the Bay of Pigs or a strategy for a presidential campaign, there is much in "WWR" that reflects groupthink: regular panelists know each other well, support rather than criticize one another's views, defer to the occasional newcomer to the group, respond to suave leadership, and conform to the imperatives of the ritual drama. One other phenomenon appears in "WWR" that reflects groupthink, one not discussed in the groupthink of policy officials or political aspirants, that is, the presence of the inside-dopester.

In a widely read book published in 1950 entitled *The Lonely Crowd* the authors argued that the character of American society was changing.[15] The social cement of America was no longer tradition, that is, people no longer took traditional values very seriously in their behavior. Nor was it a single moral code instilled in people early in life to which they subsequently adjusted their behavior. Rather, the basis of society had become the tendency of people to conform to the expectations and preferences of one another, that is, to what "they," "he," or "she" thinks. This shift in the character of society holds political implications. In a society governed by tradition people can be indifferent to politics, chiefly because traditional values dictate solutions to political problems. Action by individuals is minimized or unnecessary. Or in a society held together by a commitment to a single moral code, moralizing is the key to politics, that is, the course of action with moral sanction is the one to follow. But in a society without tradition and moral code on which to fall back, there are no pat solutions to political problems. Herein lies the rise of the inside-dopester, the person who does little to try to change politics but seeks to understand it or, if trying to solve a political problem, does so by learning and conforming to what insiders in politics urge. The inside-dopester may crave to be in the inner circle of government or, if not that, know those who are on the inside.

For the inside-dopester knowing what is going on in political circles and why and then being able to report it is frequently more satisfying than taking political action itself:

The majority of inside-dopesters take no active part in politics, but there are those who do. Thus, we find many government and party officials who handle the political news in the way encouraged by their jobs, in fragments of office gossip. There are political newsmen and broadcasters who, after long training, have succeeded in eliminating all emotional response to politics and who pride themselves on achieving the inside-dopesters' goal: never to be taken in by any person, cause, or event.[16]

"WWR," as are many forums of groupthink, is an ecology of inside dope. Panelists bring to their weekly discussions a wealth of assumptions, speculations, and factual fragments gleaned from news sources and contacts in the inner sanctums of official Washington. Sometimes "WWR" panelists name these sources, sometimes they do not. In either event viewers of the program receive the impression that they, too, are on the inside, and that the political realities mediated each week on "WWR" are authentic. To that degree, the inside-dopesters of "WWR" are gatekeepers of official truth, informed agents of Minitrue (Orwell's Ministry of Truth).

What political realities emerge from "WWR"? To answer that question, we examined the content of all weekly airings of "WWR" in a period covering the first 100 days of the administration of President Ronald Reagan, January 23, 1981 to May 1, 1981. The purpose was to explore the rhetorical visions generated in seven and one-half hours of group discussion among leading political journalists. What appeared was a recurrent pattern of consistent political visions, two principal realities/fantasies of "WWR's" inside-dopesters.

The Great Communicator

As one might expect in the opening days of a presidential administration, the "WWR" group absorbed itself in part by profiling the character of the Reagan persona. What manner of man is this? The vision that emerged bore a close resemblance to the areas stressed by the sixteenth-century political philosopher Niccolo Machiavelli. As noted in Chapter 2, for Machiavelli *virtu* (character traits) and *fortuna* (luck) fortify a prince faced with *necessita* (political problems). "WWR" panelists gave Reagan high marks for virtu and fortuna in the face of necessita.

From the week of his inauguration "WWR" fashioned a consistent rhetorical vision of Reagan's virtu as a communicator. "Great" and "good communicator" symbolized the president's demeanor. The

"WWR" consensus was that Reagan as a speaker possessed "perfect instinctive timing." He "brims with confidence" while "his voice is right and he comes off well." Here stood a man who "means what he says" and exhibits it in "act, statement, and style." Proof? The president on his first day in office signed an order cutting back on federal employees and making several other moves he "said he would" during his campaign. In early February after Reagan's first televised address as president, "WWR" concurred that his TV performance was "riveting" as he outlined his economic program. "Nobody else" could have stood there for twenty-seven minutes and "held the nation's attention." By late February panelists noted that Reagan as communicator was even better "in his own way" than the "dazzling" Kennedy as president. By mid-March, with his economic proposals reaching Congress, "WWR" foresaw Reagan's skills as a communicator as the key to "forge a mandate for change."

But in the "real" world of "WWR," the vital test of Reagan's greatness as a communicator came less over his efforts to push an economic package than in the way he conducted himself after the attempt on his life in late March. By cracking jokes, showing optimism, and behaving "as a much younger man" following his gunshot wound, the president "lifted the nation's spirits." Panelists solemnly nodded assent as one member observed, "The long and the short of it is that the system works. There was a happy ending to a dark time for the country when the president was shot." And by mid-April, "in spite of his injuries," Reagan is planning a TV address on his budget because "he is the best spokesman and best salesman for the budget cuts."

The Great Communicator emerged from the assassination attempt as Superpatient. Inside dope prophesied less than five days following his shooting that Reagan would fully recover and be back at his desk in "two or three months." One week later "word" had it that the president would return home and be in bed for ten days. "WWR" witnessed a recovery "like a man in his fifties." The only danger was in Reagan's trying to be "too active." Yet another week passed and the inside dope was that Reagan was in the Oval Office "two to three hours a day," putting a good face on it but still weak from being shot. One more week goes by and the Superpatient legend grows—he has been on the telephone "since he got out of the hospital" pushing his budget, he has "remarkable recovery powers" like those of a "young, tough man." There had been a "close shave with death," yet he is "almost back to normal." Finally, four weeks after predicting Reagan would be back at his desk "not before" two or three months (that on April 3), "WWR's" inside-dopesters noted (May 1) that Reagan was "back in charge" having "caught the country up in his gallantry."

In the first 100 days of the Reagan administration, the "WWR" groupthink attributed other traits to the president that reinforced the Great Communicator vision. Repeatedly, the reality of Reagan's persona was of a "good politician," a man "relaxed on the job" but who "hit the ground running" and "fighting for his economic program." Less than a month in office and Reagan was "comfortable in the presidency" and had "laid a good foundation for his programs." Pushing his programs he "woos" the media and Congress. Insiders had it that Reagan talked "literally to EVERYBODY" to bolster support. Two months in office and Reagan won major budget cuts, he "undid thirty years of social legislation in three days!"

A typical "WWR" construction of political reality took place in two consecutive programs, those of February 13 and February 20. In the first, viewers were provided the inside dope on the budget process—there is a "ritual" in which harsh cuts are proposed, cries of protest arise from "the wounded," appeals are made to the president, he takes the middle ground. Reagan, however, is breaking that tradition! One week later the vision was fixed. Reagan was "like Babe Ruth in his amiable audacity. He points to the bleachers and says he's going to hit a home run there—then HE DOES IT!"

But it was not skill alone that brought Reagan's first 100 days of greatness. Fortune smiled. Lady Luck smiled first with the election of Reagan, a "landslide victory" that demonstrated a "consensus in the country" for Reagan's policies. Indeed, "the nation is behind Reagan more than any other just-inaugurated president." The theme repeated throughout February and March: "The consensus in the country has reached Washington. Reagan has momentum on his side!" Fortune also came with the release of the U.S. hostages held captive in Iran. Reagan, "WWR" said, will experience "a second inaugural when the hostages return to the United States." Again, there was good fortune in Reagan's appointment of David Stockman as head of the Office of Management and Budget, "bright, talented, works nineteen hours a day, a loose cannon" who reinforces Reagan's "can do" on budget cuts. The "peril of Poland" was also a plus for Reagan. Seemingly troops of the Soviet Union poised on the Polish border justified Reagan's hardline foreign policy declarations. Even the assassination attempt turned out to be good fortune: "There will be a tremendous rally to the president, especially to support his budget programs. He can have anything he wants for the next few months. The honeymoon has been extended indefinitely." Meanwhile, repeated frequently in the fifteen weeks of "WWR" programs was the verdict of "Democrats in disarray." Virtually leaderless in Congress, unable to agree on alternatives to Reagan's proposals, threatened by the "consensus in the country,"—the opposition party was no match for the Great Communicator. Finally, Reagan was even a beneficiary of the first flight of the U.S. space shuttle—a "sense of pride and a sense of success" was in the presidential interest.

With virtu and fortuna on his side, at least as far as "WWR" viewed it, President Ronald Reagan faced necessita, that is, taking the necessary steps to cope with political problems. This produced the second "WWR" vision of the first 100 days, the New Directions theme.

New Directions

The Reagan administration is a "new beginning both nationally and internationally." So opined the five journalists appearing on "WWR" three days following the inauguration of the nation's fortieth chief of state. A week later, "new beginning" had been supplanted by "New Directions," but the rhetorical vision was the same. Recall from Chapter 2 that "Often the emergence of a rhetorical vision is indexed by the term *new*. Such labels as the 'New South,' the 'New Deal,' and the 'New Left' are shorthand ways of referring to rhetorical visions which have emerged clearly enough so people can refer to them and understand the basic elements of the vision when they are so characterized."[17] Presidential candidates, as we noted in Chapter 2, typically strive to project the image of newness. And, if they win, the label *new* is a means of symbolizing a clear break with their predecessors. So it was with the Reagan forces; they spoke much of new beginnings prior to the inauguration. Indeed, they went so far as to shift the swearing-in ceremonies to the west front of the Capitol rather than hold them on the traditional east side.

As noted earlier, the inside-dopester's goal is "never to be taken in by any person, cause, or event." But the "WWR" team accepted the rhetorical theme of the Reagan administration and for the first 100 days helped chain that fantasy out to the program's viewers. The theme of New Directions appeared in many guises: the Reagan administration is a "cut with the past" (January 30); an "economic renaissance" had begun (February 6); a "flurry of change" (February 13); a "philosophical sea change" (February 20); and, repeatedly, a "consensus in the country" for change. From the "WWR" grab bag of labels, two elements emerged to characterize the overall New Directions vision—Reagonomics and toughspeak.

Reagan's "economic revolution" was the priority item for "WWR" discussion for the first 100 days just as the Reagan administration had endeavored to make economic policy the priority domestic concern. On programs of January 23 and January 30 "WWR" group members projected the upcoming scenario. First, the Reagan administration would hold off conservative and right-wing demands to move quickly on social issues—abortion, prayer in public schools, busing, and so on—and focus instead on budgetary and economic policies. Social issues were too divisive, hence, might threaten the "consensus in the country" for economic change. Second, within the economic priority, the Reagan White House would ignore budget cuts initially and seek instead a 30 percent three-year cut in income taxes; later, in the next fiscal year, the administration would seek budget cuts. Shortly after "WWR" had constructed that scenario, Reagan addressed both budgetary and tax cuts. "A bold approach," agreed "WWR" panelists. But would it work? Only partly. On budget cuts: if Reagan can pull off even two-thirds of it, the results will be more sweeping than anything the country has ever seen—"even FDR." On tax cuts: there will be cuts, but nothing like Reagan proposes!

For the remainder of Reagan's first 100 days, panelists on "WWR" stuck with their initial script. But there was one change, that is, it became obvious that the initial projection that tax cuts would precede budget cuts was incorrect. The Reagan White House was going after both. How could this be reconciled with the earlier vision? The inconsistencies were adjusted in two ways. One was to increase talk of Reagan, the Great Communicator. His virtu and fortuna made it possible for him to cope with the necessities involved in getting his economic package through Congress. Second, the "WWR" vision of Reagan's budget-cutting proposals assumed a warlike character. "Revolution" (apparently provoked by "consensus in the country" and "momentum for change") became "War." Military metaphors were commonplace in "WWR" exchanges: the "budget-cutting blitz," a "counterattack on the budget"; a "public relations fusillade" to win the propaganda victory; Reagan says 'damn the torpedoes, full speed ahead on budget cuts"; Reagan learns in the "budget battle" that "it's a lot easier to throw a grenade than it is to catch one"; and in the end "he may just win the battle of the budget."

By marshalling virtu and fortuna, then, Reagan could win the war of the budget. Thus, "WWR" panelists revised their original rhetorical vision. But the panel remained adamant throughout the first 100 days that he could not have his tax cut. In mid-February "WWR" members concurred there would be no large tax cut ever, that Democrats in Congress would reshape the tax-cut proposals (they would be "able to get together on this one") in favor of the poor and middle-income groups. A month later it appeared Reagan would get his spending cuts, thought "WWR," but tax cuts would be "worked over heavily by Congress." Another month goes by and "WWR" remains firm: tax cuts would be *much* smaller than Reagan wanted; any cuts Congress would approve would come one year at a time, *never* over a three-year period ("No Congress would do that"), and, unlike the budget, the tax proposal "has little support in the country" and will have much more trouble in passage. On August 3–4, 1981, Congress passed a three-year tax cut on individual incomes—5 percent on October 1, 1981; 10 percent on July 1, 1982; and another 10 percent on July 1, 1983.

The second element in the New Directions rhetorical vision consisted of toughspeak. Reagan, "WWR" journalists agreed, had "talked tough for years and he is talking tough again." Throughout the first 100 days "WWR" mentioned Reagan's tough talk on the economy: "Reagan has tough medicine for the country to swallow to cure the economic ills of the country," noted Paul Duke in introducing "WWR" on February 6, a theme that repeated itself frequently thereafter. But Reagan the Tough emerged primarily in the area of foreign policy. The inside dope was clear: Reagan believes the Russians are engaged in world revolution and is determined to stop them! This determination, toughness, would be demonstrated in increased defense spending ("giving the Pentagon a blank check") and in firmness in U.S.–Soviet relations ("war of words").

For "WWR" panelists toughspeak seemed to be paying off by late February. The Reagan administration, panelists noted, "beat the Soviets over the heads with two-by-fours and now the Russians are panting for a summit." But toughspeak must be backed by toughact. Where might actions speak as loudly as words? "WWR" thought it was in El Salvador, where the Reagan administration vowed to slow the supply of military arms to rebels. "El Salvador is so terribly important to Reagan because it is a symbolic signal to the Russians on adventurism," explained one "WWR" inside-dopester. He then went on to imagine that Reagan had said to his administration on taking office, "Find a just war we can win and declare it." A month later, however, "WWR" rethought the effectiveness of toughspeak. Panelists concurred it had failed in the case of El Salvador. How did they know? "Polls show there is no support in the country for intervention in El Salvador," viewers of "WWR" learned. Toughact would be opposed. But then, in groupthink fashion, "WWR" panelists reconciled the contradiction between successful toughspeak (February 27) and failed toughspeak (March 27) by implying that toughspeak had *not been tough enough*: "The problem with El Salvador is that the administration has failed to make all the *right sounds* about the killings of missionaries in El Salvador. If they had just said the *right things*, they could have turned opinion in their direction."

"WWR" Reviewed

We single out "WWR" for extended comment not to belittle the intentions of such public affairs TV programming. Rather, we contend that "WWR" illustrates how groupthink occurs in a small group, contributes to the fashioning of rhetorical vision, provides a key link in the chaining of derived fantasies to larger audiences, and thereby joins group- and mass-mediated political realities. Whether Ronald Reagan is Reagan the Great Communicator, Reagan the Tough, Reagan the Amiable, Reagan the Good Politician is open to question. Whether an economic war was won and a revolution solidified remains to be seen. In any event, these were the realities presented viewers of "WWR"— "mandatory viewing for official Washington."

WHOSE REALITY?

Groupthink, then, may develop in any political setting—among public officials, political candidates, political journalists. When it does, there are intriguing consequences. Individual judgment yields to group pressure. Hardheaded, critical thinking gives way to wishful fantasy chaining. The potential for human fallibility, something the framers of the U.S. Constitution took for granted and the effects of which they sought to control, is multiplied. One reason for this is that group members become insulated from outside, contradictory information. To be an inside-dopester is to be inside, hence, frequently cut off from the views of outsiders who might challenge the reigning consensus.

Two political scientists, David L. Paletz and Robert M. Entman, have noted how mass-mediated politics insulates power holders from public accountability.[18] The insulation derives from many sources: public officials (say the Supreme Court) bar the news media from their deliberations or decisions; skewed coverage that ignores an institution (such as Congress) and fails to spotlight goings-on; or, too much coverage, as in making television cameras a pulpit for presidential promotion of pet programs. Add to such mass-mediated insularity the group-mediated isolation that flows from groupthink. The potential exists for officeholders to be shielded from public accountability, office seekers to misread the electorate's preferences, and for journalists to misguide audiences. The result is that there are indeed multiple visions of reality, but visions so insulated from each other as to make living in a commonly perceived world unlikely. The answer to the question "Do you see what I see?" is a resounding "No." Separate groups, separate groupthoughts, separate realities, separate worlds. We probe the implications of that separation after exploring three other cases of group mediation: pack journalism, religion, and conspiratorial politics.

NOTES

1. George Orwell, *Nineteen Eighty-Four* (New York: Harcourt, Brace and Co., 1949).

2. Erich Fromm, "Afterword," in George Orwell, *Nineteen Eighty-Four* (New York: New American Library, 1961), p. 267. (Signet Classic Edition)

3. For other examples, see Claus Mueller, *The Politics of Communication* (New York: Oxford University Press, 1973); Herbert Marcuse, *One-Dimensional Man* (Boston: Beacon Press, 1964); Murray Edelman, *Political Language* (New York: Academic Press, 1977).

4. William Safire, *Safire's Political Dictionary* (New York: Ballantine Books, 1978), p. 6.

5. Orwell, *Nineteen Eighty-Four* (Signet Classic Edition), op. cit., pp. 32–33.

6. Irving L. Janis, *Victims of Groupthink* (Boston: Houghton Mifflin Co., 1972), p. 9.

7. Robert F. Bales, *Interaction Process Analysis: A Method for the Study of Small Groups* (Cambridge, Mass.: Addison-Wesley Publishing Co., 1950).

8. Joseph H. de Rivera, *The Psychological Dimension of Foreign Policy* (Columbus, Ohio: Charles E. Merrill Publishing Co., 1968), chap. 6.

9. Ernest G. Bormann, "Fantasy and Rhetorical Vision: The Rhetorical Criticism of Social Reality," *Quarterly Journal of Speech*, 58 (December 1972): 396–407.

10. Janis, *Victims of Groupthink*, op. cit., pp. 14–49.

11. See de Rivera, *The Psychological Dimension of Foreign Policy*, op. cit., Chap. 6.

12. Philip E. Converse, Aage R. Clausen, and Warren E. Miller, "Electoral Myth and Reality: The 1964 Election," *American Political Science Review*, 59 (June 1965): 321–336.

13. Elizabeth Peer, "Washington's Press Corps," *Newsweek* (May 25, 1981): 92.

14. These data are based on a content analysis of "WWR" conducted by the authors.

15. David Riesman, Nathan Glazer, and Reuel Denny, *The Lonely Crowd* (New Haven: Yale University Press, 1950).

16. Ibid., p. 211.

17. Ernest G. Bormann, "The Eagleton Affair: A Fantasy Theme Analysis," *Quarterly Journal of Speech*, 59 (April 1973): 143–159.

18. David L. Paletz and Robert M. Entman, *Media Power Politics* (New York: Free Press, 1981).

Pack Journalism
Group Mediation of Political News

President Richard Nixon, following the resignation of Vice President Spiro Agnew on October 10, 1973, nominated Gerald Ford to be the first appointed vice president in American history. Congress agreed and Ford was confirmed. TV anchor Walter Cronkite, following a flurry of speculation at the Republican National Convention on July 23, 1980, about who would be Ronald Reagan's vice presidential running mate, nominated Gerald Ford as the first former president to seek a copresidency. Reagan did not agree, and George Bush was selected.

The phantom nomination of Gerald Ford in 1980 illustrates a form of groupthink peculiar to the news media, that of pack journalism. As a preliminary to describing pack journalism's role in group-mediated politics, let us consider briefly the details of what took place on that mid-summer night in 1980. Rumors began circulating about the possibilities of a Reagan-Ford "dream ticket" early in the week of the Republican National Convention. They seemed to receive credence on Wednesday morning, July 23. CBS correspondent Dan Rather reported that Reagan preferred Ford to other possibilities. That evening Rather reported that Reagan would consider no other name until Ford gave a "final, unequivocal no." Within minutes Cronkite, in a previously scheduled interview with Ford, asked the former president about the rumors. "If I go to Washington—and I'm not saying I'm accepting," said Ford, "I have to go there with the belief that I will play a meaningful role across the board. . . . I have to have responsible assurances." Cronkite speculated about a copresidency. "That's something Governor Reagan really ought to consider," responded Ford.

The fantasy chained out rapidly. Rather complimented Cronkite on "one of the outstanding interviews in your long and distinguished career," then filed three reports within an hour that George Bush had been told he would not be Reagan's choice, that the Secret Service detail assigned to Ford was preparing a ready room, and that aides of Reagan and Ford said "the deal has been cut," and that "the best source I have had all day long" said Reagan had met all of Ford's demands. ABC's Barbara Walters set up a TV interview with Ford leading to more speculation. On the convention floor Reagan's lieutenant, Congressman Robert Michel, learned from fellow delegates and from journalists that Reagan and Ford were about to arrive in the convention hall. Michel asked where such reports came from and learned that it was from Dan Rather's report. Michel then set off to find Republican Chairman William Brock to seek confirmation and ran into Rather. Rather phoned his producers to report that Michel was trying to see Brock, the implication being that the deal had, indeed, been struck.

The fantasy reached its turning point at 10:10 P.M. EDT. Cronkite announced to CBS viewers that "CBS News has learned that there is a definite plan for Ronald Reagan and the former President of the United States, Gerald Ford, who will be his selection as running mate—an unparalleled, unprecedented situation in American politics . . . to come to this convention hall tonight to appear together on this platform for Ronald Reagan to announce that Ford will run with him." Cronkite was not alone in mediating that reality: the *Chicago Sun-Times* headlined, "It's Reagan and Ford," the Associated Press (AP) and United Press International (UPI) wire services reported the fantasy as fact, and it was the story in newspapers in Cleveland, Charlotte, Raleigh, Shreveport, and other cities, as well as the lead account on late evening TV newscasts.

It took some time for the fantasy to evaporate. At 10:30 P.M. NBC's Jessica Savitch interviewed Senator Paul Laxalt, a close Reagan confidant. Laxalt reported he had just talked to Reagan and no deal had been made. Yet six minutes later NBC's David Brinkley noted that reliable sources confirmed Reagan would come to the convention hall, apparently with Ford; NBC coanchor John Chancellor underscored the likelihood of the arrangement, noting that never before had a former president accepted the vice presidency. Another eight minutes and Rather interviewed a pollster who had more inside dope, "There is no doubt that there will be a Reagan-Ford ticket." It was to be yet another hour before a reporter broke out of the pack. At 11:54 P.M. NBC's Chris Wallace, after overhearing a Reagan aide shouting, "It's Bush, it's Bush," confirmed the story with a second source and then reported it just one minute before CBS's Leslie Stahl did so; five minutes later ABC News fell in line with the latest reality. Ronald Reagan would, as the old saying goes, "let George do it."

RUNNING IN PACKS

Gerald Ford's nomination in 1980 by the news media reveals several things about the fine line between fiction and fact. It indicates how reporters under pressures to scoop competitors rush to report what has not been adequately confirmed. Moreover, it suggests how correspondents and news organizations feel compelled to emulate one another; for example, if CBS interviews Ford, so must ABC. The story also exemplifies how politicians being covered by the news media provide information to reporters that, as it often turns out, the politicians have received from the press. Then, because what the correspondents have already reported is fed back to them, they take that as validation of journalistic accounts (as in the exchange between Michel and Rather). And there is another point, namely, politicians plant stories with reporters for self-serving purposes. Who is to say that the Reagan, Ford, or Bush forces were not exploiting the rumors circulating through the news on that July evening?

But most of all, the Ford fantasy was an exaggerated case of pack journalism. The phrase is obviously a metaphor; it likens journalists running together in packs to be like dogs, wolves, or coyotes. In one form or another the practice is ancient. For example, the first systematic effort to examine how correspondents report political news from the nation's capital described a widespread practice in the tradition of pack journalism.[1] The practice is carbon sheeting. If a reporter assigned to cover a story could not (or simply did not want) to do so, he would ask a reporter from a rival newspaper for a carbon copy of the competitor's account. Then, with a few minor changes, the reporter would file the rival's story as his or her own. This worked to everyone's advantage—to the reporter who did cover the story (for if the account appeared in altered form in a competing newspaper, it validated the authenticity of the reporter's account) and to rival publications (publishing the same details as other journals confirmed not only the facts but also one's news judgment). In short, pack journalism is cooperative competition/competitive cooperation in the news business.

The notion of pack journalism was most widely publicized in Timothy Crouse's informative and entertaining book that described how the press covered the 1972 presidential election, *The Boys on the Bus*.[2] During a presidential campaign a group of reporters from a variety of news organizations follow a single candidate for several weeks or months. They are, writes Crouse, "like a pack of hounds sicked on a fox."[3] The fox is the candidate, the packlike behavior of the reporters derives from the fact that they travel on the same bus or plane; eat, drink, and make merry together; and share notes and impressions.

They are friendly rivals both competing and cooperating in efforts to cover the story, namely, the candidate.

The womblike coexistence is a source of some of the conditions of groupthink described in Chapter 7. Those conditions are reinforced by another facet of pack journalism, pool reports. Each day on the campaign trail one or two members of the pack comprise a pool of reporters designated to be close to the candidate. The pool constitutes the eyes and ears for the other members of the press entourage who cannot be with the candidate—say on the candidate's private plane, at small enclaves, during motorcades, and so forth. Members of the pack take turns serving in the pool. When in the pool a reporter writes an account of the candidate's activities; that account then is available to all members of the pack. In filing his or her own article on the candidate, a pool reporter is not supposed to include anything not included in the pool report. Needless to say, TV, newspaper, and newsmagazine accounts of the campaign derived from pool reports have a groupthink uniformity to them—as any regular reader or viewer of campaign news knows.

The similarities of pack journalism to groupthink extend to the tendency of pack members to identify themselves as a unit engaged in common endeavor. A leading member of the pack covering the 1972 presidential campaign, James M. Perry, wrote a book on his impressions. He titled it *Us & Them*.[4] "This book," he said, "is about *us*, the political reporters, including me, and *them*, the people who wanted to be President in 1972."[5] Perry was not modest in describing what "us" did:

We are filters. It is through our smudgy, hand-held prisms that the voters meet the candidates and grow to love them or hate them, trust them or distrust them. We are the voters' eyes and ears, and we are more than that, for, sometimes, we perform a larger and, some would say, a more controversial function. We write the rules and we call the game.[6]

In short, the pack mediates political reality.

In covering presidential campaigns the journalistic pack is a group of elite members of the press. Crouse specifies the pecking order. At the top are national political reporters—experienced correspondents of prestige newspapers, the wire services, national newsmagazines, and television networks. At the bottom are the representatives of smaller newspapers and organizations. Among the top elite by 1980, the print journalists had far less star quality than did TV network correspondents. But regardless of the identity of the leading actors in the pack drama, the groupthink atmosphere in campaign coverage in 1980 remained much as Crouse had described it in 1972:

They all fed off the same pool report, the same daily handout, the same speech by the candidate; the whole pack was isolated in the same mobile village. After a while, they began to believe in the same rumors, subscribe to the same theories, and write the same stories.[7]

Politicians, ever mindful to the ways of the pack, take advantage of current groupthink trends. By 1980 this certainly meant capitalizing on the elevated status of TV correspondents, their needs, and their expectations. The "good picture," for example, is a must for the TV journalist, producer, and news organization. Candidates go out of their way to assure good pictures. But, writes one observer, "Those TV pictures, however, depicted a different reality from what an onlooker witnessed." Thus, "raw footage of a typical Reagan campaign day revealed that the crowds always seemed much larger than they actually were."[8] Why? Because at each stop on the campaign trail the Reagan staff placed a raised camera platform close to the speaker's rostrum, then jammed the crowd between the two, thus, leaving the visual impression of Reagan speaking to a vast throng.[9] The electorate's reality, the visual reality mediated by TV news, was, thus, the reality the candidate's managers wished.

Pack journalism is not limited to coverage of political nominating conventions and electoral campaigns. A pack can form in reporting any story. Running in packs is most likely to occur when two conditions prevail, that is, when editors assign reporters (1) to regular beats and (2) to cover stories about largely predictable events. The White House press corps, for example, consists of reporters with long-term assignments from their news organizations to cover the scheduled briefings, appearances, and actions that derive from presidential comings and goings. Because they are scheduled and predictable in outcome, news organizations can plan their coverage of such events, a fact that makes any newspaper or newsmagazine correspondent or editor or any TV journalist or news producer more secure in the daily task of gathering the news. Politicians recognize this and manipulate both events and accounts of them to suit their own and journalists' requirements. A close monitoring of political news would reveal the result, that is, from one-half to two-thirds of front-page stories of major newspapers or lead stories in network TV news originate from official sources. Thereby pack journalism serves both government and press interests.[10]

But pack journalism need not have the optimal conditions of regular assignments of reporters to predictable events in order to thrive. Packs form in the coverage of unexpected events as well. Symptoms of groupthink follow. Recall the accident at the Three Mile Island (TMI) nuclear power plant described in Chapter 1. Many of the reporters assigned to the story for the major news organizations found themselves housed in the same hotel, eating at the same restaurant, drinking at the same bar. Relatively few were versed in the technical operations of nuclear facilities. Their pluralistic ignorance contributed to the same responses that Crouse found among "the boys on the bus." TMI correspondents shared the same rumors, constructed common fantasies, reported the same stories. A good example concerned the fictional hydrogen bubble. Following the initial accident, officials at TMI learned of a hydrogen burn that had flashed through the plant's containment building. They assumed a 1,000-cubic-foot bubble of gases containing hydrogen had formed. A question arose about the potential for an explosion of this hydrogen bubble. It was the alleged potential for such an explosion that contributed to the "horror tonight" coverage of TMI described in Chapter 1. As it turned out, there was no hydrogen bubble and fears of an explosion were groundless. The failure to make that clear was in large measure that of government officials. But the journalistic pack contributed to the misunderstanding as well. First, pack members shared the view that there was deep conflict and disagreement among government officials regarding what was happening at TMI. Consequently, when the chief government spokesman (Harold Denton of the Nuclear Regulatory Commission) declared at a press conference that no combustible mixture existed in the containment building or reactor vessel, reporters discounted his words and news stories continued to stress an explosion potential. Second, being uninformed in nuclear technology, pack members simply did not know how to ask the appropriate questions of officials, questions that might have confirmed or refuted rumors of conflicts, danger, and panic.

Crisis coverage—where authentic accounts of what is happening and why are hard to obtain—promotes pack journalism virtually as much as the routine coverage of scheduled events. Rumors and fantasies abound; eyewitness, firsthand accounts confirming or denying such tales are rare. During the Vietnam War, reporting about the Tet Offensive in 1968 (see Chapter 1) bore an aura of pack journalism. Evidence and official interpretations to the contrary, journalistic accounts of the Tet crisis constructed a common vision, one of U.S. disaster. The author of a voluminous study of press coverage of Tet argues that "The generalized effect of the news media's contemporary output in February–March 1968 was a distortion of reality—through sins of omission and commission—on a scale that helped shape Tet's political repercussions in Washington and the Administration's response."[11] Whether "distorted" is the appropriate designation for Tet coverage is questionable. Rather, in considering pack journalism, it is more accurate to say that a single, uncontradicted version of reality derived from accounts of

Tet, providing readers/viewers with no opportunity to conceive of alternatives.

Similarly, during the Iranian hostage crisis a form of pack journalism emerged. Like the hydrogen bubble and the Tet disaster it consisted of a story that fed on itself without refutation. During the 444 days of captivity there was much journalistic speculation regarding the likely psychological state of U.S. hostages once released from captivity. Would they suffer from the Stockholm syndrome? As noted in Chapter 1, this malady consists of painful psychological disturbances produced when captives are freed from their captors. Allegedly, after long confinement captives grow dependent on their guards, so much so that ultimately winning freedom produces high anxieties and stress at the very thought of being apart from captors on whom prisoners have been dependent. Dire predictions of such psychological pain were made regarding the hostages in Iran—in news reports, on TV talk shows, in editorials and columns. So widespread did the speculation become— and so widely did the Stockholm syndrome fantasy chain—that the American Psychological Association took a stand. The association noted that the reactions of individual captives would obviously vary greatly and that broad generalizations might be without foundation. Indeed, the whole notion of a Stockholm syndrome derived from a limited study of a few hostages held captive in that city, scarcely grounds for proving a theory.

In addition to flowing from both the coverage of scheduled and crisis events, pack journalism can stem from efforts to report other nonscheduled, noncritical happenings. Billygate in 1980 was a case in point. For three weeks in the mid-summer of 1980 newspapers and television trumpeted accounts of how President Jimmy Carter's brother, Billy, had received a six-figure loan from Libya, a nation not friendly to U.S. interests. There were rumors that the loan was actually a payment for covert oil deals arranged by Billy Carter. And there were hints of a White House cover-up and of obstruction of justice by the attorney general, perhaps even the president. Recalling the scandal of the Nixon presidency, segments of the press speculated that Billygate might be another Watergate. As it turned out, the two were poles apart. Watergate evolved into a political tragedy, Billygate into a news comedy— with the journalistic pack cast as much in the role of fools as the president's brother. With rare exceptions, neither newspaper headlines and articles nor TV news accounts noted, let alone emphasized, that no evidence appeared that Billy Carter had influenced U.S. policy toward Libya or that the president was guilty of anything worse than bad judgment. Both points were left to be made by a congressional investigation.

CONVENTIONS OF PACK JOURNALISM

Such is the nature of the herd instinct in the group mediation of political realities by the press, a few forms pack journalism takes, and some of the conditions that help spawn it. Pack journalism, as with any type of reporting, has its customs, rituals, and tried-and-tested procedures called conventions. Wrote Walter Lippmann:

Every newspaper when it reaches the reader is the result of a whole series of selections as to what items shall be printed, in what position they shall be printed, how much space each shall occupy, what emphasis each shall have. There are no objective standards here. There are conventions.[12]

One such conventional practice in pack journalism is to follow the leader. Because a journalistic pack has by definition a pecking order, it has its leaders, that is, key reporters from whom other members of the pack take their cues. The leader plays a crucial role in creating and chaining out the journalists' group-mediated fantasy. Frequently, the leader is a highly respected reporter of national standing. Walter Cronkite, reputedly named the most trusted person in America in nationwide polls, played a leadership role for a generation. There was little wonder that Cronkite's interview with Gerald Ford at the 1980 Republican National Convention provoked a fantasy about Ford's accepting the vice presidency on a ticket with Ronald Reagan. After all, it was Cronkite who had declared a war ended in Vietnam in 1968, the all clear for residents to return to homes at TMI in 1979, and John B. Anderson a viable presidential candidate in 1980. His judgment had been followed before, there was no reason for floor reporters and rival anchors to ignore it in Joe Louis Sports Arena in Detroit in July 1980.

TV journalists are not the only pack leaders. Reporters for major metropolitan papers also set the tone of mediated politics. In 1972 the press acknowledged Senator Edmund Muskie of Maine as front-runner for the Democratic presidential nomination. On the eve of the New Hampshire primary, David Broder, national political correspondent of the Washington Post, proclaimed that such a front-runner would need at least half of the primary votes (there were more than a half-dozen candidates) to claim victory. Other reporters repeated Broder's judgment. When Muskie received "only" 46 percent and George McGovern showed "surprising strength" with 37 percent of the vote, the mediated reality was "a damaging loss" for Muskie, "a moral victory" for McGovern.

In reporting major stories the news dailies and TV networks usually lead off their accounts with essentially the same information about what happened. There is a twofold reason why such story leads are frequently identical. First, they originate from the same source—the lead sentence in the story prepared by the wire service reporter, either AP or UPI, on the spot. What Crouse found in 1972 still holds, "Thus the pack followed the wire service men whenever possible. Nobody made a secret of running with the wires; it was an accepted practice."[13] Second, the wire service lead is an editorial standard against which the accuracy and veracity of an account is judged. If newspaper or TV reporters file an account with a different lead or that tells a story different from that of the wire services, their editors are reluctant to publish it or put it on the air. Crouse relates an incident in the 1972 California primary between Democrats George McGovern and Hubert Humphrey that illustrates this pack convention. The two candidates engaged in a televised debate. Reporters were hard put to find much of substance, that is, a story, in it. The AP wire service reporter, a respected member of the pack, filed a "Wallace" lead—saying both candidates would refuse to accept George Wallace as a running mate. Other news organizations, for example NBC and CBS, followed suit. But *New York Times* reporters led with a "fool" lead—that is, Humphrey apologizing for having called McGovern a fool earlier in the campaign. The *Times* editor quickly called from New York demanding to know why his reporters had not selected the "Wallace" lead.

As follow the leader shades into follow the lead, another journalistic convention comes into play, that of shared news judgment. What events are newsworthy? What realities deserve mediation? As Lippmann noted, there are no objective standards for answering those questions. Instead, what is news turns out to be a matter of consensual validation, namely, news is what the news media agree on as such. In the case of TMI related in Chapter 1, news organizations narrated different melodramas, but they agreed that TMI was the lead story (the most newsworthy event) of the period. Here, again, the wire services play a major role. Each day they notify their subscribers of what the wires deem the most newsworthy stories. Editors and TV producers are free to ignore that judgment, but they rarely do. The consensus on what is reportable reality is not limited to daily accounts in newspapers and on television. Rival newsweeklies, *Time* and *Newsweek* especially, agree from week to week on lead stories.[14] Moreover, there is a high coincidence on weekly features, a coincidence that extends even to the front covers of the newsmagazines. Thus, in 1981 (as in many previous years) *Time* and *Newsweek* featured virtually the same front cover approximately one-quarter of the time.

The fantasy chaining that derives from pack journalism owes much to another convention, that is, Newspeak. Recall from Chapter 7 that Newspeak constituted the official language of George Orwell's fictional society of *Nineteen Eighty-Four*. As a set of linguistic conventions, Newspeak bears a close relation to groupthink. In pack journalism Newspeak consists of a jargon and a style that leaves readers and viewers with a sense that reporters are objective observers who know what is "really going on" (are inside-dopesters). The words and the style of current pack Newspeak imply that pack-mediated reality is "the real thing."

A student of political language, William Safire, refers to journalistic jargon as journalese. His tongue-in-cheek definition of journalese is replete with examples of Newspeak buzz words:

At the BACKGROUNDERS held by AUTHORITATIVE SOURCES, which can be MEDIA EVENTS in themselves, members of the FOURTH ESTATE— evoking the public's RIGHT TO KNOW—refuse to settle for NO COMMENT or OFF THE RECORD. Instead, reporters protected by a LID and on a NOT FOR ATTRIBUTION basis probe the SOURCES for material for their TICK-TOCKS and KEEPERS, sometimes seeking to enliven MEGOS with the technique of RULE OUT.

Meanwhile, some PUNDITS—anxious for LEAKS but suspicious of PLANTS and scornful of HANDOUTS—reportedly write such infuriating DOPE STORIES, THINK PIECES, THUMBSUCKERS that they wind up on the ZOO PLANE.[15]

We need not further define each bit of journalese to make the point (definitions are readily available in *Safire's Political Dictionary*). Phrases that appear repeatedly in news accounts—such as "usually reliable sources," a "Pentagon spokesman," "sources close to the White House," and so on—mark the reporter as someone who knows what is going on, the eyes-and-the-ears of the citizen inside government circles.

Newspeak has a distinctive style as well as jargon. If the jargon provides the impression of the journalist as objective inside-dopester working on the citizen's behalf, so does the style. In fact, the Newspeak style reinforces the image of the reporter as citizen's representative by saying, in effect, "I work on your behalf because I think, write, and talk like you; my reality is your reality." Like everyday conversation, Newspeak is straightforward, to the point, clear, with no room left for ambiguity. Reports are brief, with short, clipped sentences and simple words (aside from the insider's jargon that lends an air of mystery); accounts are succinct, compact, devoid of frills. Metaphors are familiar ones—elections are horseraces, economic conflicts are "battles of the budget," weapons systems are "hardware," the president's cabinet is his "family," political party leaders "squabble," and so forth. And stories are structured (most important information first, secondary information next, details later, interpretation last), balanced to "give both sides" (as if there is but a two-sided reality), and fast paced (as if to ad-just to the America-on-the-move image).

The words and rituals of Newspeak influence the visions of reality available through pack mediation. Other rituals do so as well. One such convention has developed to aid journalists with a particularly troublesome kind of event, one designated as tainted. Journalists rec-ognize that many alleged newsworthy events are staged solely for their benefit. If the events were not to be reported, they would not occur at all. Political campaigns, protest movements, presidential efforts at molding public opinion—all are filled with events designed to be re-ported by the news media. Yet, even though journalists know the event is staged, they cannot ignore it. Editors want copy, TV producers want film, rival news agencies are reporting it, something unexpected might happen, a reporter might get scooped—all are pressures on the journalist to cover the tainted affair. To put the best face possible on what should not be covered at all, the journalist uses a coping strategy. This consists of distancing oneself in a rhetorical way from the non-newsworthy news event. Communication scientist Mark R. Levy calls this disdaining the news, a technique by which the reporter says, in effect, "Yes, I define this phenomenon as news. But my story is a bit troublesome for me in my role as journalist."[16] For example, during the Iranian hostage crisis in 1979 NBC carried a televised interview with one of the hostages. There were strong suggestions that the Iranians wanted the interview staged. Hence, the NBC correspondent intro-duced the interview by noting that the Iranians agreed to the interview on the condition that it be aired in prime time and that it include a statement from the Iranians but that NBC insisted on no limitations on the interview and that the network have editorial control. The inter-view appeared. Then, the correspondent told viewers to decide for themselves what the Iranian motives had been, that NBC had pre-sented "what we can get."[17] In at least one respect the convention of disdaining the news adds a new wrinkle to pack mediation of reality. By alerting readers and viewers to the tainted quality of an event, news persons imply that it is *not* real and, thus, by further implication, that mediated versions of other events *are* real. One is reminded of the labeling of foods, drugs, and other substances as "may be dangerous to your health"; does this imply those not so labeled are thereby healthful?

Sometimes tainted news is not so labeled, not for audiences and not even for the editors of the news organs that publish it. In 1981, for example, a Pulitzer Prize—a much coveted award for journalistic, artis-tic, and literary merit—was awarded to a *Washington Post* reporter for a feature entitled "Jimmy's World." The story mediated the reality of an eight-year-old heroin addict. The *Post* returned the prize and fired the reporter when it came to light that reality was fiction, that is, Jimmy was fabricated by the correspondent. Also, in 1981 the *New York Daily News* published a feature depicting how a troop of British soldiers had shot a Catholic teenager in Northern Ireland. The story went on to tell of Christopher Spell, a British trooper who was involved in the incident and had seen a comrade shot. An inquiry revealed that a Catholic boy had been shot but that no Christopher Spell existed, no comrade could have been shot, and that facts in the story regarding the month the troop had arrived in Northern Ireland and its route on the day of the shooting were wrong. The reporter admitted making up the questioned details. And, on yet another front, an associate editor and editorial writer for the *Portland Oregonian* admitted fabricating quotes for a news article reporting an interview with Governor Dixy Lee Ray of the state of Washington. The reporter had tape recorded the interview, but the recorder had malfunctioned. So, the journalist reconstructed quotes. But the governor had also recorded the interview. On reading the news article, she played back her tape and discovered numerous inaccuracies in the news account.

We are not saying that pack journalism is a pack of lies. The realities of pack journalism are versions of what might have been, not usually intentional efforts to deceive. But there are instances (how common or rare is simply unknown) when the pressures on correspondents to cover their assignments, scoop their rivals, protect their bylines, garner time on camera, and rise in the pecking order may contribute to fictional accounts. Because journalists must, under the conditions of deadlines and limited space and time, be selective in the story they tell, the account is never pure fact. But even though selective in the information provided, it need not be pure fiction either. The "problem of journalism," notes news media critic and political scientist Edward Jay Epstein, is that it lies "between fact and fiction."[18] The realities of that vast territory are hard enough to verify without adding the endless expanse of intended fiction as well.

In addition to following the leaders and the lead, Newspeak and news rituals, there is another of the many conventions of pack journalism that should be singled out. That is the increasingly common practice of *polltalk*. There are few political fantasies as enduring as that labeled public opinion. Banner headlines tell us "Public Opinion Supports President" or "Candidate Courts Public Approval." Editorials, columnists, and commentators purport to say what the public thinks. Scholars write texts and monographs defining public opinion and charting its changes. Children learn in school that democracy is government by public opinion. But public opinion is a shibboleth—a catchword thrown around to cover a range of vastly different things. Certainly people have opinions. Some, but not all, are about political matters. And people's views conflict, even contradict one another. Rarely do they concur, at least to the degree that we can speak with confidence about a single public opinion.

Given the diverse nature of people's views, how can one say what public opinion is regarding a political figure, issue, or event? Many means have been used. One of the most common is to assume that public opinion is precisely what the news media say it is, what a scholar more than four decades ago dubbed the "journalistic fallacy," the fantasy that "the item which one sees represented in print as 'public opinion,' or which one hears in speeches or radio broadcasts as 'public information' or 'public sentiment,' really has this character of widespread importance and endorsement."[19] Polltalk is the contemporary version of the journalistic fallacy. It consists of the tendencies of journalists and news agencies to label as public opinion the popular views and sentiments on political questions that opinion polls measure in a statistical fashion.

No major news organization in the country is now without its pollster. Polling may be the in-house operation of the news agency or, more frequently, the agency may hire the services of a prominent pollster. News services often collaborate in conducting polls. Thus, during the 1980 presidential election, CBS and the *New York Times* worked together, as did NBC and AP. *Time* magazine used the services of pollster Daniel Yankelovich, *Newsweek* of George Gallup, ABC of Louis Harris. Throughout the campaign, virtually on a weekly, then nightly basis, readers and viewers were innundated with news accounts purporting to show which candidate was leading in the race, how people felt about issues, who would or did win debates, and so on.

But how real is the pollsters' reality of public opinion? Critics suggest that there are possibilities for fantasy.[20] To begin with, any nationwide poll purports to measure public opinion on political affairs by questioning a small sample (typically fifteen hundred persons) selected in accordance with scientific criteria that assure a representative cross section of the population. But in any sampling procedure a certain degree of error will intrude. Take, for example, a sample of eighteen hundred eligible voters asked for whom they would vote on November 4, 1980; assume 47 percent said Ronald Reagan, 44 percent said Jimmy Carter, and the remainder were undecided or favored another candidate. A sample of eighteen hundred persons has an error of 3 percent, that is, any reported percentage might be in error 3 percent plus or minus. Hence, in this hypothetical poll anywhere from 44 to 50 percent might favor Reagan, 41 to 47 percent Carter. The surface reality, then, would show a Reagan lead; taking possible error into account, however, the reality is of a dead heat. Such, in fact, was what happened to the pollsters' realities in 1980. *Time*, the *New York Times*/CBS, and

Newsweek polls all predicted a very close presidential election. Instead, Reagan defeated Carter 51 to 41 percent, a margin not indicated by any major news poll.

Another problem with the pollster's reality is that people do not always have opinions on public affairs, yet express views under the pressure of questioning. Studies show that when people are asked their opinions on such nonexistent matters as the "Metallic Metals Act" or the "Public Affairs Act of 1975" or on such obscure issues as the "Agricultural Trade Act of 1978," from one-third to two-thirds polled will volunteer a view. Crafted into a news item such pseudo-opinions provide a mediated fantasy of public opinions.[21] How questions are worded makes a difference, too. Faced with the proposition that, "The right of a woman to have an abortion should be left to the woman and her doctor," almost three-fourths in nationwide polls agree. But asked, "Do you support legalized abortion up to three months of pregnancy?" as many disagree as agree.

Nor is it always clear in news polls who the public is that pollsters are talking about. In preelection polls, for instance, some pollsters sample all eligible voters, others all likely voters, and still others all registered voters. These populations differ substantially from one another and the mediated realities based on them differ markedly as well. Because we know that Republicans vote in higher proportions than Democrats, a poll reporting a Democratic lead among eligible voters may foretell an illusory reality when on election day the unregistered and apathetic do not vote.

But problems of error, pseudo-opinions, question wording, and the identity of the public notwithstanding, polltalk abounds in political journalism. Polltalk reinforces the tendency of pack journalism to fashion a reality and hold to it. For example, recall that in Chapter 2 we noted that candidates running in presidential primaries not only compete with one another but also with "Expected," that is, the share of votes that polls show candidates are expected to receive on election day. A candidate not living up to expectations defined by news polls suffers a "crippling loss"; one who exceeds poll-mediated expectations pulls off a "startling upset." Moreover, the widespread use of exit polling (questioning voters outside the election precinct after voting) can reinforce a pack judgment. Whether the issue of confidence in the integrity of rival candidates was on the minds of Democratic primary voters or not, one cannot say. However, after every Tuesday's primary in the spring of 1980 Lynn Sherr of ABC News dutifully reported the degrees of confidence voters in exit polls had expressed in candidates Jimmy Carter and Edward Kennedy, thus highlighting concerns over the latter's handling of the 1969 Chappaquiddick accident.

Political scientists David L. Paletz and Robert M. Entman point to another area in which polltalk reinforces pack journalism. During each presidential administration news accounts assess how well the incumbent performs. Our discussion of the assessments made by correspondents on "Washington Week in Review" (see Chapter 7) are one such example. Paletz and Entman argue that, in the case of the presidency of Jimmy Carter, the journalistic pack contributed to a negative assessment through news reports; these reports influenced the president's standing in opinion polls; the pack, then, used Carter's low popularity as further evidence of his failures. "Pack journalism contributed to his decline," they note. "Stories about the president's inadequacies (real and imagined) punctuated by regular, well-publicized surveys charting his falling public approval (but not explaining why people lacked confidence in him) appeared frequently," they go on. Finally, "Each defeat in Congress, each defensive speech was linked to the theme of incompetence and waning popularity, thereby contributing to his descent—or doing nothing to brake it."[22]

PACKTHINK: LIMITING CITIZENS' POLITICAL REALITIES

The descent of Jimmy Carter in press and polls raises a question of the long-range impact of pack journalism on group-mediated politics. There are many consequences, but we shall illustrate their importance by focusing on one—that is, packthink's contribution to the seasonal ritual of elevating and lowering esteem for presidents.

Presidential Melodramas

In Chapter 2 we noted that presidential election campaigns are seasonal rituals. That is, as recurring dramas, they play themselves out in cyclical ways. Another seasonal ritual occurs once a victor occupies the presidency. It is a ritual not limited solely to American politics. To illustrate that point we consider parallel melodramas, those of President Jimmy Carter, 1976–1980, and France's President Valery Giscard d'Estaing, 1974–1981. Each has three acts, each involves pack journalism.

The first act in the melodrama of the rise and decline of presidential prestige consists of the bestowal of a mystique on the president. The bestowal is the joint effort of the news media and the president. The second act strips that mystique away; glimpses of the private man reveal an illusory public face. The final act reconciles the contradictions between public and private: the president is but a self-serving politician devoid of greatness. He must be replaced, hence, the seasonal ritual of election, then incumbency begins anew.

The opening act is one of appearances. The Italian political philosopher Machiavelli, in the sixteenth century, wrote that any true prince

should possess all the qualities his followers would deem good—
generosity, mercy, humaneness, honesty, strength, decisiveness, and
so on. But the conditions of life do not permit that. So a reputation (the
modern term is image) for positive qualities must replace the possession. The quest for reputation begins early. For example, as early as the
caucus and primary campaigns in 1976, a consistent theme developed
in the candidacy of Jimmy Carter, an evolving and single mediated vision of Carter. Put briefly it was that Carter was unknown, an outsider,
sweeping his party by storm; he was unstoppable. The "media burst
forth with stories about the family, background, and rustic life in the so
evocatively named Plains, Georgia."[23] Stories not consistent with that
mediated vision, namely, of Carter's career as a practical politician, his
agribusiness fortune, and his banking/commerce connections were relatively rare. For Carter this favorable mediation of reality continued
well into the early months of his administration. In part this reflected
the seemingly inevitable honeymoon scene of the opening act of the
presidential melodrama: "The time for stories about the president, his
family, closest associates, decision-making processes, and goals."
These stories "are almost invariably favorable, recounting, as they do,
foibles, cute traits, the human interests of the new faces."[24] (Of course,
we saw this honeymoon scene played out in press coverage of the first
100 days of the Reagan administration in our discussion in Chapter 7.)
The news media spawn a large portion of the vision, but the president
benefits from his own calculations as well. The Carter administration
took great pains to exploit the reputation-enhancing coverage of the
press—an inaugural walk down Pennsylvania Avenue, the presidential
suitcase and garment bag carried on and off Air Force One by the president himself, the publicity given construction of a tree house for
daughter Amy. The result was an image of generosity, openness, faith-
fulness—a gentle, religious, humane, loyal, family man.

The melodramatic presentation of reputation enhancement is not
confined to the United States. Consider how one journalist recalled the
early incumbency of French President Giscard d'Estaing: "A 'new style'
simplicity had entered the Elysée: scaled down formalities, business
suits instead of frock coats, a slower paced "Marseillaise," the July 14
parade moved to another site, dinners in the homes of ordinary people." Here was "a go-getting, supposedly simple, president, the candidate who set out to discover France and the 'people' in the course of a
successful election campaign...modest...of the working class."
Again the image-building involved the joint efforts of news media and
politician for "behind the forced simplicity a tortuous design was at
work."[25]

The second act, the unveiling of the private man—thus, exposing
the public face—derives from the conjunction of several forces. Fortuna

(recall our discussion in Chapter 7) plays a role, that is, events occur that the president seems at first to control, but they turn out to be unmanageable. Conflicts seemingly dormant during reputation enhancement burst full bloom. But the news media enter in as well. The journalistic pack begins writing not of events but of presidential efforts to manipulate news about those events:

The president has a special aura of authority that can lend weight to any policy he endorses. But much of this weight is reduced by the way journalists have taken to reporting presidential forays into opinion management. What their reports do is to strip the aura away by placing his actions firmly in a political context. He becomes another politician seeking to retain and enhance his power, not a special leader.[26]

For Jimmy Carter fortuna frowned when oil prices soared, inflation boomed, living standards dropped. Suddenly the greatness the pack had found in Carter evaporated: "Having helped raise expectations of the president's performance, the mass media then helped contrive the chorus of dismay and disillusion when Carter's effectiveness was found wanting—wanting against standards of action and achievement propounded and promoted by presidents and the press."[27] So, also, fortuna no longer smiled on Giscard d'Estaing. The French journalistic pack was quick to note that etiquette and protocol, once due for simplification, returned to old rules that reserved formal roles for the president. There was "an imperious appetite for the trappings of sovereignty."[28] Reports of regal intent replaced those of gentle simplicity: a penchant for elaborate hunting outfits, a tracing of ancestry, a casting about for a coat of arms. And, as in the case of Carter, the press took a hard look at Giscard's efforts to mobilize support. Witness this review of one of the president's television appearances: "Giscard's fake demonstration with marker pen and writing board . . . paid the usual attention to this image . . . use of the pedagogical skills he is often credited with . . . treated his interviewers and TV audiences to a short course on statistics . . . an old and durably effective method, but stale, all the same."[29]

In sum, the first act of the presidential melodrama is one of ascendancy that romanticizes and mythologizes presidential greatness and power; the second act is one of descendancy that deromanticizes and debunks. The final act is one of role reversal, that is, the once special leader, the once great man is now a mere politician. It was on precisely this role reversal that the managers of Ronald Reagan's 1980 campaign against Jimmy Carter capitalized. So successful were they that, if we are to believe their poll data, Reagan's image evolved as more presidential than that of the incumbent.[30] And note how one journalist summed up the Giscard image as the president entered his reelection campaign in 1981: "The image that has improved is that of Giscard the politician, a man who, when all's said and done, faced up to a political situation and survived it."[31] The label politician, whether intended for good or ill, carries with it an attitude, a way of thinking about public figures. It reflects the end of the seasonal ritual, the view that things have died and decayed. It is time for a new season to begin, a rebirth of flora and fauna. So, in 1980 Ronald Reagan challenged Jimmy Carter with a campaign slogan appropriate for the season, that is, "A NEW BEGINNING." In 1981 François Mitterand successfully challenged Giscard d'Estaing with a slogan equally appropriate for the season, "IL FAUT UN PRESIDENT," which implies France must have a president, not a politician.

Why Great Men Are Not Chosen President

Writing more than a century ago, a leading analyst of American politics, James Bryce (an English scholar who became Lord Bryce), pondered why great men do not become president of the United States. By great he meant two things: a great man is (1) someone who would have been remembered even if he had not ever become president and (2) someone who displays rare qualities in the office of president. By and large, he determined, few presidents measured up to either standard of greatness. He spelled out several reasons: American politics attracts few men of first-rate ability, there are few ways in politics to become memorable, eminent men make enemies and are, thus, not electable, and so on. But another reason, wrote Bryce, is that "the ordinary American voter does not object to mediocrity.... He likes his candidates to be sensible, vigorous, and above all, what he calls 'magnetic,' and does not value, because he sees no need for, originality or profundity, a fine culture or a wide knowledge."[32]

Whether Bryce's judgment of American voters is too harsh is not at issue. Rather, mediated politics, at least in the fashion of pack journalism covering the presidency, makes the *discovery* of mediocrity the plot line of the melodrama. In the act of ascendancy the news media focus on the qualities Bryce notes—the sensible, vigorous, magnetic side of candidates. It is for the act of descendancy to expose the mediocre, at least if that term refers to ordinary, and for the act of role reversal to convert ordinary into ordinary politician.

Can more be expected of mediated politics, more particularly of pack mediation? Journalist Walter Lippmann, whose counsel we have cited frequently, was not optimistic. "The press is no substitute for institutions," he wrote. Instead, "it is like the beam of a searchlight that moves restlessly about, bringing one episode and then another out of darkness into vision." But, "men can not do the work of the world by this light alone. They can not govern society by episodes, incidents, and eruptions. It is only when they work by a steady light of their own that the press, when it is turned on them, reveals a situation intelligible enough for popular decision."[33] Are there light-focusing groups and institutions that can sharpen vision of political journalism, thus sharpening realities for popular decision? Let us now turn to two areas, religious politics and conspiratorial politics, where efforts have been made to direct such a focus. We will find that the light that shines may be the light that blinds.

NOTES

1. Leo C. Rosten, *The Washington Correspondents* (New York: Harcourt, Brace and Co., 1937).

2. Timothy Crouse, *The Boys on the Bus* (New York: Ballantine Books, 1974).

3. Ibid., p. 7.

4. James M. Perry, *Us & Them* (New York: Clarkson S. Potter, 1973).

5. Ibid., p. 4.

6. Ibid., p. 4.

7. Crouse, *The Boys on the Bus*, op. cit., p. 8.

8. Joel Swerdlow, "The Decline of The Boys on the Bus," *Washington Journalism Review*, 3 (January/February 1981): 6.

9. Ibid.

10. Leon V. Sigal, *Reporters and Officials* (Lexington, Mass.: D. C. Heath & Co., 1973). See also Michael Baruch Grossman and Martha Joynt Kumar, *Portraying the President: The White House and the News Media* (Baltimore: Johns Hopkins University Press, 1981).

11. Peter Braestrup, *Big Story* (Garden City, N.Y.: Doubleday & Co., 1978), p. xi. (Anchor Books).

12. Walter Lippmann, *Public Opinion* (New York: Macmillan, 1922), p. 354.

13. Crouse, *The Boys on the Bus*, op. cit., p. 23.

14. See Herbert Gans, *Deciding What's News: A Study of CBS Evening News, NBC Nightly News, Newsweek, and Time* (New York: Random House, 1980). (Vintage Books).

15. William Safire, *Safire's Political Dictionary* (New York: Ballantine Books, 1980), p. 351.

16. Mark R. Levy, "Disdaining the News," *Journal of Communication*, 31 (Summer 1981): 24–331.

17. Ibid.

18. Edward Jay Epstein, *Between Fact and Fiction* (New York: Random House, 1975), passim (Vintage Books).

19. Floyd H. Allport, "Toward a Science of Public Opinion," *Public Opinion Quarterly*, 1 (Spring 1937): 7–23.

20. See Albert H. Cantril, ed., *Polling on the Issues* (Cabin John, Md.: Seven Locks Press, 1980); and Albert E. Gollin, ed., "Polls and the News Media: A Symposium," *Public Opinion Quarterly*, 44 (Winter 1980): 445–597.

21. George F. Bishop, Robert W. Oldendick, Alfred J. Tuchfarber, and Stephen E. Bennett, "Pseudo-Opinions on Public Affairs," *Public Opinion Quarterly*, 44 (Summer 1980): 198–209.

22. David L. Paletz and Robert M. Entman, *Media Power Politics* (New York: Free Press, 1981), pp. 74–75.

23. Ibid., p. 37.

24. Ibid., p. 71.

25. Noel-Jean Bergeroux, "Standing on a Contested Record," *Le Monde* (English Section), reprinted in the *Manchester Guardian Weekly*, March 18, 1981, p. 11.

26. Paletz and Entman, *Media Power Politics*, op. cit., p. 64.

27. Ibid., p. 72.

28. Noel-Jean Bergeroux, "But Can It Win an Election?" *Le Monde* (English Section) reprinted in the *Manchester Guardian Weekly*, March 22, 1981, p. 11; see also Paul Farba, "Why Can't We Hear the Whole Story?" *Le Monde* (English Section) reprinted in the *Manchester Guardian Weekly*, March 29, 1981, p. 11.

29. Bergeroux, op. cit., p. 11.

30. Richard Wirthlin, Vincent Breglio, and Richard Beal, "Campaign Chronicle," *Public Opinion*, 4 (February/March 1981): 43–49.

31. Bergeroux, "Standing on a Contested Record," op. cit., p. 11.

32. James Bryce, *The American Commonwealth* (New York: Macmillan, 1896), p. 60.

33. Lippmann, *Public Opinion*, op. cit., p. 354.

9

The Fantasies of Religious Movements

Political Perspectives of Contemporary Evangelicals

The year was 1620. A small band of Puritans approached the shores of what was to become Massachusetts. On the evening before landing their leader, John Winthrop, told them, "For the worke wee have in hand, it is by mutuall consent through a speciall overruleing providence, and a more than an ordinary approbation of the Churches of Christ to seeke out a place of Cohabitation and Consorteshipp under a due forme of Government both civill and ecclasiasticall." He exhorted the faithful, "the eies of all people are upon us," for "we shall be as a City Upon a Hill." The scene now shifts forward in time three and one-half centuries. Ronald Reagan accepts the nomination of the Republican party for the presidency of the United States. He says, "Can we doubt that only a Divine Providence placed this land, this island of freedom, here as a refuge for all those people in the world who yearn to breathe freely?" In his campaign Reagan promises to restore "the city on a hill." After taking the oath as fortieth president he says, "We are a nation under God, and I believe God intended for us to be free."

For over 350 years the refrain has continued: "Divine Providence," "city upon a hill," "a nation under God." So close has been the tie between political and religious rhetoric that one could hardly ignore the importance of organized religion as a mediator of political realities.[1] Yet, many Americans do. Because they lead their daily, secular lives in a rough-and-tumble world, they sometimes forget the role religion

182

plays in their politics and economics. Many, for example, think America a blessed land, which links the political community with the Almighty. Yet, those same people regard government as corrupt, politicians as crooks. Real politics and ideal religion seem far removed from each other for a large number of citizens.

This is not the case, however, for groups intensely committed to a theological view of the world. Such groups elaborate, for their own and the world's benefit, an explanation of all things, including politics, entirely in rhetoric derived from religious belief. Scripture and revelation combine in a rhetorical vision of history and politics—past, present, and future. The world of politics becomes part of a cosmic melodrama as an agent of God's purposes and design in history. What nations and politicians do reveals the workings of Divine Providence. The wicked, as agents of Satan, also have a role in the grand drama. This revelatory and apocalyptic articulation has been a strain in Christianity since St. Augustine, and it survives in many religious groups in America today—such as Mormons, Jehovah's Witnesses, and Southern Baptists. This chapter focuses on the rhetorical vision of that contemporary religious movement in America variously labeled the Christian Right, fundamentalism, the born again, or the evangelicals. The discussion permits an account of both the techniques by which that movement mediates political realities and of the overriding rhetorical vision involved. Moreover, it serves as a brief prologue to a consideration of another form of group-mediated politics in Chapter 10, that is, conspiratorial politics.

The revelatory and apocalyptic vision of politics is most associated with so-called evangelical churches and movements. The evangelical branch of American Christianity is ancient and tenacious, often more of a movement than a church. American revivalism—the great awakenings of our history—come and go, often in conjunction with, and in reaction to, social change and mass disillusionments. Thus the 1920s, 1950s, and 1970s witnessed the revival of evangelical Christianity, including the elaboration of a rhetorical vision simplifying confusing social and political changes for the benefit of the faithful. In the post-Vietnam and post-Watergate world of the 1970s, evangelical Christianity and the simple and powerful explanatory power it offers acquired new salience. Although very much in the tradition of the nondenominational, fire-and-brimstone, repent-for-the-end-is-at-hand tradition of Dwight Moody and Billy Sunday, the new evangelical movement adds new features—including a higher degree of politicization—and new twists to the old rhetorical vision of politics.[2]

The evangelical Christian movement that emerged in the 1970s was theologically not much different from the predecessors of the "sawdust trail." Proselytizers were fundamentalist, believing in the inerrancy of the Bible, active soul winning, and being born again, contemptuous of mainstream churches, the social gospel, and ecumenicalism. And they assured, yet once again, that the world was in the premillenial last days. The group fantasy evoked a Christian drama that has survived since Augustine. But the character of the faithful was different: rather than rural folk who flocked in to large tent meetings to hear the word, they were now often urbanized and part of the new industrial and technological society. Too, the group was not linked together by their physical presence in the tent, but rather by their technological linkage: television.

THE MASS-MEDIATED WORLD OF THE ELECTRONIC CHURCH

The melodrama of religious revival in its most recent form is not enacted in tent meetings, river baptisms, or remote country cinder-block churches. Rather the enactment is in slick television productions, choreographed and produced with professional skill. Massive media audiences are in attendance—in their own homes. Estimates of the numbers of people across America who attend the programs of the electronic churches through TV are staggering: every week, evangelists such as Jerry Falwell, Pat Robertson, Oral Roberts, and Rex Humbard reach an estimated 128 million viewers. Another estimate is that 47 percent of the American people are members, potential or actual, of electronic churches; that is, they view the TV shows. Although some public opinion analysts think these figures are exorbitant, nevertheless the growth of the electronic church has been phenomenal. Religious programs, Christian-oriented radio and television stations, and even Christian broadcasting networks are replete with news, talk shows, game shows, kiddie shows, even soap operas. Christian broadcasting is the media manifestation of an evangelical subculture that serves the entertainment function for that mass-mediated group and, indeed, probably is the only institution that holds this physically dispersed group together. That this nationwide group pays to keep this plethora of Christian programs on the air is an indication of its existence and loyalty. (There is now some evidence that many of the more ambitious TV evangelical programs and preachers have overextended themselves and are in great financial straits.[3])

The rhetorical vision of the electronic church includes not only what they overtly say but also what they implicitly suggest. Whether a particular evangelical program is political or apolitical—and they run the gamut of politicization—they all conform to the media logic of television, using structural and personal settings and styles appropriate to the medium.[4] Oral Roberts, in bringing the evangelical message, for example, is cool, avoiding the fire-and-brimstone, repent-or-ye-be-damned message that curled the hair of tent-meeting audiences of yore. The Roberts show is upbeat, with soft-rock gospel tunes sung by the World Action Singers—lovely girls with long hair and stylishly dressed—and with Oral in a three-piece suit delivering a comforting message ("Something *good* is going to happen to you"). Robert Schuller of the "Hour of Power" offers a spectacular crystal cathedral and grounds, ministers in academic robes, stunning visual effects, and an optimistic and nondenominational message (possibility thinking). Rex Humbard includes singing by his wife and children in beautiful pastoral settings, shots of his grandchildren, and the Cathedral of Tomorrow with a huge neon cross on the ceiling.

Similarly, the more overtly political evangelical shows utilize television logic to communicate with their audience. Pat Robertson of the "700 Club" uses the Johnny Carson–style talk-show format and affects an "Aw shucks" style that is low key and nonthreatening. Jerry Falwell's "Old Time Gospel Hour" is directly political. His program is perhaps the most strict and demanding because he communicates a commitment to a moral and political agenda much more specific than the other TV evangelists. Indeed, Falwell uses distinct themes to communicate avowed political appeals.

The "Old Time Gospel Hour" employs the format of a church service set in a relatively spartan Protestant church setting. Although there are songs, celebrity guests, and features, the authority figure of Falwell dominates. The format and preaching style of the show is distinctly political. First, the program communicates *community*. The viewer has a sense of being part of a unified community that is orderly, respectable, and purposeful. If one is fearful that the world is chaotic and contemptuous of one's values, Falwell offers an alternative. One can identify with the pseudocommunity of the show through parasocial interaction, vicarious and undemanding identification with an appealing group.[5] The fantasy is one of belonging to a primary group, the church family, through television. Belonging to a church in one's own hometown is messier, beset by the ambiguities and human failings of any actual group. But with the Falwell family, one can fantasize an idealized community without having the responsibilities of belonging to a local church. The media entertainment draws large audiences who find uses and gratifications in watching, but the pseudocommunity is also unstable. TV audiences may grow tired of the program, quit watching and contributing to it, thus undermining the church's media base.

The "Old Time Gospel Hour" also communicates *piety*. The pseudocommunity is pious, whereas the world outside—including mainstream churches—are impious. The people in the pews are quiet, respectful, and prayerful. The youth choir consists of young men and women who are clean-cut, neatly dressed, and responsible. The procession of speakers, singers, and prayers are all pious. The hushed tone communicates a group that believes in the power and presence of God. The TV viewer can feel secure that in an impious world there is somewhere a pious community of believers who keep and respect the faith.

The Falwell message is one of *authority* as well. The program is a religious service, not a talk show. There is no audience participation, aside from a few invoked responses, such as applause on occasion and "Amens." The show service is tightly run on schedule and revolves around the command of Falwell. His style as well as his message is authoritative. No one disputes his authority or the truth of his assertions about God or government; the TV audience can easily conclude that the religious community of the media-extended Thomas Road Baptist Church is unified in belief and support of Falwell. His assertive style and confident, even arrogant, air helps communicate certainty in a world of confusion. He brooks no insubordination ("with no one moving about or disturbing the service in any way . . . "), asserts the absolute authority of the Bible and himself, and condemns critics who question that authority (homosexuals, liberals, women's rights groups, etc.). For the sympathetic viewer the assertion of authority comes as a welcome alternative to moral relativism and competing claims of freedom, diversity, and secular humanism.

In this regard it is interesting to note how Falwell runs his church-affiliated school, Liberty Baptist College. Students need administrative consent before dating, and dates are chaperoned. Students can and are suspended for dancing, swearing, reading pornography, being in the dorm of a member of the opposite sex, or drinking; one is expelled automatically for using drugs, joining a demonstration, or immoral behavior. Dorm officials inspect rooms daily, strictly enforce curfews, conduct mandatory prayer sessions, forbid listening to rock music (which Falwell calls "the devil's anthem"), and sign students in and out. The school hires only born-again faculty, enforces orthodoxy in teaching (evolution is not taught in biology), censors carefully what the library contains, and fires those who teach unwelcome ideas. If Liberty Baptist College is a model of what Falwell would like America to become, then it will be strict on discipline.[6]

Finally, the mass-mediated religious service communicates *growth*. The church is always filled to overflowing. The organization is constantly on the move; Falwell is always announcing his speaking tours all over the country. The numbers of viewers, of young preachers sent out to start soul-winning churches, and of those won to Christ are flaunted as evidence of the growing movement spreading across and changing America. Falwell reminds viewers that the Thomas Road

Baptist Church was built from nothing, a religious success story very much in the American tradition of business entrepreneurship and the Protestant ethic. Although rooted in traditional values and a small town, the church is very much up to date, exploiting the latest media technology, showmanship, and computer mailout campaigns to run a flourishing business. Falwell, the church leadership, and the congregation all appear prosperous, the benefactors of a thriving business bringing in money and experiencing success. They are the corporate executives of a successful religious enterprise that appeals to an ever larger audience.

These messages—community, piety, authority, and growth—are implicit in the *structural fantasy* of the program. They are also politically charged because the high political profile of Falwell suggests what the rest of the country should be like—a replica of the "Old Time Gospel Hour."

THE RHETORICAL VISION OF THE CHRISTIAN RIGHT

The newly politicized Christian Right—led by TV celebrity preachers and the media organizations they command, yet rooted in evangelical Protestant denominations in the American hinterland—has developed a loosely stated rhetorical vision about politics. This vision is a mediated reality both for the groups that form the constituency of the Christian Right and for the larger political order as well. The fantasy themes that comprise the vision are not necessarily consistent, articulated in the same way, or even totally shared by everyone who participates in this group. In general these themes and the entire vision stem from the Christian drama of history as stated by St. Augustine, in which the elect of God must struggle against Satan's hordes as a church militant. The Augustinian vision makes one very much aware of the sin and corruption that stems from Satan. Not all Augustinians believe that sin can and should be controlled by the elect. But with the spread of Calvinism—to, for example, the United States—the idea persisted that Christians should apply moral standards to society and control vice and folly. In some measure both liberal reformism (feminism, abolitionism, and progressivism) and conservative reformism (blue laws, book banning, and Prohibition) stem from American Calvinism. The roots of the Christian Right are in both the Augustinian and Calvinist traditions as modified by their experience in American history. Although the rhetorical vision of the Christian Right thus rests on the old-time religion, it has taken a new form and salience in recent years. The evangelical and reformist zeal of old has been revived, but the nature of the drama has been changed. Let us review the dramatic logic of the politico-religious scenario of the Christian Right.

The Christian Right views itself involved in a theological moral drama, fighting a holy war against Satan and his earthly agents. Satan's hordes include a wide variety of villains and fools—liberals, feminists, proabortionists, pornographers, television executives, homosexuals, and others. They may wittingly contribute to the evil (such as *Playboy* owner Hugh Hefner allegedly does) or they may be unwitting dupes and fools, for example, churches that ordain women ministers (Satan "welcomes sermonettes by preacherettes," says Falwell). In any event, the Manichean war against Satan's hordes includes the Calvinist use of political power to defeat Satan and legislate God's moral laws. "We're fighting a holy war," says Falwell. "What's happening to America is that the wicked are bearing rule. We have to lead the nation back to the moral stance that made America great. . . . We want to bring America back . . . to the way we were."[7] The holy war fantasy contains both a promise and a threat. To the extent America is ruled by righteous men, it is blessed; to the extent that America is ruled by the wicked, it is cursed. Because God is on the side of the holy, He assures their victory but expects of them struggle against the damned. Although evil is strong, the fantasy goes, it can be defeated by the ardent—critics would say fanatical—zeal of the righteous. Control of the State becomes crucial to the enforcement of morality and to the control of the unholy.

The theological/moral drama of the Christian Right is historical. America experiences political, economic, and social difficulties because it has drifted away from fundamentals. It has turned away from traditional morality and the family, from the economic fundamentals of capitalism, and from social responsibility. Adherents imagine a nostalgic world of an American past devoid of present problems because of the commitment of our forefathers to fundamental principles. From a golden age, America has descended to the present state. Part of the reason for this immoral and irresponsible condition is a secular government that has led the way in the abandonment of fundamentals through welfare-state measures, accommodation with Communist states, and the extension of rights to women, homosexuals, and others. If we put "God back into government," such policies will be undone, and we shall return to fundamentals and God's blessing will be restored.

The political goal, therefore, of the Christian Right is to *Christianize* America. Secular and pluralistic America will be transformed into a sacred and monistic culture unified by fundamentalist Christian values and institutions. Capitalism, which is biblical, would be transformed into a benevolent and altruistic force governed by Christian principles. Society would cease to be materialistic, yet would be prosperous. Prayer would return to public schools and school textbooks (which are "destroying our children's moral values") would paint a positive picture of America. Pornography, dirty Hollywood movies, and immoral TV shows would disappear. Some persons on the Christian Right advocate ministerial moral boards to pass on the acceptability of books, movies, school curricula, and so forth. Like the Marxist utopia, the Christian America envisioned is a bit vague in its details. But it would certainly be a different society and government than now.

In Chapter 10 we shall note that certain ideological groups develop elaborate conspiracy theories to explain political events. The Christian Right has traditionally shared the conspiracies and enemies of the secular Right, which we shall also detail in Chapter 10, but more recently it has fashioned a more nebulous, but equally nefarious, conspiratorial group: secular humanists. Secular humanism, in this view, is an anti-Christian creed that has become the substitute religion of America and responsible for all its ills. Like the witches of Salem or the Communists of the 1950s, secular humanists must be purged from the community and their influence eliminated from textbooks, classrooms, and pulpits. The secular humanist conspiracy has a long history. Historical co-conspirators include Aristotle, Machiavelli, St. Thomas Aquinas, Rousseau, Marx, Bertrand Russell—indeed, a breathtaking array of intellectual talent spanning virtually the entire Western tradition. Tim LaHaye, author of *The Battle for the Mind*, scores Michelangelo for sculpting a nude David: "The Renaissance obsession with nude 'art forms' was the forerunner of the modern humanist's demand for pornography in the name of freedom."[8] Although there are only about 275,000 humanists in the United States, nevertheless "they occupy key positions of leadership, where they exercise an inordinate influence on America."[9] This group forces on us the teaching of evolution, sex education, socialism, situation ethics, critical history, pornography, and all the ills that flow from such things. The holy war to Christianize America, then, will identify secular humanist enemies and purge them from the garden.

This crusade is made all the more urgent because we are in the last days. The world will end soon, apparently in a gigantic war in the Middle East involving Israel, the Arab states, and the Soviet Union. As with St. Augustine, one might think that Christians should give up reforming the damned or realizing a Christian American Dream. But the rhetorical vision of evangelical Christianity posits the necessity of action by the elect to prepare for the imminent apocalyptic end of history. If America is Christianized, it will yet be blessed at the end of time, which is now upon us. Signs and omens portend the end— earthquakes, volcanic eruptions, famine, unusual weather, as well as the appearance of false prophets and Satan worship. Writers such as Hal Lindsey envision a final battle, Armageddon, involving the world's major powers in a nuclear holocaust that kills a large portion of the human race but in which Christ returns at the peak of the battle. One observer has termed this vision of the last days as the "Gunfight at the Armageddon Corral," in which Jesus intervenes like a Western gunfighter to zap the bad guys and rescue the good guys.[10] The climax to history is near, and the believer can feel part of a grand drama that will soon end with the victory of the good guys.

The rhetorical vision of the Christian Right is very old wine in new bottles. It is an old popular strain in Christianity redefined and given new salience in the 1980s. Christians have predicted that the end of time was at hand since the first century A.D. Various groups—Romans, Jews, Moslems, Nazis, Communists, Catholics—have been identified as part of Satan's hordes. Every generation since time immemorial has cast some world figure as the Antichrist. Zealous efforts to Christianize communities through conversion or force have been tried many times. And it is certainly wishful thinking to believe that a society like America in the late twentieth century can be returned to a nostalgic preindustrial, preconsumer, smalltown past. Holy wars to restore some set of fundamentals have been waged before (by both Christians and Moslems), and they are more war than holy. With the possibility that the Christian Right's social and historical vision might not come true, it behooves us to assess where their rhetorical vision might lead them in the years ahead.

THE LENGTH OF THE FANTASY CHAIN: FAITH AND FANATICISM

Theologians like to distinguish faith from fanaticism. Not all evangelicals identify themselves with the Christian Right nor are they all fundamentalists. Using polling techniques in nationwide surveys, the Gallup organization has endeavored to estimate the size of the two groups, that is, evangelists and the Christian Right. To be classified as evangelist, a person must respond in the affirmative to three questions: (1) Are you a born-again Christian or have you had a born-again experience? (2) Do you encourage other people to believe in Jesus Christ? and (3) Do you believe in a literal interpretation of the Bible or at least with the proposition that the Bible is the inspired word of God, but not everything in it is to be taken literally, word for word? Using this standard, the Gallup organization estimates that approximately one of every five of those surveyed in nationwide polls (19 percent) is in the evangelist category. The Christian Right category is only slightly larger—23 percent. Persons so labeled are Christian in religious preference, describe themselves as "very religious," place themselves on the right on a liberal/conservative scale, and say they are biblical literalists. Yet, although the proportion of Americans in each of the two groups is roughly the same, the same people do not comprise the two categories. Nor do those identifying with the Christian Right always hold the same views as the evangelicals. For instance, the Christian Right are considerably more Republican and pro-Reagan than evangelicals as a group. And there are sufficient differences on certain issues—banning abortions, allowing homosexuals to teach in public schools, and so on —to suggest that evangelicals and identifiers with the Christian Right would find it hard to constitute a single voting bloc, let alone an overbearing political force.[11]

The contemporary Christian Right, thus, draws its strength less from rank-and-file evangelicals than from the devotion of more fanatical followers. In that sense the Christian Right is simply an American version of the worldwide fundamentalist movements (such as the Shiite Moslems of Iran) that are "militantly antimodern, fanatical, and hold in contempt the separation of church and state."[12] Hence, the Christian Right is more of a movement than a church and counts on the fanatical zeal of its followers to bring about the creation of a Christian America. It may also be the case that the Christian Right is antimodern, at least insofar as it imagines the creation of a nostalgic world of smalltown and pastoral virtue devoid of the problems of urban and technological modernity. And, certainly, the rhetorical vision of the Christian Right does not include a wall of separation between church and state.

If this is correct, then the rhetorical vision of the Christian Right stands outside of the traditional contract between state and church in America. As Roderick P. Hart has pointed out, this contract is rhetorical and not legal, involving not only political obeisance to sacred symbols but also the understanding that politics will remain secular. This contract has persisted through the putative agreement of mainstream churches and the political establishment. But, as Hart notes, the contract is tentative and subject to the strains of time and circumstance. The mainstream churches are organizations of faith and are not activated by either religious or political fanaticism. But in troubled times that is not enough for many people who desire a more intense and tribal religion with a radical political agenda. Hart warns that we may have to face a future reality of a totalitarian tribal religion in demonic form.[13]

The politicization of religion can produce a fantasy of a politics of redemption. American politics hitherto has largely been a politics of accommodation, based on a political rhetorical vision of compromise, toleration, and laissez faire. But the politics of redemption turns politics into a moral crusade that accepts no accommodations. Armed with a vision of absolute values and a belief that one is on the side of God, the movement formulates a rhetorical vision that sees the use of political power as necessary for the completion of the theological/moral drama. The politics of redemption is a much more ambitious agenda than the politics of accommodation because people have to be converted and mobilized, and institutions transformed into moral agencies. The ancient fantasy that morality can be legislated, people made moral, and monistic agreement on values and policy maintained is revived again.

A Christian politics of redemption would be tempted, as are all political movements, with the use of power to enforce the agenda. Such a quest can become infected by the same intoxication of power that is the political sin of all such movements. The use of power ironically becomes demonic, a zealous nationalism and moralism that enforces tribal unity and the moral law. Power is used with fanatical zeal to redeem the world through the destruction of the wicked.[14] America would be Christianized by a holy war that purges its enemies and integrates its citizenry into an enforced monism. Realizing the rhetorical vision would require a political idolatry of secular salvation beyond the restraints of the Gospel and constitutional law.[15]

Fantasies of moral perfection in a Christian America die hard, but failure to achieve political goals could well bring alteration in the Christian Right's world view. The result may be a retreat into a disillusioned Augustinian quietism that sees the world as unregenerate; hence one must look after one's own soul. Or the result could be a less ambitious religious grouping that accepts the terms of the church-state contract. Symbolic crusades often adapt to institutionalized settings, devoid of the zeal that once moved them.[16] Whatever the result, however, the Christian Right stands today as a prime mediator of political realities for a growing, or perhaps diminishing, cadre of followers.

NOTES

1. Roderick P. Hart, *The Political Pulpit* (West Lafayette, Ind.: Purdue University Press, 1977), offers an excellent summary of the rhetorical dimensions of civil religion in the United States.

2. The transitional figure in this development is Billy Graham. See Marshal Frady, *Billy Graham: A Parable of American Righteousness* (Boston: Little, Brown & Co., 1979).

3. Albert R. Trost, "Old-Time Religion in the New Electronic Church," *The Cresset*, 52 (April 1979): 20–22; Charles E. Swann, "The Electronic Church," *Presbyterian Survey* (October 1979): 17–20; Johnathon Kaufman, "An Evangelical Revival Is Sweeping the Nation But with Little Effect," *Wall Street Journal* (July 11, 1980), p. 1.

4. David L. Altheide and Robert P. Snow, *Media Logic* (Beverly Hills, Calif.: Sage Publications, 1979).

5. Donald Horton and R. Richard Wohl, "Mass Communication and Para-Social Interaction: Observations on Intimacy at a Distance," *Psychiatry*, 19 (1956): 215–229.

6. "Falwell's College Denies Independence, Free Inquiry," *The Torch,* October 5, 1981, p. 10. (Published by Valparaiso University, Indiana.)

7. Eileen Ogintz, "Evangelists Seek Political Clout," *Chicago Tribune,* August 31, 1980, sec. 2, pp. 1–2.

8. Tim LaHaye, *The Battle for the Mind* (Old Tappan, N.J.: Fleming H. Revell Co., 1980), p. 30.

9. Ibid., p. 179.

10. John Wiley Nelson, "Hal Lindsey and the Late Great Planet Earth: Uncivil Civil Religion." Paper delivered at the 1980 meeting of the Popular Culture Association March 1981, Pittsburgh, Pa (Unpublished).

11. Martin E. Marty, "Fundamentalism Reborn: Faith and Fanaticism," *Saturday Review,* 7 (New Series) (May 1980): 37.

12. George Gallup, Jr., "Divining the Devout: The Polls and Religious Belief," *Public Opinion,* 4 (April/May 1981): 20–21.

13. Hart, op. cit., p. 65.

14. See Robert Jewett, *The Captain America Complex: The Dilemma of Zealous Nationalism* (Philadelphia: Westminster Press, 1973).

15. Ernest B. Koenker, *Secular Salvation* (Philadelphia: Fortress Press, 1965); Eric Hoffer, *The True Believer* (New York: Perennial Library, 1966).

16. Joseph R. Gusfield, *Symbolic Crusade* (Urbana: University of Illinois Press, 1966).

10

Devils and Demons
The Group Mediation of Conspiracy

John Wilkes Booth. Lee Harvey Oswald. James Earl Ray. History books, commissions of inquiry, and courts of law record that these three men acted alone as assassins of Abraham Lincoln, John Kennedy, and Martin Luther King, Jr., respectively. Not everyone agrees. Periodically people raise doubts. They argue that each assassination was not the act of a single murderer but the final scene in an elaborate conspiratorial plot planned and executed by persons unknown. The doubters demand that investigations be reopened. Sometimes they are successful. Congressional investigations have examined anew the circumstances surrounding the deaths of John Kennedy and Martin Luther King, Jr.; the results reassured some skeptics, confirmed the suspicions of others, but more frequently simply raised new questions. In any event the inquiries failed to answer the fundamental question, that is, were the deaths of such political figures the ill-gotten gains of conspiratorial politics?

One requirement of democratic politics is that government be conducted in the open. Leaders present proposals up front for public scrutiny and debate. The election and appointment of public officials, the adoption of public policies, the turnover of political regimes—all are to occur openly. People who believe in conspiratorial politics think things work otherwise. For them assassinations of political leaders are not aberrations of the body politic but the realities of conspiratorial power seeking. Their suspicions are not restricted to assassinations. Electoral outcomes, executive actions, legislative logrolling, judicial decisions—for doubters of the open society all government derives from a base of conspiracy.

194

What is the source of this mediated reality of conspiracy? Among a variety of sources, one is key, that is the tendency of political groups to create fantasies about the world "out there" more or less shared by members of the group. The process of the creation, maintenance, change, and decay of such shared world views is complicated. Some groups develop elaborate rhetorical visions of the political world that are strange and illogical to outsiders. Strange or not, the political vision ardently persists if the group regards itself as righteous—the soldiers in a crusade for a noble cause. Moreover, the political fantasy intensifies, perhaps fanatically, if the group is remote from the centers of power and resides on the political extremes. The fantasy under such circumstances is not likely to be refuted by the group's everyday political reality, hence, group members reinforce each other in a shared vision. Through an elaborate form of groupthink, self-righteous groups on the far periphery of power contrive a fantasy of politics of both past and present. Such rhetorical visions evolve in groups on both the right and left of the political spectrum. However, to illustrate the group mediation of conspiratorial politics, we shall focus on the American Right, relegating the fantasies of the American Left to a concluding note.

POLITICAL IDEOLOGY AND RHETORICAL VISION

Political scholars often note that the major appeal of communism to many politically conscious people is its dramatic quality rather than its philosophical sophistication. In its development on the political fringe during the nineteenth century, many adherents were attracted by the dramatic fable of the rhetorical vision of communism: that history is a drama of class conflicts, all of which bring nearer the final struggle of My Lord Capital and the Collective Worker (the last villain and hero of history, respectively), whose outcome produces the final, utopian stage of man's long quest. Probably unconsciously derived from the Judaeo-Christian eschatological tradition, the Communist rhetorical vision offered a mighty struggle of the forces of good and evil wherein a providential force mysteriously works to insure, after long suffering and strife, that good triumphs over evil in the last act and that the drama's denouement is a happy ending.[1] In some measure, Nazi believers in the 1930s developed their rhetorical vision of a Thousand-Year Reich in the same circumstances of political isolation.

Political theorists often label such groups as Communists or Nazis as ideological. This is not to say mainstream political groups—the Democratic party, say—do not have an ideology discernible in party documents, speeches by party leaders, and in the hearts and minds of good Democrats. Most of us could sit down and elaborate our political ideology, at least in the sense of the political ideas and images we hold and try to articulate. But with members of a politically active group, who value and share the political perspective of that group, people usually acquire a political vision from the ideological leanings the group produces. In speeches, position papers, books, films, and so on, political groups develop an official ideology. This is their *forensic* ideology, the "elaborate word systems, formulated at a rather abstract level, which constitute the language of political discussion in times of severe political stress and strain."[2] There may be latent variations on the articulated political doctrine of the group, but its forensic ideology is there for group, and public, consumption.

Even though a forensic ideology may be abstract on the surface, behind its ideology (the logic of its abstract ideas) is a dramatic rhetorical vision that, as we noted above, gives the political world an emotional significance well beyond logical abstractions. Like the Judaeo-Christian story, modern political ideological groups remote from power can envision themselves as part of a grand drama, the historical struggle of the forces of good versus the forces of evil, whose outcome is both in doubt but ultimately certain. To paraphrase Lenin, groups regard themselves on the side of right, but the inevitable victory of right still requires commitment to struggle and strife.

THE DEMONIC MELODRAMA IN HISTORY

In a classic American movie, *All About Eve,* two sophisticated New York theater people are having a lover's quarrel. At one point in the argument, she asks petulantly, "Is this going to be a bad melodrama?" He replies, "My dear, the first twenty years of human history was a bad melodrama." This reference to the Genesis story of the expulsion from Eden is a play on words. Bad means not only poor quality, but rotten in the sense of Eve's seduction by the Devil, Adam's seduction by Eve, and so forth. The story is the root of a rhetorical vision on which many religious, economic, and political movements have since drawn to cast themselves as actors in a mighty historical struggle of good versus evil, the forces of the godly versus the forces of Satan.[3] As in St. Augustine's famous formulation, history is a cosmic drama that people envision as a war of light and darkness, wherein one's enemies, real or imagined, are demonic.

In the ancient biblical version, of course, enemies are literally demonic, conscious agents of Satan. The demons that would subvert good are part of the grand conspiracy of Satan that gives shape to history. Satan's hordes, in this vision, subvert morale, social institutions, and the Church in an effort to defeat and destroy God's people. But these demons can and will be defeated by the militancy of those committed to God's side. The drama involves the agents of God rooting out and destroying the agents of Satan, who are among us, either as palpable beings working to undermine good or by possessing innocent people invisibly. Satan's ingenuity and energy are boundless, and the righteous must be eternally vigilant to prevent simple backsliding and more complex concessions to the temptations of evil.

In this view history, including any contemporary political struggle, is a fight against an unregenerate enemy who is eternally cunning and resourceful and with whom compromise is impossible. This notion translates the processes of history from cold economic and political conflicts into a drama of destiny, peril, and heroic strife against the forces of evil. This shared myth has persisted both in sacred and secular forms in the West. As a recurrent and reformulated group fantasy, it has played a large role in solidifying the activities of religious and political groups. If group members see themselves as acting in a historic drama, then identifying the demons—the villains of the piece—is a large part of the recognition scene of the drama. This makes the play *a demonic melodrama*.[4] Bad melodrama, after all, draws the characters as totally good and evil, retains a sentimental faith in the triumph of good, sketches plots of the intense peril of the triumph of evil (which is foiled by action), and intersperses elements of adventure, mystery, romance, and nightmare. The adventure is the heroic defeat of evil; the mystery is identifying the conspirators; the romance is love winning over hate; the nightmare is the menace of evil.[5]

The power of this rhetorical vision is evident enough. The tradition of the Antichrist has haunted religious folk down to the present. Each generation, it seems, identifies important political figures as the current candidate for the job—in our century, Kaiser Wilhelm, Stalin, Hitler, Mao, or some abstract force, such as fascism or communism. The elaborate myths about demonology—societies of witches, the Witches' Sabbath, devil possession, sacrifices of virgins and babies, and so forth —have haunted the Western mind down to the present. One historian of the late medieval period has cast doubt as to whether societies of witches ever really existed at all![6] Certainly a good bit of witch hunting was hysterical fear stimulated by immediate circumstances (e.g., economic distress, puzzling social change), and many "witches," as in the famous Salem witch trials, were simply scapegoats.[7] Jews, of course, were convenient targets for pogroms throughout history, and the myth of an international Jewish conspiracy persists to the present.

The recurrent revival of the Jewish conspiracy fantasy in new form is an example not only of the astonishing persistence of such rhetorical visions but also of the secularization of conspiracy. In recent times, visions of conspiracy have become more earthbound, stemming from some group or movement that can be cast in the role of villain. In troubled times the alleged conspirators may be little more than a class or group plotting to take power and enslave—the French aristocrats, the Norman ruling class, Bolsheviks, Jewish bankers, the British Empire, the Yellow Peril, and so on. However, these secular conspiracies retain in our fantasies satanic qualities and evil designs. The Nazi fantasy about the Jewish conspiracy, for instance, is rooted in the religious anti-Semitism of the past, but it secularizes the conspiracy into a plot of bankers, industrialists, and politicians pulling the strings in every country. The Nazis produced documents, such as the famous *Protocols of the Elders of Zion*, that "proved" the existence of the conspiracy.[8] Hitler once remarked, "Behind England stands Israel and behind France and behind the United States."[9] So the Jew, once a religious conspirator, became a secular conspirator, two temporal fantasies stemming from the same persistent myth. (The myth is still around, if latent: when "Holocaust" appeared on TV, one popular reaction was that somehow "they" deserved it, including, presumably, the approximately one million Jews under eight years of age who were executed.)

Conspiracy theories are especially attractive to political movements. A movement's followers often see the movement as the symbolic bearer of a new faith that will save the world. Hence, their rhetorical vision often casts their enemies as demonic. Norman Cohn, in his book *The Pursuit of the Millenium*, notes that past "revolutionary millenarians" were characterized by:

The megalomanic view of oneself as the Elect, wholly good, abominably persecuted yet assured of ultimate triumph; the attribution of gigantic and demonic powers to the adversary; the refusal to accept the ineluctable limitations and imperfections of human existence, such as transience, dissent conflict, fallibility whether intellectual or moral; the obsession with inerrable prophecies . . . [as well as] ruthlessness directed towards an end which by its very nature cannot be realized—toward a total and final solution such as cannot be attained at any actual time or in any concrete situation, but only in the timeless and autistic realm of phantasy.[10]

Political movements (by definition not in official power), thus depend heavily on the power of their rhetorical vision to sustain true belief. "'Things which are not,'" wrote Eric Hoffer, "are indeed mightier than 'things that are.' In all ages men have fought most desperately for beautiful cities yet to be built and gardens yet to be planted."[11] The rhetorical vision of millenial movements almost invariably includes an imagined idealized past or future. The conspiracy that bedevils the present did not hold sway in that glorious past that will be restored in the future with defeat of the conspiracy. The mission of the political group, therefore, is transcendent, something higher than the petty squabbles of mainstream politics. This sense of mission has two consequences.

First, the group sees itself as above politics, and, thus, the compromises and deals of ordinary politics corrupt and, indeed, are proof of the power and duplicity of the conspiracy. Second, the group is in principle justified in using any means, including those violating current political rules of the game, to attain its ultimate goals. Because the mission is transcendent and the enemy demonic, any means, regrettable and nasty though they may be, are justified to attain one's higher ends.

The rhetorical vision of political movements imbued with millenarian imagery carries with it a principle of perfection.[12] Because the demonic melodrama casts "us" as the bearer of an absolute principle that is to be realized through us, it logically casts "them" as the underminer of that principle. In such rhetorical visions there is an impulse to fantasize about the perfection of both the principle for which one fights and the characters in the melodrama. The principle will be perfected in the envisioned future devoid of the conspiracy. There is also a tendency to perfect heroes and villains. Such group fantasies include a perfect enemy whose capabilities and evil are boundless. Satan, the Antichrist, international Jewry, whoever—one must not underestimate the power and pervasiveness of the conspiracy. By perfecting the enemy, groups make the force seem awesome, something that can only be conquered and slain by holy warriors.

The perfection principle leads the group into demonic irony. The demonic conspiracy is of such magnitude and strength that it can only be fought on its own terms. This justifies the forces of good using the tactics of the demonic, to fight fire with fire in order to be equal to the mighty task. Ironically, then, the good must imitate their perfected enemy by being as mean and ruthless as they envision evil. In pursuit of the defense and furtherance of a higher principle, the forces of light must be as demonic as the forces of dark to triumph. The gravity of the evil demands no less. Part of the irony is the extent that crusaders admire, both openly and secretly, the ruthlessness of the fantasized enemy. Satan, Jews, Masons, the Papacy, or whoever—all are perceived as more disciplined, dedicated, and singleminded than "us," who are endangered by sloth and lack of zeal. Thus, the Jesuits tried to be more ardent than Satan's hordes, the Nazis more ruthless than the Jews, the anti-Communist more dedicated than the Communist. In any case, it is nothing less than ironic that one projects on one's enemy perfected attributes of evil that one must then emulate in order to defeat the potent enemy. By becoming as bad as they are, rivers of blood flow. Inquisitions, pogroms, purge trials, lynchings, death camps—all are created by the fantasy of a perfect enemy.

The rhetorical vision of such groups is temporal with a full-fledged philosophy of history. The conspiracy is the causal force in history, explaining why everything is going to hell. The conspiracy is historical, oftentimes having a long continuity and being responsible for a wide variety of historical events. It was, and is, directed by unseen directors and has its tentacles in many institutions. The historical goal of the conspiracy is sinister, amounting to nothing less than world control. The climactic struggle is in the present, for which we must gird ourselves. The fantasy foresees an imminent denouement, the final battle, exposure, defeat, and victimization of the conspiracy, followed by the glorious victory of the group. The demonic melodrama is done, replaced by an angelic one.[13]

The rhetorical vision described here in general terms receives substance in a wide assortment of well-developed conspiracy theories. There are many other themes in conspiracy theories we could mention, but the ones noted suffice to suggest the dramatic elements in a variety of political visions. The "ideo-logic" of political groups includes a vision articulated by the group that gives the dramatic power of a grand struggle in the spirit of *Paradise Lost* and *Paradise Regained*. Such a grandiose vision certainly puts one on the side of the angels. Now consider selected American political groups with conspiratorial theories as contemporary examples of an ancient American tradition.

AMERICAN CONSPIRATORIAL TRADITION AND THE CONTEMPORARY RIGHT

Contemporary political groups of the Right or Left continue a long tradition of groups in America that have espoused conspiracy theories containing dramatic elements. Historian Richard Hofstadter has called this the paranoid style in American politics. He refers not so much to the clinical, pathological sense of a paranoia and persecution mania as to a more generalized perception of the way the political world works and the melodramatic features attributed to it.[14] Americans have been receptive to conspiracy theories throughout their history. They are adept at creating rhetorical visions of conspiracies. From the beginnings of the Republic, pamphlets and books exposed the alleged conspiratorial activities of Catholics, Masons, and other groups. John Robison's book on "the Illuminati conspiracy" in 1797 was an early example.[15] Political groups, often with patriotic or nativist impulses, conjured up visions of conspiracies, and the anti-Masonic party, Know-Nothing Party, and Ku Klux Klan espoused the presence of a foreign cabal bent on controlling the United States. In the present this tradition of fantastic conspiratorial thinking continues.

The tradition received considerable impetus with the advent of the Soviet Union as a world power and the spread of communism as a twentieth-century political ideology. Communism, of course, did espouse world revolution and calculated means to obtain power. In the demonology of many Americans, Communists have replaced Masons, Catholics, and Jews as the source of the grand conspiracy of tradition. Reds were an easily perfectable enemy: centered in a vast and mysterious land (Russia), advocating values that were economically and socially repugnant, politically aggressive and calculating, alleged to have committed atrocities and enslavements—all in all a good candidate for a demonic conspiracy. After World Wars I and II, America had two Red scares fed by monstrous fears of domestic communism.

Out of the Red scare following World War II, the rhetorical vision of the American Right evolved. Like the Puritans of Salem in the seventeenth century, the enemies suddenly appeared. Rather than explain the widening appeal of communism as an ideology as derived from long-range historical forces, fears dramatized the doctrine as an insidious conspiracy with tentacles reaching to the heart of America. Senator Joseph McCarthy accused Secretary of State George Marshall in 1951 as being part of a "conspiracy so immense, an infamy so black, as to dwarf any in the history of man."[16] J. Edgar Hoover of the FBI, always quick to pick up on an issue of symbolic significance at the moment, abandoned the fight against organized crime for the fight against domestic communism.[17] The Red scare gradually abated as a popular concern, but the fears it generated added zeal to people attracted to conspiracy theories. The Red menace and godless communism helped create and sustain groups of the recent New Right, such as the John Birch Society, the Liberty Lobby, the Christian Anti-Communist Crusade, and others. In the best tradition of conspiratorial rhetorical visions, these groups developed distinctive theories of a demonic conspiracy. These right-wing groups have perhaps the most highly developed of contemporary political conspiracy theories, rhetorical visions of conspiracy that warrant our focus.

The membership corps of groups such as the John Birch Society have developed elaborate explanations for why the political world is as they believe it to be. Monolithic communism for them is a secular but demonic force, a perfected enemy of uncanny guile and zeal, whose historic scheme is to undermine the United States by isolating it abroad and subverting it domestically from within. The Communist conspiracy, directed from Moscow, has had such success that most of the world is, or soon will be, in the Red orbit. Only a few staunchly anti-Communist states—Chile, Taiwan, Rhodesia—have stood firm against the tide, but they, too, either have or soon will be swept away with the tide. At home Communist infiltration into the government was rife, or so it seemed to conspiracy theorists in the 1950s and 1960s. Such figures as President Eisenhower, Chief Justice Earl Warren, and Secretary of State John Foster Dulles were labeled conscious agents of international communism. Leaders of major church bodies, corporate and banking executives, mass-media moguls, and, of course, labor unions were also included in the conspiracy. In 1973 Robert Welch, the founder of the John Birch Society, said that their "scoreboard shows that the United States is 60 to 80 percent influenced by communism."[18] Every major policy innovation—Medicare, Occupational Safety and Health Administration, environmental protection—was actually a plot to expand government control and the overall aims of the conspiracy. Every foreign policy involvement was actually designed to aid the Communists. The Vietnam War, for example, was fought to help the Communist cause in Asia. And, of course, every desire for social change (e.g., civil rights) and every popular fad (e.g., rock 'n' roll) were Communist inspired to undermine order and morality.[19] Communism, then, was perfect for a conspiratorial rhetorical vision: it was a movement that could be attributed demonic overtones and conspiratorial ubiquity with a historic mission and the power to manipulate events, institutions, and elites.

The original Bircher rhetorical vision was supposedly documented in John A. Stormer's widely circulated *None Dare Call It Treason*.[20] Published during the Goldwater movement of 1964, it codified the fantasy of widespread Communist influence in virtually every facet of American life. Throughout the book, the formula is the same: some area of life—the churches, media, unions, government—is infiltrated by Communists, identifiable by having belonged to some pro-Communist organization or supported some pro-Communist position, which explains why changes have occurred inimical to U.S. interests. Good people have been duped by Communist cunning into supporting things that the Kremlin wants. Villains have wormed their way into positions of power to subvert institutions and morals. For example, theologians with "records of support for communist causes" advocated destructive changes in the Revised Standard Version of the Bible.[21] Mental health is not designed to help the mentally ill but rather to "re-educate the world's population using psychological procedures to create a new breed of amoral men who will accept a one-world socialistic government. They hold the weapon of commitment to a mental institution over the heads of those 'reactionaries' who rebel at accepting the 'new social order'."[22] The private, elite foreign policy organization, the Council on Foreign Relations, controls American foreign policy and aims at a world government that will expand the Communist empire.[23] And so it goes. It is a conspiracy of design in which each part fits the blueprint for takeover and control. "The communists," we are told, "are extremely close to total victory."[24] The demonic threat is imminent; only a holy crusade can defeat it now.

In the 1960s the Birchite conspiracy fantasy grew more ambitious and inclusive. Birch literature integrated the Communist conspiracy into a larger and longer-running conspiracy. Although communism was an ideological conspiracy, the new vision consisted of a historical conspiracy that exploits ideological movements, such as communism and fascism, but has no ideology itself, only the pursuit of sheer power over the world. Robert Welch noted:

In the upper circles of this conspiracy, there is no slightest trace of noble purpose, or of the misguided idealism by which members of the lower echelons are sometimes deceived. There is only sordid self-interest of the most Faustian variety. For two centuries ruthlessly ambitious criminals, whom we shall call the "Insiders" have been helping themselves, and each other, to the prestige and wealth and power which were the only real objectives of their lives. They have been held together in all of these activities, however, and their efforts have been given coherence and direction, by their concerted dedication to the ultimate goal of world leadership for the "Insiders" of a later day. And that day is now almost upon us.[25]

The "Insiders" are the international elite attempting to control the world. It can be traced at least to the Bavarian Order of the Illuminati, formed in 1776 and dissolved by the Bavarian government in 1785. (The American Opinion bookstores of the John Birch Society carry reprints of Robison's 1797 book on the Illuminati.) Birch researchers have tried to document the activities of the Illuminati and its founder, Adam Weishaupt. The order appears to have been an Enlightenment rationalist movement with links to Freemasonry. Both Robison and Welch (two centuries later) entertain the fantasy of moral degradation as both practice and goal of the Order. Robison saw the Illuminati as "a libertine, anti-Christian movement, given to the corruption of women, the cultivation of sensual pleasures, and the violation of property rights."[26] Welch charged that Weishaupt seduced the sister of another leader of the Order and then had her murdered.[27] Such gossipy tidbits about the fantasized immoralities of the enemy provide a recurrent theme in conspiracy theories, dating at least to the medieval fantasies of orgiastic activities during the Witches' Sabbaths.

In the Birch theory, the Illuminati survives and prospers, all in virtual secrecy, save for a few who see through their scheme. The Illuminati were behind the French Revolution, hired Karl Marx to write *The Communist Manifesto*, engineered Bismarck's social legislation in Germany, and brought about the Federal Reserve System, the graduated income tax, and the direct election of U.S. Senators to further nefarious schemes. They financed the Bolshevik Revolution in Russia, planned all the major wars of the twentieth century, started the United Nations for their ultimate purpose of a world government, are responsible for every great upheaval, such as the civil rights movement and the assassinations of key political figures. Their domestic agenda in the United States is subversive, to corrupt and eventually control through a variety of means, including fluoridating water, destroying religion, teaching socialism in the schools, presenting morally undermining fare in the movies, music, and other entertainment industries, managing the news, inflating currency, even spreading disease. (Russian flu was germ warfare!) Their success is truly fantastic, a triumph of secret organizational manipulation and cooptation.

This international power elite has no national or ideological loyalties. Nations are to be destroyed to realize conspiratorial goals; ideological agendas are simply tools in conquest. In the widely circulated update of the conspiracy theory, Gary Allen's *None Dare Call It Conspiracy*, the author notes that "finance capitalism is the anvil and communism the hammer to conquer the world."[28] The Council on Foreign Relations remains the key American institution for the conspiracy, but international bankers, such as Rockefeller and Rothschild, are now at the top of the great conspiracy. The conspirators (dubbed Bilderbergers, after the hotel where they first met in Holland in 1954) meet annually to plot the latest moves, meeting at some secret resort site. They include politicians, industrialists, intellectuals, and other powers, all united in their secret loyalty to the conspiracy. The meetings plan policy; subsequent world events can be explained as carrying out the grand design. When Nixon introduced wage and price controls in 1971, for instance, the conspiracy was given advance notice, making it possible for them to profit from the policy move. Every recent American president, apparently from Woodrow Wilson on (with the exceptions of Harding and Coolidge) has been under conspiratorial control, including Presidents Carter and Reagan. Carter was "taken inside" by Rockefeller as governor of Georgia; Reagan "sold out" at an unspecified time.

The institution that is key to the conspiracy is Rockefeller's Trilateral Commission formed in 1972. The Commission is, in the John Birch Society's view, the foreign ministry of the Council on Foreign Relations. It carves out spheres of influence around the world. When Carter became president, his appointment of people with Trilateral ties to high office fed the fantasies of conspiracy theorists. Although Reagan is not a member, Vice President Bush is, as is Secretary of Defense Caspar Weinberger and others in Reagan's administration. Bush and Secretary of State Alexander Haig attended a meeting of the Trilateral Commission the night before the attempt on President Reagan's life in March 1981, undoubtedly stirring speculation that the power elite wanted him dead. Important foreign members of the conspiracy are often not openly members of such groups for reasons of secrecy but allegedly have included such strange bedfellows as Nikita Krushchev, Mao Tse-Tung, Josef Tito, Charles de Gaulle, Fidel Castro, and many others. Notable Americans members include Henry Cabot Lodge, Margaret Mead, Edward Kennedy, Marlon Brando, Otis Chandler, publisher of the *Los Angeles Times,* and William Paley of CBS.[29]

The conspiracy theory casts Edward Kennedy as one of the ultimate villains, a man conspirators hope to make president of the United States someday. Zad Rust's book *Teddy Bare* says that "the Force of Darkness" conspired to cover up the Chappaquiddick affair because Kennedy is "one of the prominent operators chosen by the Hidden Forces" to lead us to (returning to a traditional image) "the enthronement of the Antichrist."[30] There is often speculation among Birchers that events occur because of internal conflicts and intrigues *within* the conspiracy. Thus, Kennedys (John and Robert) were killed for reasons internal to the conspiracy. Watergate occurred because of a split within the conspiracy. Even wars, the speculation goes, occur because of divisions within the conspiracy.

The conspiratorial elite approaches ever nearer victory. The John Birch Society stands alone—with the heroic symbol of John Birch, a missionary in China, who was apparently executed by the Communists—as a strong force with a sense of missionary rectitude and an urgent recognition of the immediacy of the climactic apocalypse—the approaching secular Armaggedon in which the grand conspiracy will be either victorious or defeated. The society advocates action—educating youth to the "truth" in summer camps, becoming active in local politics, holding seminars and lectures to educate the public, and so forth. The contemporary political world is a drama in which the hidden villains must be unmasked if the great mass of fools (the public) are to see the existence and perfidy of the conspiracy.

How do we evaluate such a grandiose theory? As with any fantasy it feeds on assertions that seem true enough or are at least credible: it is true that there is an international power elite, there are secret meetings of international figures in secluded spas and nobody really knows what goes on, there is a Trilateral Commission with ties in high places. But that this constitutes proof of a "conspiracy" is debatable. How a vast conspiracy could make such gains and exercise such power without anyone ever really breaking the silence is puzzling. The theory assumes a causal and controlling force in history, but it is equally as plausible that the world is disorganized with no one in charge. If a conspiracy is running the world, people might well say it is doing a pretty bad job of it! If it is not, then that may be even worse, proving no one can deal with the vast problems the world will experience in the future.

Yet, we can understand the appeal of such a theory to many persons. The people drawn to conspiracy theories do not fit any particular psychological profile, so the appeal of a conspiracy theory cannot be explained solely as mass paranoia. People gather in groups, we have said, and through fantasizing create a satisfying rhetorical vision of the world. For a variety of reasons, persons attracted to right-wing political groups have developed a common fantasy about the political world, one that provides them with a powerful dramatic explanatory device. Ernest G. Bormann notes:

Against the panorama of large events and seemingly unchangeable forces of society at large or of nature the individual often feels lost and hopeless. One coping mechanism is to dream an individual fantasy which provides a sense of meaning and significance for the individual and helps protect him from the pressures of natural calamity and social disaster. The rhetorical vision serves much the same coping function for those who participate in the drama and often with much more force because of the supportive warmth of like-minded companions.[31]

Orrin Klapp, speaking of crusading groups in general, notes that *dramatic rituals* enhance the solidarity and satisfaction of group members.[32] It is likely that an elaborately articulated conspiracy theory —discussed and applied within the group and disseminated to the world outside—is such a ritual drama for the group. As group members dream a collective fantasy about the conspiratorial structure of the political world, they achieve the kind of satisfaction that only theater can provide—identification of the nature of the world, personification of roles, and catharsis through the knowledge the play brings.[33] The group dramatizes the political world, giving it a sense of "inside dope," of knowing what's "really" going on, transforming the impersonal world of historical change into an understandable drama, pitting "us" against those archfiends who threaten what we believe in, "them." The group can take considerable satisfaction in identifying and personifying itself as the hero of the drama; members can experience a thrill over knowing the true nature—and even for some the outcome—of the play; and they can share anxieties over the satanic challenge they face.

The John Birch conspiracy theory is a bad melodrama. It is a rhetorical vision in the demonic tradition with the villains clearly unregenerate, even satanic, and morally degraded in every way. The Rockefellers, Kennedys, and other villains could scarcely be more nefarious if they played the evil landlord in a nineteenth-century stage melodrama. The richest and most privileged men in the world, the greatest beneficiaries of Euro-American capitalism, are ironically the ones who are trying to destroy it. But someday the first shall come last, and the last first. The moral force of ordinary people will topple the temples of Mammon, slay the Philistines, and restore the moral community. The *adventure* of the melodrama is the quest to expose and defeat the conspiracy; the *mystery* is who is in it and what they are up to; the *romance* is the preservation of values—family, church, town; the *nightmare* is the possibility of the conspiracy gaining control of the world. The rhetorical *logic* of the conspiracy drama impels it toward a story denouement very soon, the children of light versus the children of darkness; and the *perfection* of the conspiracy's villainy and the extent of its power leads to the advocacy of demonic means to fight adequately against its imminent success. One may only wonder whether in the course of redeeming the world, the saviors, imbued with the logic of their own rhetorical vision, will become as demonic as those they fantasize as the conspiratorial enemy. Armed with a rhetorical vision, political groups sometimes gain the power to impose their fantasies on reality whether they are true or not. The logic of the vision leads to a quest for redemption through the victimization and purgation of "the conspirators;" reality must live up to the logic of the mediating rhetorical vision.

FANTASY CHAINS ON THE RIGHT

Rhetorical visions about world conspiracies and current events are not restricted exclusively to group members. Indeed, the groups that create such fantasies are generally eager to disseminate them through ever larger populations. Through group propaganda, the fantasies thus chain out. Using radio, television, books, magazines and pamphlets, newspapers, ham citizen's band radio, and word of mouth, various right wing groups propound their group fantasies for the masses. The John Birch Society, for example, has a morning "news report" carried on many small-town radio stations. Books, such as Allen's *None Dare Call It Conspiracy*[34] or Hal Lindsey's apocalyptic *The Late Great Planet Earth*,[35] are widely circulated free, financed by donations. Politically active celebrity preachers comment on politics on syndicated television shows.

Perhaps the best-known and feistiest publication on the American Right is the Liberty Lobby's weekly newspaper, *The Spotlight*, the *National Inquirer* of the Right. The headlines of weekly issues in 1980 and 1981 illustrate the flavor of a sensationalist fantasy: "Cuba Building Nuclear Bomb," "Will Superthief Rockefeller Be Ruined by Illicit Loans to the Shah?," "U.S. May Quit U.N.," "New 'Pot' Epidemic Looms," "World Police Force Formed," "You'll Wait in Line for $2 Gas," "Rockefeller Blocks Deal for Release of Hostages." *The Spotlight* entertains readers with a variety of fantasies, focusing on recurrent subjects such as the Rockefellers and the Trilateral Commission, the alleged attempts by the U.S. Government to stop gun ownership, why "citizens" should resist the draft, answering census questions, and paying taxes, why and how to invest in gold and silver, and how to survive the coming breakdown of civilization. The advertisements, too, give an idea of the fantasy world of the readers. One can buy survival foods, join survivalist communities hidden away in the West, purchase laetrile and other miracle drugs, water distillers, a machine that replenishes "vital negative ions" in the air, protection devices, and hear various prophecies, religious and political, about the apocalyptic era about to unfold. The Liberty Lobby has been accused of being anti-Semitic. Why? The paper constantly attacks Israel, Zionism, and Jewish involvement in international banking. The group outraged Jewish-Americans by claiming that the Nazi Holocaust was a hoax—a propaganda ploy to make Christian Americans feel guilt and self-hatred and to extort millions of dollars to finance Zionist aims, such as the creation of the state of Israel. Indeed, the Liberty Lobby even offers a $50,000 reward for anyone who can "prove" that the Holocaust occurred! The lobby holds "revisionist conferences" where "scholars" demonstrate there were no Nazi "genocide" policies, concentration camps, gas chambers, and mass murder. *The Diary of Anne Frank*[36] the lobby alleges to be a fraud. *The Spotlight* offers a widespread fantasy of hostile feelings about Jews, one that will not admit that a Christian nation like Germany could commit mass murders.

The Christian Right (as noted in Chapter 9), a loose array of media church organizations, has developed political fantasies in line with their religious views. Celebrated right-wing divines such as Billy James Hargis, Jerry Falwell, James Robison, and others, mingle religious belief with politics. They are active in movements against the Equal Rights Amendment, censoring TV shows, suppressing pornography and homosexuality, outlawing abortion, and electing "acceptable" politicians to office. They fantasize that we are in the "last days" before the Second Coming and that America needs to be "saved" by cleansing it of sin—including apparently political sins such as unbalanced budgets and the Panama Canal treaty. Many followers believe in a satanic conspiracy's attempts to undermine the United States morally and politically. Falwell and others talk vaguely of a conspiracy of secular humanists in positions of influence in the mass media, universities, and government. It is these humanists who have led us astray from biblical truth and moral order. When sufficiently chained out, such fantasies can lead to action. A high school teacher in Maryland was fired, apparently under pressure from fundamentalist activists, for having students read Aristotle's *Politics* and Machiavelli's *The Prince*, two archvillainous figures whose books are supposedly in the satanic tradition of secular humanism! (Machiavelli would no doubt be pleased that his book still stirs the controversy—and attempts to suppress it—that has characterized its history; Aristotle would probably be mystified.)

Some groups on the Christian Right even fantasize that the Illuminati conspiracy is linked to Satan's plans to control the world. One publication asserts:

Satan's attack through politics and finance comes through a well-organized undercover group called "The Insiders" or the Illuminati (the enlightened ones who follow the angel of light, Lucifer).

It has been reported, says the publication, that this international group is controlled by the House of Rothschild:

> They control international banking. . . . They financed and built up both the Nazi party in Germany and the Communist party in Russia. . . . War is very good business so they get involved in planning and financing wars. . . . Political parties are controlled. Hardly anyone goes into high office without their approval. It has been said that they control and direct the fighting of the Right and Left wings in politics. . . . Satan's super politician (the Beast or Antichrist) spoken of in the Bible (Rev. 13) will come into power through the Illuminati. . . . All this is interwoven with (Masonic) lodges and traced back to Nimrod's idea for one world government. . . . Satan has stacked the deck.[37]

In such a way, apocalyptic religious views are linked to a rhetorical vision of politics. Right-wing fantasies also chain out through more informal mediated ways, including simple rumor mongering. These rumors chain out across the country in a variety of publications, talk among the like-minded, and deliberate rumoring. In 1963 the U.S. Army began anti-guerrilla maneuvers in Georgia and invited small groups of officers from friendly nations to observe. Before long, rumors had chained out about a plot to seize Georgia as the first step in a takeover of the United States by the United Nations in league with NATO and the U.S. Arms Control and Disarmament Agency. The invasion force included 20,000 Congolese troops supported by 30,000 Mongolians who were sweeping through Georgia. In addition there were 35,000 Chinese troops in Baja California, ready to strike San Diego. Apparently this rumor spread over the country through right-wing media, but the rumor went far beyond those circles and soon police, public officials, and congressmen were beset by calls and letters from frightened people who had heard the rumor. The Army finally altered its maneuver plans and congressmen and editorial writers denounced the rumor mongers.[38] In 1980, Republican presidential candidate George Bush, campaigning in the Texas primary, was forced to run ads and release memos to the press and public explaining why he was once a member of the Trilateral Commission because right-wing groups were conducting a mailout and whispering campaign accusing Bush of being part of the international conspiracy.

With the spread of amateur radio capabilities, there now exists an ultraconservative "Liberty Net" (3950 kHz) on which operators share fantasies about the world three nights a week. A listener in 1980 heard talk of resistance to the census, that CBS is the Communist Broadcasting System, calls for taking back the Panama Canal and invading Cuba, speculation about the coming Depression, demands for bombing Iran, and similar fare. This long-distance fantasy chaining centers around conspiracy and the world as run by international bankers. Foremost, education in the United States is a conspiratorial scheme: pupil test scores, for instance, are confidential because the government is trying to advance its plan for regimentation.[39] Thus, new technology helps create fantasy groups among people remote from each other in space but bent on sharing and sustaining a rhetorical vision.

A NOTE ON THE CONSPIRACY FANTASIES OF THE LEFT

Ideological groups on the American Left also structure fantasies about the existence and machinations of political conspiracies. Several groups on both the traditional Left and the New Left, for example, explain political events as derived from a reactionary conspiracy centered in a power elite, a ruling class that governs America—and the world—in its own interest. Some commentaries of the Left perceive conflict between elite power groups. One theory holds that political conflict centers around two elite coalitions, the Yankees (bankers, corporations, universities, and unions connected to the Eastern liberal establishment) and the Cowboys (new centers of power in the Sunbelt).[40] Other commentaries detect considerable elite consensus at the top. In either case fantasies abound about who is doing what to whom from and within the secret councils of economic and political elites.

Many Left-conspiracy theorists agree with tenets of conspiracy theories on the Right. Like the Right, the Left agrees that the Trilateral Commission and the Council on Foreign Relations are key institutions in elite rule and that the Rockefellers, the Rothschilds, and the Bilderberg group are key actors in elite planning, largely in their own interest. Both assume elite solidarity and communication, although the Left does not give power elites a historical continuity or a link to Satan, the Masons, the Illuminati, or even a tight conspiratorial unity in the way that the Right does. The Left, however, does fantasize that many events can be explained in terms of elite activities. Both Left and Right tend to believe that assassinations are not the work of lonely and deranged individuals but are planned for conspiratorial purposes. Watergate was explained on the Left as the "tip of the iceberg" of a vast elite struggle between the Yankees and the Cowboys.[41] In any case, although there are differences between the political explanations of Left and Right, they share the group impulse to dramatize the political world in a rhetorical vision that includes the menace of a conspiracy at the top. Poles apart on the ideological spectrum, the neo-Marxist Left and the paleoconservative Right share a fantasy about who are the villains—but not the heroes. And both Right and Left deem those who do not pay a penny for *their* thoughts to be fools.

BAD MELODRAMA AS ENTERTAINING THEATER

The group impulse to dramatize history by transforming it into a grand conspiracy—and a struggle of heroes, villains, and fools in a demonic melodrama—personalizes, simplifies, and renders understandable confusing and complex, contradictory realities. Groups yielding to that impulse explain history in an entertaining way by imbuing it with the attributes of a theatrical play. History is as an uncompromising war in which the source of evil and travail has been unmasked, wherein the causal power has been identified, and where the victory or defeat of the conspiratorial enemy is imminent in the apocalyptic present—the culmination of history. It is good theater even if bad melodrama. To the skeptic, it may all be a castle in the air, but one with considerable appeal.

In one way the conspiracy fantasy of the American Right is a popular philosophy of history. Academic philosophers of history vigorously debate how history works. Most scholars speak of history as blind, as a chaotic succession of events over time, as a process of impersonal forces and chance elements that propel history onward toward no discernible goal. Such a view of history is not only frightening, it is also unsatisfying. To explain historical chaos as simply chaos does not appeal to dramatic sensibilities. History is much more understandable, interesting, and exciting if it is a grand romantic melodrama, full of adventure, mystery, peril and threat and wherein there is a moral to the story.

NOTES

1. See Robert Tucker, *Philosophy and Myth in Karl Marx* (Cambridge: at the University Press, 1961), pp. 221–224.

2. William T. Bluhm, *Ideologies and Attitudes* (Englewood Cliffs, N.J.: Prentice-Hall, 1974), p. 10.

3. See Norman Cohn, *The Pursuit of the Millenium* (New York: Oxford University Press, 1970).

4. Discussion of the presence of the demonic may be found, variously, in Ernest Becker, *Angel in Armor* (New York: George Braziller, 1969); Robert Jewett and John Shelton Lawrence, *The American Monomyth* (Garden City, N.Y.: Doubleday & Co., 1977), pp. 210–216 (Anchor Books); Dan Nimmo and James Combs, *Subliminal Politics* (Englewood Cliffs, N.J.: Prentice-Hall, 1980), pp. 242–243; James Combs, *Polpop: Politics and Popular Culture in America* (Brunswick, Ohio: King's Court Communication, 1982).

5. Earl F. Bargainnier, "Hissing the Villain, Cheering the Hero: The Social Function of Melodrama," *Studies in Popular Culture*, 3 (Spring 1980): 48–56;

David Thornburn, "Television Melodrama," in Horace Newcomb, ed., *Television: The Critical View* (New York: Oxford University Press, 1979), pp. 536–553.

6. Norman Cohn, "Was There Ever a Society of Witches? Myths and Hoaxes of European Demonology," *Encounter*, 43 (December 1974): 26–42.

7. Hugh Trevor-Roper, *The European Witch-Craze of the 16th and 17th Centuries and Other Essays* (New York: Harper & Row, 1969) (Torchbooks); Norman Cohn, *Europe's Inner Demons: An Enquiry Inspired by the Great Witch-Hunt* (New York: New American Library, 1977).

8. Norman Cohn, *Warrant for Genocide: The Myth of the Jewish World-Conspiracy and the Protocols of the Elders of Zion* (New York: Harper & Row, 1969). (Torchbooks)

9. Adolf Hitler, quoted in Hermann Rauschning, *The Voice of Destruction* (New York: G.P. Putnam's Sons, 1940), p. 237.

10. Cohn, *Pursuit of the Millennium*, op. cit., pp. 283–284.

11. Eric Hoffer, *The True Believer* (New York: Harper & Brothers, 1951), p. 73.

12. Kenneth Burke, "Definition of Man," in his *Language as Symbolic Action* (Berkeley: University of California Press, 1968), pp. 16–20.

13. The tradition of the Grand Conspiracy is traced to biblical revelation by Robert Jewett, *The Captain America Complex: The Dilemma of Zealous Nationalism* (Philadelphia: the Westminster Press, 1973), pp. 113–141.

14. Richard Hofstadter, *The Paranoid Style in American Politics* (New York: Random House, 1964), pp. 3–40. (Vintage Books)

15. John Robison, *Proofs of a Conspiracy Against All the Religions and Governments of Europe* (1797).

16. Joseph R. McCarthy, "America's Retreat from Victory" Congressional Record, June 14, 1951, 9A Reprint, p.1.

17. Richard Gid Powers, "J. Edgar Hoover and the Detective Hero," *Journal of Popular Culture*, 9 (Fall 1975): 257–278.

18. Phillip Nobile, "Welch Still Sees Lefties on the Right," *Chicago Sun-Times Midwest Magazine*, September 16, 1973, p. 38.

19. Seymour Martin Lipset and Earl Raab, *The Politics of Unreason* (New York: Harper & Row, 1973). (Torchbooks)

20. John A. Stormer, *None Dare Call It Treason* (Florissant, Mo.: Liberty Bell Press, 1964)..

21. Ibid., p. 128.

22. Ibid., p. 155.

23. Ibid., pp. 209–217.

24. Ibid., p. 229.

25. Robert Welch, *Birch Society Bulletin* (July 1968): 4.

26. Hofstadter, *The Paranoid Style in American Politics*, op. cit., pp. 11, 31–32.

27. Lipset and Raab, *The Politics of Unreason*, op. cit., p. 254.

28. Gary Allen, *None Dare Call It Conspiracy* (Rossmoor, Calif.: Concord Press, 1971), p. 125.

29. See such Birch articles and books as Gary Allen, "Investigating the Great Conspiracy: 13 Clues," *American Opinion*, 26 (May 1979): 23–38; John Rees, "Beware the Trilaterals: An Exclusive Interview with the Leading Authority on Trilateralism," *Review of the News*, 27 (February 1980): 39–54; Alan Stang, "What the Trilateralists Want from You," *American Opinion*, 27 (May 1980): 5–14; Anthony C. Sultton and Patrick M. Wood, *Trilaterals over Washington* (Phoenix: The August Corporation, 1979).

30. Zad Rust, *Teddy Bare* (Boston: Western Islands, 1971), p. x.

31. Ernest G. Bormann, "Fantasy and Rhetorical Vision: The Rhetorical Criticism of Social Reality," in John F. Cragan and Donald C. Shields, eds., *Applied Communication Research: A Dramatistic Approach* (Prospect Heights, Ill.: Waveland Press, 1981), p. 20.

32. Orrin Klapp, *Collective Search for Identity* (New York: Holt, Rinehart & Winston, 1969), pp. 292–295.

33. See Richard Merelman, "The Dramaturgy of Politics," in James Combs and Michael Mansfield, eds., *Drama in Life* (New York: Hastings House, 1976), pp. 288–289.

34. Allen, *None Dare Call It Conspiracy*, op. cit.

35. Hal Lindsey, *The Late Great Planet Earth* (Grand Rapids, Mich: Zondervan, 1970)

36. Anne Frank, *The Diary of a Young Girl* (New York: Modern Library, 1958).

37. "Angel of Light," vol. 9 of "The Crusaders" (Chino, Calif.: Chick Publications, 1978), p. 29. (A comic book)

38. Tamotsu Shibutanti, *Improvised News* (Indianapolis, Ind.: Bobbs-Merrill Co., 1966), p. 80.

39. Stephen G. Esrati, "Liberty Net: Unofficial Voice of the Far Right," *Chicago Tribune*, June 11, 1980, sec. 3, pp. 1, 10.

40. Carl Oglesby, *The Yankee and Cowboy War* (Berkeley, Calif.: Berkeley Publishers, 1977).

41. See such works as G. William Domhoff, *The Higher Circles* (New York: Random House, 1970). (Vintage Books); Thomas R. Dye, *Who's Running America* (Englewood Cliffs, N.J.: Prentice-Hall, 1976); Holly Sklar, ed., *Trilateral Commission and Elite Planning for World Management* (South End Press, 1980); and the classic, C. Wright Mills, *The Power Elite* (New York: Oxford University Press, 1956).

Conclusion

Fantasyland

The Idols of Politics

Miss Sherwin of Gopher Prairie was a fictional character. But she represents all of us who live in a mediated world. Howard Beale was also a fiction, that is, the leading character in the 1976 film *Network*. The movie depicted the operations of the news division of the UBS Television Network, an organization that simply obliterated any distinctions between news and entertainment programming. Beale, anchorman for the UBS nightly news, warned his audience what was happening. Imagine one of his real-life contemporaries for ABC, CBS, or NBC saying, "We deal in illusions, man. None of it is true." Beale chastised, "But you people sit there day after day. Night after night. All ages, colors, creeds. We're all you know. You're beginning to believe the illusions we're spinning here. You're beginning to think that the tube is reality and that your own lives are unreal. You do whatever the tube tells you." So audience members dress, eat, raise their children like "the tube." And, even worse, "you even think like the tube. This is mass madness! You maniacs!" Beale pleaded, "In God's name, you people are the real thing. We are the illusion."

Should Americans take the fictional Howard Beale seriously? If readers have received the message of this book, the answer is an unequivocal yes. We have argued that the political realities of most Americans derive not from direct, firsthand experience with politics but from the mediation of mass and group communication. Given the limits on the time, resources, interests, and so on, of most people, direct involvement in political life is too taxing for vast numbers of citizens. Vicarious participation through the mass media—news, popular magazines, film, entertainment programs, sports, and so on—is at least a convenient, even if not always perfect, substitute. And even for persons who live their daily lives in politics—officeholders, political candidates, political journalists, group members, and others—groupthink frequently provides only an illusion of firsthand knowledge of politics. Hence, what Howard Beale said of "the tube" holds for a considerable portion of mass- and group-mediated politics. If the dependency theory outlined in Chapter 1 makes sense, then, more people than TV anchors should be heard saying, "We deal in illusions, man."

So, in this closing chapter of our account of mediated politics, let us take Howard Beale seriously. Doing so poses at least two questions: (1) What are the consequences of mediated politics? (2) How can we live in a land of fantasy?

THE WAR OF THE WORLDS

On Sunday evening, October 30, 1938, countless Americans were enjoying what was becoming the nation's most popular form of entertainment, that is, listening to the radio. As the night wore on many tuned to one of the season's moderately successful programs, "The Mercury Theater on the Air." They heard an announcer introduce the program, "The Columbia Broadcasting System and its affiliated stations present Orson Welles and 'The Mercury Theater on the Air' in 'The War of the Worlds' by H. G. Wells." Orson Welles moved immediately to the script, noting that earthlings now realized there was a time when they had been observed by other beings of a superior intelligence. He described how things were in the nation on October 30 in the "thirty-ninth year of the twentieth century:" the economy was improving, the war scare was over, and 32 million were listening to their radios, according to latest Crossley ratings. The program then cut away to an apparent weather broadcast, followed by a program of orchestra music from the "Park Plaza Hotel in New York City." Suddenly the orchestra music was interrupted by a "special bulletin from the Intercontinental Radio Service." Allegedly, "Professor Ferrell" at an astronomic observatory in Chicago had just spotted "incandescent gasses" spouting "from the planet Mars." The radio announcer identified the gas as hydrogen and moving toward Earth. From that point the "War of the Worlds" broadcast continued a fictional tale in a news format, telling of the invasion of Martians, the destruction of America's defending armies, the devastation of cities, the slaughter of human beings, and widespread panic. Ultimately the Martians died—they were not immunized against common human illness. But only listeners staying around until the end of the broadcast were to learn the happy ending.

Anyone tuning in late—at the time of the initial weather report rather than at the show's introduction—could have been misled into believing the first half-hour of the program was a legitimate newscast.

According to later news accounts many Americans were indeed misled. Newspapers reported that a "tidal wave of terror swept the nation." Other news reported that New Jersey highways (near the locale of the fictional invasion) were jammed with hysterical people; farmers joined in vigilante groups; prayer meetings hastily gathered; people fled cities; others committed suicide. Supposedly college students in North Carolina fainted at the news; a woman in Boston claimed she saw the fire of the invasion; rumors spread of people being killed by the thousands; and one story told of a man in Reno, Nevada, rushing back home to aid the wife he had gone to Reno to divorce!

The 1938 "War of the Worlds" broadcast and the reaction to it have become legendary. We take note of the broadcast and its aftermath because the events surrounding "The War of the Worlds" indicate how difficult it is to learn how people respond to mediated realities, realities surely fantastic in character. The Mercury Theater's fictional newscast was a mediated reality for many of its listeners. But news accounts of how people responded to the broadcast's real-fiction mediated yet another reality, that is, the fantasy panic. Legend has it that Welles's production created not only a mass fantasy but also a mass panic as well. But did it? Studies undertaken following the broadcast suggest otherwise. Estimates are that only about 12 percent of the adult population actually heard the program (the much more popular radio program featuring "Edgar Bergen and Charlie McCarthy" was broadcast on NBC during the same hour). And, of those who did hear "War of the Worlds," only 28 percent believed the news bulletin was authentic rather than part of the drama. Only 2 percent of the entire American population could be described as "excited" by the program and even a smaller fraction responded with any action, let alone fear and flight.[1]

Similarly in 1973 a Swedish radio broadcast revolved about a tale of a fictitious nuclear accident at an as yet to be constructed power plant at Barseback. The broadcast employed a "War of the Worlds" motif, that is, the real-fiction of a newscast with a lead bulletin, easily recognizable radio announcers, sirens, authentic sounds, and so on. Within an hour of the broadcast (and well into the following day) national and international news agencies reported widespread panic. The reaction to the simulated newscast provoked heated debate within Swedish news organizations and even within the Swedish Parliament. Unquestioned in those debates was the assumption that there had indeed been mass panic. A team of Swedish sociologists, however, examined the effects of the broadcast. They found that only 20 percent of the adult population in the locale of the fictional accident (a failure in the plant's cooling system that resulted in a radioactive leak containing gas that was carried by winds over populated areas) heard the broadcast. Only one in ten of those took it for other than a fictional account, only about 7 percent were frightened at all, and only 1 percent reacted to the program. The researchers uncovered not a single case of panic flight.[2] The impression of mass panic derived from a relatively few telephone calls to police and fire stations. These officials created a fantasy of widespread fear, the fantasy translated into news fact, and soon the Barseback fantasy had chained out to the nation and the world.

The 1938 and 1973 broadcasts were avowed fictions. What of events that actually happen? Can more accurate accounts of how these influence human responses be made? Apparently not, at least if the case of the accident at Three Mile Island (TMI) (see Chapter 1) is any lesson. As with "War of the Worlds" and Barseback, the news media generated and chained out a panic fantasy. On March 30, 1979, ABC–TV reported people "on the verge of panic" and in "momentary panic." NBC–TV filmed firetrucks moving through the deserted streets of small towns, the implication being of people having fled their communities in fear of a radioactive holocaust. CBS–TV stood alone in reporting "no panic," only fear and confusion. One week after the TMI accident had passed *Time* reported that "thousands of people fled the area." One week later *Time* wrote that "100,000 or so of the area's 650,000 residents who had left started to trickle home." *Newsweek* was more conservative, that is, "an estimated 60,000 residents moved out voluntarily."

But the panic fantasy chained out by the national news media was not shared by the local press. In Pennsylvania the *Lebanon News* reported, "No Panic Noted in Wake of Nuclear Crisis at TMI" on March 29 and "Realtors Report No Panic Selling Since TMI Crisis" on April 6. The director of the Lebanon County Emergency Management Facility estimated only eighteen hundred people actually left the area. The Pennsylvania State Police noted that weekend traffic in counties around the plant was not unusually heavy. Local police officials in towns within a five-mile radius of TMI recorded no extraordinary exodus.

What these cases—two fictional and one actual—of mediated realities suggest is that it is very difficult to know what effects fantasies have on individuals, both on those who share them and those who do not. News stories are certainly unreliable indicators of such effects. There is a reason for that. Precisely because a news account is a *story* (i.e., story journalism rather than information journalism as distinguished in Chapter 1), dramatic logic requires that individual behavior be described in ways conforming to the imperatives of the narrative. The "War of the Worlds," Barseback, and TMI are clear examples. Each is a technological fable—a tale that appeals to the fear that some powerful and evil force armed with mysterious technological superiority will invade and destroy our Edenic existence, even our lives. By design or accident technological demons disrupt the fabric of ordinary life. The fable stands as a recurrent theme in popular culture—witness the enduring popularity of the Frankenstein story, science-fiction tales, fictions of mad scientists, and accounts of endless technological conspiracies (as, for instance, the cloning of Hitler in the film *The Boys from Brazil*). And a key element in the technological fable is the implication that the monster can never be laid to rest, never destroyed. Hence, the only recourse is flight in panic. Whether told through pseudonewscasts or actual news accounts, the technological fable plays out its full scenario. Thus, the newsmaking process, once defining a situation as a technological fable as in the case of "The War of the Worlds," Barseback, and TMI, finds, accepts, and magnifies "facts" consistent with the dramatic logic of the panic fantasy even in the face of actual serenity and calm.

A NATION OF TRIBES IN A GLOBAL VILLAGE

In the face of a dearth of systematic, empirical studies on the effects of fantasy chaining and fantasy sharing on the behavior of people, we simply are unable to judge the consequences of mediated politics for individuals. And we can but speculate about the impact of mediated realities on groups as well. Recall that in our introductory chapter we noted the role played by pluralistic ignorance in the creation and transmission of fantasies. Pluralistic ignorance consists of people in groups being uninformed of the opinions, views, and perceived realities of persons in other groups. Group members frequently talk to one another, thus socially validating their shared views of things. More rarely do they transcend their group identities to discover what is on the minds of nonmembers or of members of other groups. There is, thus, potential at least for Americans to separate and isolate themselves through the fantasy groups with which they affiliate. The result is a nation of tribes, that is, people talking only to affiliates with whom they agree (perhaps reinforcing the fantasies derived from their groupthink) while remaining blissfully ignorant of the multiple, even contradictory, realities of others in a pluralistic society.

What unifies these disparate islands of fantasy are the illusions confessed to by Howard Beale, namely, the mediation of realities by mass communication. In his widely read work, *Understanding Media*,[3] the late Marshall McLuhan argued that the electronic media have transformed not only personal lives but society as well. Because of the capacity for instantaneous and simultaneous communication, the electronic media make it possible for people scattered throughout all parts of a nation, even the world, to share intimately in a common, single experience. Whether it be the assassination of a political figure, the playing of the Super Bowl, the discovery of "Who shot J. R.?," or the telecast of "Roots," literally millions of individuals can experience at the same time the same event in the same way. For McLuhan the electronic media represented a paradoxical opportunity, that of reclaiming the intimacy of people sharing a common event as though they were members of a small tribal village but doing so on a global scale. The miracle of television, as it was called during its early years by its boosters, unifies a nation of tribes into a global village.[4]

There are, however, a number of dangers in such unification. To begin with—as we have stressed throughout this volume—the mass-mediated realities of electronic democracy are no less prone to fantastic content than are the group-mediated realities of interpersonal relations. The media of mass communication offer means of transcending the pluralistic ignorance of fantasy islands, but the illusions the mass media substitute for that ignorance need not be any more informative than the group isolation itself. In fact, as in the cases of the panic fantasies so frequently created by the news media, the mass illusion may simply contribute to group isolation. Certainly much of what we have said of religious fantasies (Chapter 9) and conspiratorial fantasies (Chapter 10) suggests as much.

Second, if in a media-dependent society individuals and groups must rely on mass communication to lead tribal members out of a jungle of pluralistic ignorance, they will be so led only on those matters that the news and entertainment media place on the agenda of the global village. But as Robert Cirino has demonstrated with respect to both news[5] and entertainment[6] that agenda is highly restricted and politically biased. The conventions that determine what is a newsworthy event (see Chapter 8) frequently preclude global villagers from reading, hearing, or viewing stories about crucial matters. World hunger, consumer safety, pollution, environmental deterioration, and other matters were major problems in the global village long before the press admitted them to the public agenda. And, as Cirino notes, television dramas, sports, popular magazines, cartoons, and many other forms of entertainment are much more likely to reflect libertarian or conservative ideological viewpoints than liberal or socialist perspectives.[7]

Moreover, by the overall coverage of events that are unrelated to one another and generally ambiguous in meaning, the media can build a peculiar vision of the times for global villagers, a vision that becomes so widely taken for granted as to assume the persistence and endurance of a myth. Entman and Paletz label this the Alice in Wonderland syndrome.[8] Their research indicates, for example, that throughout the 1970s news reports and commentaries routinely attributed conservative sentiments to the residents of America's global village. This consisted of reports that the trend of American opinion was to the right, the overall mood of the public was conservative, and there was a building conservative majority in the nation. Using survey data, Entman and Paletz demonstrate that the alleged conservative swing was largely a fantasy of the news media with little foundation in fact. Yet as both rank-and-file citizens and members of the nation's political elite began to take for granted this mediated reality of pack journalism, the fantasy had real-world consequences. The fantasy depiction of the political climate of the 1970s as conservative did much to create a conservative bias among political officials that resulted in the insulation of powerholders from public accountability, popular dissatisfaction with officials and institutions, and reallocations of political power among social interests. The effects of the mass mediating of realities, thus, go beyond the effects of substituting an illusion of information for ignorance, agenda setting, and mythmaking. They extend to producing changes in political alignments aand institutions.

The vast range of potential consequences of group- and mass-mediated realities suggests a final thought. If societal members grow solely dependent on mediated politics rather than involving themselves in direct political action, the possibilities emerge for a very special kind of global village, namely, a Nineteen Eighty-Four global village along the lines of George Orwell's fictional utopia (see Chapter 7). A totally mediated politics is only one step removed from a totally controlled politics, that is, a totalitarian global village of carefully calculated and manipulated fantasies. That such a potential exists, however, need not dictate its certainty. At least it need not if we are willing to surrender the illusion of single realities and step out into a world of plural possibilities.

FROM IDOLS AND PIPE DREAMS TO PLURALITY

In the seventeenth century the philosopher Francis Bacon speculated about the tendency of humans to hold to beliefs that were simply not true. He called these false notions and reasoned that there were four chief sources of such "idols."[9] First, he wrote, there are idols of the tribe. These idols spring from the false assertion that human senses and perceptions are valid sources of beliefs. Such idols are similar to those we have likened to the pluralistic ignorance that marks group-mediated politics in our contemporary nation of tribes. Persons who reject the human senses and perceptions as a touchstone of beliefs and instead think that the private reasoning capacity of the individual offers a better source of reality worship what Bacon called the idols of the cave. If one can but look into one's self, think such worshipers, true knowledge will flow not from mediation but from meditation. A third source of false notions derives from the idols of the marketplace, that is, social intercourse, group discussion, and group decision making. This is what we have described as groupthink. Finally, the source of reality for some people consists of beliefs passed down from generation to generation through tradition, philosophy, ritual, custom, convention, and so on. These are the idols of the theater and very much in the character of the melodramatic imperative of mass-mediated political realities.

Bacon provided no particular advice for how to escape such idolatry. That people still base their political beliefs on superficial impressions, meditation, groupthink, and dramatic portrayals is testimony to the endurance of the idols of tribe, cave, marketplace, and theater. The fantasies derived from the mediation of political realities constitute our modern-day idols of politics. Giving up such fantasies, no longer embracing such idols, is not merely difficult, it is sometimes too painful to contemplate. This was the lesson learned by the clientele of Harry Hope's hotel and bar.

In 1946 Eugene O'Neill, certainly one of America's greatest dramatists, published one of his last plays, *The Iceman Cometh*.[10] It is a drama about fantasies tenaciously held. It teaches us something about how the fantasies of our politics beguile and, if taken for granted as reality, can enervate, devitalize, and perhaps even immobilize the body politic. All of the action of the drama occurs in a back room of a combination hotel and saloon in New York City owned and operated by Harry Hope. It is the summer of 1912. Gathered in the bar in the very early hours of the morning are Harry and a host of regulars—most of them roomers at Harry's hotel. The regulars are not actually customers because each and every one is down on luck and has no money to buy anything. So, in a daily and nightly ritual, each sits in the back room of the bar hoping that either Harry or a rare stranger from off the street will stand them to free booze.

The cast of characters is a strange combination: Harry's brother-in-law, an unemployed one-time circus man; a one-time police lieutenant kicked off the force; an alumnus of Harvard Law School who never practiced law; a former proprietor of a gambling house; a former Boer War commando; a one-time captain of British infantry; a perennially unemployed news correspondent; a one-time editor of anarchist publications; a weatherbeaten former syndicalist-anarchist; another one-time syndicalist who fled to Harry's after informing on fellow conspirators, including his own mother. The only gainfully employed members of the clan are two bartenders and three prostitutes, all also residents of Harry's hotel.

A strange place. Says the aging syndicalist-anarchist, "It's the No

Chance Saloon. It's Bedrock Bar, The End of the Line Café, The Bottom of the Sea Rathskeller!" He surveys the regulars as they sleep off their drunks at dimly lit tables. He notes a "beautiful calm in the atmosphere." He remarks, "No one here has to worry about where they're going next, because there is no farther they can go. It's a great comfort to them." But, he says, "Even here they keep up the appearances of life with a few harmless pipe dreams about their yesterdays and tomorrows. . . ."[11] These pipe-dream fantasies, however, are the meaning of life for each person. Harry, a former ward politician, has not been outside his building since his wife died twenty years earlier. He dreams of taking a walk around the ward "tomorrow"[12] to reclaim his political power as though he had yielded it only yesterday. His brother-in-law fantasizes a return to the circus. The former police lieutenant plans to seek exoneration "tomorrow." Also "tomorrow" the lawyer will practice law, the gambler will get a new establishment, the commando and infantry officer will return to the Veldt, the news correspondent (nicknamed "Jimmy Tomorrow") will reclaim his job, the prostitutes will quit walking the streets, and on and on. And, of course, everyone will pay Harry past-due bills, "tomorrow." "The tomorrow movement is a sad and beautiful thing,"[13] says the cynical old revolutionary.

Today, however, everyone is awaiting the arrival of Theodore Hickman (Hickey). Hickey is a hardware salesman who occasionally drops in (on his "periodicals"), throws down a wad of money, buys drinks for the house, gets smashed, and indulges the regulars in their pipe dreams. The patrons eagerly await Hickey's arrival on this particular day for it is Harry's birthday. Hickey is always especially generous in buying booze each year on Harry's birthday.

After a long wait, especially for those suffering from the withdrawal symptoms of not having had a drink, Hickey arrives. He enters in the normal glad-handed, boisterous manner of "good ol' Hickey." The bartender brings drinks. There is a toast. Everybody drinks, everybody but Hickey. "You'll have to excuse me, boys and girls, but I'm off the stuff. For keeps," he declares. The regulars stare in amazed incredulity. He assures everyone that he will still buy them rounds, to their relief, but that he will have none of it: "I finally had the guts to face myself and throw overboard the damned lying pipe dream that'd been making me miserable, and do what I had to do for the happiness of all concerned—and then all at once I found I was at peace with myself and I didn't need booze anymore."[14]

The remainder of The Iceman Cometh (the iceman of reality) concerns Hickey's efforts to get the regulars of Harry Hope's to face up to their pipe dreams, recognize them for the illusions that they are and, having faced them, be goaded into doing all those things they had promised themselves for "tomorrow." Once they give up the "Palace of Pipe

Dreams" they, too, will find "true peace" and happiness. The patrons do not yield without a struggle but slowly some come around. The news correspondent finally admits that he would never be able to get his job back for he was fired for drunkenness. Others begin to face up to their pipe dreams. After years of idleness some even walk (or are shoved) out the door of Harry's bar. But Harry Hope is the hard case for Hickey. Harry has all kinds of excuses for not surrendering his pipe dream and actually going out to walk the ward—his loss of hearing, his rheumatism, the heavy traffic on the streets, and so on. But in a rage at Hickey, Harry finally relents, "If there was a mad dog outside I'd go and shake hands with it rather than stay here with you!" Out he goes but soon the bartender notes Harry is turning around. Says Hickey, "Of course, he's coming back. So are all the others. By tonight they'll all be here again. You dumbbell, that's the whole point."[15]

And they do all return. But things do not seem the same. They feel shame, especially in the face of Hickey's new-found serenity and peace. They drink and drink, but to no effect. "No life in the booze. No kick. Dishwater. Beejees, I'll never pass out!,"[16] whines Harry Hope. And at that point Hickey reveals the story of how he rid himself of his pipe dream. As he tells it, his fantasy involved his wife's love for him and her misery because of it. All she ever wanted to do, he says, was to make him happy. But she was never happy in return. The reality, Hickey says, to which he awakened, his pipe dream exposed, was the deficiencies in his own character. Those were the sources of his wife's sadness—his drinking, absence from home, chasing after other women, carousing, and so on. Having awakened to his pipe dream, Hickey asked himself how he could make amends, how he could make his wife Evelyn happy and remove her torment at loving such a louse. "I'd driven myself crazy trying to find some way out for her," he says. Then it came to him, "the only possible way out—for her sake," and "the only possible way to give her peace and free her from the misery of loving me." The regulars chorus "Who the hell cares? We want to pass out in peace!" But Hickey continues, "So I killed her."[17]

Hickey is arrested. It takes some time for things to return to normal at Harry's. But they do. Each patron picks up the old pipe dream. Harry takes another drink, then joyfully exclaims, "Beejees, fellers, I'm feeling the old kick, or I'm a liar. It's putting life back in me!" Then he opines, "It was Hickey kept it from—" Harry stops, says Hickey was crazy, possessed with "a lunatic's pipe dreams."[18] Everyone at Harry's, in contrast, is sane. So the pipe dreams are not fantasies, they are reality. That reality reinforced, all sink back into the stupor of their ritualistic lives.

Like Plato's parable of the cave with which we opened this volume, *The Iceman Cometh* testifies to the human yearnings for illusion. Hickey is but the prisoner freed from the cave to walk out and peer into the sunlight. On returning to the cave of Harry's bar, he is a threat to that reality. But like the prisoner as well, he may merely be substituting one illusion for another. *The Iceman Cometh* speaks not only of the seduction and persistence of fantasy but also something about what happens when one acts on the basis of such illusion. Hickey kills Evelyn because he follows the logic of his pipe dream to its end. His act was no illusion, however, for it had real-world consequences for Evelyn.

It is on this note that we conclude our mediated reality of mediated political realities. The logic of fantasy dictates simplified, single explanations for events; the logic of reality, however, is one of complexities and plural explanations. The logic of fantasy demands consistency or, at least, easily reconciled inconsistencies; the logic of reality is one of contradictions or, at least, of confusions. The logic of fantasy is one of certainties, the logic of reality of equally plausible possibilities. In his "Ivan Turgenieff," which appeared in *French Poets and Novelists* in 1878, Henry James wrote:

Life is, in fact, a battle. . . . Evil is insolent and strong; beauty enchanting but rare; goodness very apt to be weak; folly very apt to be defiant; wickedness to carry the day; imbeciles to be in great places, people of sense in small, and mankind generally, unhappy. But the world as it stands is no illusion, no phantasm, no evil dream of a night; we wake up to it again for ever and ever; we can neither forget it nor deny it nor dispense with it."[19]

No manner of premature closure of potential political realities will allow us, despite our store of dramatic and enriched fantasies, to avoid awakening to the political world that "as it stands is no illusion." We hope that readers of this volume will "for ever and ever" seek out and ponder alternative realities to those derived from mass- and group-mediated politics. The security of Harry Hope's is not as appealing as it might seem.

NOTES

1. Hadley Cantril, *The Invasion from Mars* (Princeton: Princeton University Press, 1940).

2. Karl Erik Rosengren, Peter Avidson, and Dahn Sturesson, "The Barseback 'Panic': A Radio Programme As a Negative Summary Event," *Acta Sociologica*, 18 (1979): 303–321.

3. Marshall McLuhan, *Understanding Media* (New York: McGraw-Hill, 1964).

4. Ibid.

5. Robert Cirino, *Don't Blame the People* (Los Angeles: Diversity Press, 1971).

6. Robert Cirino, *We're Being More Than Entertained* (Honolulu: Lighthouse Press, 1977).

7. Ibid.

8. Robert M. Entman and David L. Paletz, "Media and the Conservative Myth," *Journal of Communication,* 30 (Autumn 1980): 154–165.

9. Francis Bacon, "Novum Organum," in Edwin A. Burtt, ed., *The English Philosophers from Bacon to Mill* (New York: Random House, 1939), pp. 34–35. (Modern Library).

10. Eugene O'Neill, *The Iceman Cometh* (New York: Random House, 1957). (Vintage Books).

11. Ibid., p. 25.

12. Ibid., p. 51.

13. Ibid., p. 50.

14· Ibid., p. 79.

15. Ibid., pp. 195–196.

16. Ibid., p. 235.

17. Ibid., pp. 240–41.

18. Ibid., pp. 249–50.

19. Henry James, *French Poets and Novelists* (London: Macmillan and Co., 1878), pp. 318–319.

Author Index

227

Subject Index

in presidential elections, 48–69
in religious movements, 182–189, 219
social construction of, 10
in sports, 124–139
and subversion, 108
of technology, 119–120
in TV news, 23–46
of transcendental hope, 117–120
and values, 130
and violence, 117–120
Fantasy-building, 11
Fantasy chaining, 12, 67, 146–147, 162
of the American right, 206
evangelical, 190–192
Fantasy themes, 12, 65, 69
Father Divine, 88
Federal Aviation Administration (FAA), 43
Flight 191, TV news coverage of, 42–45
Forbidden Planet, 107
Ford, Gerald R., 31, 54–67, 78, 120, 129, 162–164, 169
Frank, Reuven, 27
"Franklin and Eleanor," 78
French Poets and Novelists, 224

Gallup, George, 174
Garagiola, Joe, 129
Gatekeepers, 152–160
Gehrig, Lou, 78, 126, 127
"General Hospital," 15, 96
Ghotbzadeh, Sadegh, 35
Gifford, Frank, 128
Giscard d'Estaing, Valery, 176–178
Global village, 218–220
God, 182, 184, 187–188, 190, 191, 196–197
Godfather, The, 121
Goldwater, Barry, 151
Gone With The Wind, 15, 73
Good Housekeeping, 97
"Good Morning America," 33
Graham, Billy, 108
Great Cabbage Hoax, 13

Great Communicator, 154–156, 158–160
Great Depression, 109–112
Great Society, 117–118
Green Berets, The, 117
Grooved responses, 66, 143
Group mediation, of political news, 162–180
Groupthink, 144–160
defined, 144
in news media, 162, 164
political, 148–160
role in mediating political realities, 145
and "Washington Week in Review," 152–160
"Guiding Light," 15, 96
Guevara, Ché, 96
"Gunsmoke," 73
Guthrie, Janet, 134
Guyana: Cult of the Damned, 87
Guyana Massacre: The Eyewitness Account, 86
"Guyana Tragedy: The Story of Jim Jones," 88

Haig, Alexander, 204
Haldeman, Bob, 77
Harding, Warren G., 204
Harper's Bazaar, 97–98
Harris, Don, 85
Harris, Fred, 55
Harris, Louis, 53, 174
Harris Survey, The, 25
Hearst, William Randolph, 29, 30, 32
Hendrix, Jimi, 118
Heroism, 72, 79, 106, 122, 127
model of the sportsman, 131
Hiss, Alger, 108
Historical biography, 78–81
Historical fiction, 84
Historical panorama, 81–83
Hitler, Adolf, 96, 197
Hitler Fantasy, 89
Hitler's Children, 113
Hockey, U.S. Olympic Team, 136
Hodges, Russ, 124